ETERNAL GOD

ETERNAL GOD

A Study of God without Time

Paul Helm

CLARENDON PRESS · OXFORD
1988

Oxford University Press, Walton Street, Oxford OX2 6DP
Oxford New York Toronto
Delhi Bombay Calcutta Madras Karachi
Petaling Jaya Singapore Hong Kong Tokyo
Nairobi Dar es Salaam Cape Town
Melbourne Auckland
and associated companies in
Berlin Ibadan

Oxford is a trade mark of Oxford University Press

Published in the United States
by Oxford University Press, New York

British Library Cataloguing in Publication Data
Helm, Paul
Eternal God: a study of God without time.
1. God. Existence—Philosophical
perspectives
I. Title
212'.1'01
ISBN 0-19-824478-9

Library of Congress Cataloging in Publication Data
Helm, Paul.
Eternal God: a study of God without time/Paul Helm.
Bibliography: p.   Includes index.
1. God.   2. Eternity.   3. God—Omniscience.   4. Free will and
determinism.   I. Title.
BL473.H45   1988   212'7—dc19   88-25236
ISBN 0-19-824478-9

Phototypeset by Cotswold Typesetting Ltd, Gloucester, UK
Printed in Great Britain by
Biddles Ltd., Guildford and Kings' Lynn

To the children,
Anna, John, Philip, and Benjamin

PREFACE

PORTIONS of this book have previously appeared in various journals in a different form. Parts of Chapters 3 and 4 first saw the light of day as 'God and Spacelessness' (*Philosophy*, 55 (1980), 211–21); part of Chapter 6 as 'Timelessness and Foreknowledge' (*Mind*, 84.336 (1975), 516–27); part of Chapter 7 as 'God and Whatever Comes to Pass' (*Religious Studies*, 14 (1978), 315–23); part of Chapter 8 as 'Divine Foreknowledge and Facts' (*Canadian Journal of Philosophy*, 4.2 (1974), 305–15; and part of Chapter 9 as 'Theism and Freedom' (*Neue Zeitschrift für Religions Philosphie*, (1979), 139–49).

Thanks are due to Norman Kretzmann who has helped me with specific points about timeless eternity, and to William Young who has provided assistance and encouragement on these themes, and much else, over many years. But I have to add, particularly bearing in mind the arguments advanced in Chapter 9, that the responsibility for the views expressed in this book is mine alone. Joan Stevenson's typing and editorial skills have been, and continue to be, quite indispensable.

The writing of the book was completed during the academic year 1985–6, a sabbatical year generously provided by the University of Liverpool.

P.H.

University of Liverpool

CONTENTS

When at the Grammar School in Aberdeen, I got hold of a volume of George Campbell, in which he ridicules, as lamentable folly, the notion that to God there is no past, present or future—to Him all are one. I remember how well I *abhorred* George Campbell for that. I thought it the most magnificent thought I had ever met with.

John Duncan, *Colloquia Peripatetica*

Introduction

THE classical Christian theologians, Augustine of Hippo, say, or Aquinas or John Calvin, each took it for granted that God exists as a timelessly eternal being. They accepted it as an axiom of Christian theology that God has no memory, and no conception of his own future, and that he does not change, although he eternally wills all changes, even becoming, when incarnate in the Son, subject to humiliation and degradation.

The position at the present time among philosophers and theologians is a very different one. For there is a widespread belief among Christian thinkers who are often otherwise in disagreement that God is in time. For example such a view is characteristic of so-called 'Process Theology', which holds not only that God is in time but that it is essential to God that he changes, that his own character matures as he experiences the love, disappointment, and frustration of his creation. In this vein a distinguished contemporary theologian, though not a Process theologian, Jurgen Moltmann, has written,

God demonstrates his eternal freedom through his suffering and his sacrifice, through his self-giving and his patience. Through his freedom he keeps man, his image, and his world, creation, free—keeps them free and pays the price of their freedom. Through his freedom he waits for man's love, for his compassion, for his own deliverance to his glory through man.[1]

From a different quarter certain biblical scholars hold that the idea of timelessness is a Greek notion and that therefore it ought to form no part of a true exegesis of the text of Scripture, nor of a truly Scriptural hermeneutic. While they are prepared to allow that certain expressions of Scripture are anthropomorphic—God does not have hands, or feet, or a

---

[1] *The Trinity and the Kingdom of God*, 56.

nose, though Scripture says that he has all these—such figures of speech do not extend to divine activities. God only metaphorically has feet, but he literally remembers, or changes his mind, or grows weary.

This consensus among scholars is enlarged by current work in what is called 'analytic philosophy of religion', rigorous philosophical reflection upon the corpus of beliefs known as Christian theism. With few exceptions philosophers of religion in this tradition are united in dismissing the idea of God's timeless eternity.

There are two main reasons for this dismissal. The more prominent and central reason is that the view that God exists timelessly eternally is incoherent, not because timeless existence as such is incoherent, for perhaps propositions and numbers exist timelessly, but because the idea of an intelligent being, the creator and sustainer of the universe, existing timelessly, is incoherent. How could such a being be a person, with a life of thoughts and purposes?

A rather less central reason for dismissing divine timeless eternity is that it allegedly coheres less well, and perhaps not at all, with other elements in a developed theism. Despite Boethius' celebrated claim in *The Consolation of Philosophy* that divine eternity provides a ready solution to the problem of divine foreknowledge and human freedom, contemporary philosophers of religion have generally not followed him in this but have instead 'made a place' for human freedom by supposing God to limit his own knowledge. The chief conceptual virtue of the idea of God's being in time is that it permits not only this idea of God abridging his own knowledge, but also the idea of God responding to what he newly learns as free human decisions are made.

In fact an interesting and surprising contrast can be drawn between current attempts to resolve the anciently alleged incompatibility between divine omniscience and human freedom and the attempt made by Boethius. Boethius was bent on safeguarding divine omniscience and human freedom in a situation in which God is not envisaged as interacting with his human creatures but as eternally commanding and decreeing. Boethian theology at this point is a kind of Platonic deism. By contrast current philosophers who tackle the alleged incompatibility are more anxious to safeguard human freedom in a situation in which God interacts in time with his free creatures. They do so at the expense of certain divine attributes hitherto regarded as essential to God, notably changelessness and omniscience. Or so, at least, I shall argue.

Apart from the first chapter, which discusses some of the issues raised by deciding whether a text does or does not teach or imply a particular concept, this book is wholly concerned with the arguments of analytical philosophers of religion. In this sense it is both reactive and reactionary; but this stance is imposed by the terms of the debate. To the claim that a particular concept is incoherent there is no alternative but to try to show its coherence by rebutting the opposing arguments. This is inherently unsatisfactory, because by it the best that can be hoped for is the verdict that the incoherence is 'not proven', for there is no argument or type of argument by which one might establish the coherence of the idea of divine timeless eternity *de novo*, and conclusively. There is no alternative, therefore, to a patient consideration of what are claimed to be the chief arguments against the idea of divine timeless eternity.

But there is a more positive side to things. For in addition to trying to maintain the coherence of the idea of timeless eternity an attempt is made to draw out some of its consequences for each of the traditional *loci* of that somewhat arbitrary abbreviation known as 'classical theism'. In particular I try to show that some of the allegedly more calamitous consequences of an unattenuated version of divine immutability and divine omniscience for human freedom and responsibility are either not calamitous or are not consequences. In particular an attempt is made to argue that given certain assumptions which in other contexts are plausible enough, assumptions about determinism, divine omniscience and human freedom can cohabit amicably, and that to ascribe timeless eternity to the creator does not lead inevitably to Spinoza's pantheism. Nevertheless although Spinozism can be avoided it can be anticipated that the Spinozistic flavour of the resulting brew will be too much for most stomachs, but that cannot be helped. In the final chapter, in an attempt to effect a *rapprochement* between the God of the Philosophers and the God of Abraham, Isaac, and Jacob, I venture beyond the metaphysics of theism to discuss the question of how one might identify and refer to a timelessly eternal God.

The mention of metaphysics is worth dwelling upon. There is a school of philosophical thought which claims that the ascription of eternity to God is the first move in the language-game of religion. On this view what it means to say that God is eternal is that certain types of question about God cannot be raised within religion; that to try to raise them betokens a misunderstanding of the 'grammar' of religion. Well, if God is timelessly eternal then of course it makes no sense to raise certain questions about him, or, for that matter, to make certain statements about him. But not being able to raise these questions, or make these statements, is a consequence of divine timeless eternity, it is not what divine timeless eternity is. It follows that whether God is timelessly eternal or not is a fact about reality in general, about how things are; it is not merely a remark about the linguistic phenomenology of religion.

Although the central chapters of the book deal with a family of issues in the metaphysics of theism, principally omniscience, immutability, and freedom, it would be a mistake to think that the ramifications of timeless eternity are confined to these issues, important as they are. The idea of God as timeless, as the changeless ground of all that changes, has profound implications for the character of human spirituality, for the focusing of faith, hope, and love in what is unseen and eternal rather than what is visible and transient. John Milton gave expression to such spirituality when he wrote of the prospect of triumphing over death and chance and time. Such an idea of God also has consequences for trinitarian theology, for the Father's eternal generation of the Son, which in the Christian Church has usually been taken to mean more than that there was no time when the Son was not.

I
The Issue of Divine Eternity

THIS book aims to provide a sympathetic account and defence of the idea that God exists in a timeless eternity, rejecting the idea that God exists at some or at all times, and to do this as a contribution to the philosophy of the Christian religion.

Such an aim runs up against a number of immediate difficulties. One is the seeming remoteness and scholasticism of the whole area of discussion. But the answer to that can only be provided in the substance of the argument of the whole book, in the way in which it draws attention to the ramified philosophical and theological consequences of either ascribing timelessness to God, or of denying it.

Another difficulty is the charge that the debate about God and his relation to time arises out of an unwarranted use of Greek thought-forms and concepts in the service of Christian theology, and particularly that the idea of timeless eternity comes from Plato or neo-Platonic sources. 'The doctrine of God's timelessness seems to have entered Christian theology from neo-Platonism, and there from Augustine to Aquinas it reigned.'[1] It is claimed that if instead we stick to the biblical data we shall discover that to a man the biblical writers thought of God as being in time. For them God acts and reacts and changes. Hence the debate is not a legitimate Christian theological debate, but represents an attempt by Athens to incorporate Jerusalem.

These claims raise large and complicated issues in the history of ideas already much discussed from many angles. To follow them up would require encyclopaedic resources. Nevertheless the charge ought to be taken seriously in a work such as this. And so this opening chapter offers two general

[1] Richard Swinburne, *The Coherence of Theism*, 217.

arguments which, if convincing, will enable us to ignore the results of the debate regarding Greek influence upon biblical ideas whatever those results turn out to be. If these two arguments succeed they will together answer the question of why timeless eternity is worth arguing about.

The first argument is that there is nothing unbiblical about the idea of a timeless God and therefore no reason why a timeless God should not be an element in Christian theology. But even if this argument succeeds, it does nothing to show why the idea of an eternal God is worth pursuing. So it is necessary to consider a second argument which has to do with the reasons for insisting that God is timelessly eternal.

First, then, the argument about the biblical data. It may be alleged that almost any ascription of an action to God, and the Bible is full of such ascriptions, indicates that God is in time. God speaks (Genesis 12: 1), he redeems and judges (Exodus 13: 3, 12: 29), and, most significant of all, he responds to human action or inaction by action of his own. Actions are events, they are datable, they take time, and so God is portrayed as being an agent in time. And since no individual can both be in time and outside time, and God is in time, he cannot exist timelessly, not, at least, if we are to remain faithful to the biblical portrayal of him.

But may not such representations of God be anthropomorphic (or anthropochronic) in order to render his relations to his creation more intelligible to us? For it is agreed that there are anthropomorphisms in the Bible. God does not have ears, or a mouth; indeed he does not have a face, or feet, or a body of any kind. But anthropomorphism must stop somewhere, and while it is patent that God cannot have an ear, otherwise he would have to have a body and to occupy finite space and so be finite, it is not so obvious that he cannot be a spirit in time who represents himself, for vividness and convenience, as having a body. References to God being in space are anthropomorphic while references to him being in time are, apparently, not anthropomorphic. Is there prejudice here? Certainly not all statements about God can be anthropomorphic, for this would result in an obvious form of reductionism. But what, if we are to take the language of Scripture about God seriously, is to prevent such reductionism? Perhaps God is only an enlarged and magnified human being. Surely some argument is needed to show why God may be in time but not in space, and why he may have passions and a memory but lack feet and a heart.

And what about those biblical data which appear to ascribe timelessness to God? 'Before the mountains were brought forth, or ever thou hadst formed the earth and the world, even from everlasting to everlasting, thou art God.'[2] Is this not a fair representation of the idea that God timelessly *is*, that he exists timelessly while the creation he brings forth is subject to time and change?

To this it is possible to imagine two sorts of reply. The first would be to say that the language of the psalm is a piece of poetic licence, understandable hyperbole, but hyperbole nonetheless. What the Hebrew poet is doing is drawing attention to a contrast between the stability of the creator and the instability of the creation, but nothing more than that. Alternatively it could be retorted that the poet is not teaching the doctrine of divine timelessness, because he says that God existed *before* the mountains were brought forth, at a time before the time the mountains were created. So God is in time.

So even expressions which seem prima facie to sanction timelessness cannot be regarded as conclusively doing so. And those, such as Augustine, say, or Calvin, who do argue that Psalm 90 implies timelessness can be dismissed on the grounds that they are influenced by Greek learning and are (no doubt unwittingly) importing their presuppositions into the exegesis of the text.

This comment is based upon the assumption that the developed concept of timelessness is a Greek idea, stemming from Plato and the neo-Platonists, which entered Christian

---

[2] Ps. 90: 2. Other biblical texts which could be cited are Mal. 3: 6, John 8: 58, Jas. 1: 17.

theology probably via Origen (*c.* 185–254), Augustine (354–430), and Boethius (*c.* 480–524).[3] If this is so then it follows that the New Testament writings (with the possible exception of the Gospel according to St John) are not influenced by such ideas, and *a fortiori* nor are the Old Testament writings.

But what does this absence of influence mean? It means, at the least, that the biblical writers did not take over and use the Greek idea of timelessness. Yet this does not imply that they could not have turned over the idea in their minds as an abstract possibility (one not received from the Greeks) and rejected it. Did they turn over this abstract possibility in their minds and accept it? Again, there is no evidence of such acceptance of the concept of timelessness arrived at independently from Greek influences and accepted by the biblical writers. But if there is no evidence of either the acceptance or rejection of the abstract idea of timelessness then what this allows one to infer is not that the biblical writers *rejected* the idea of timeless eternity but that they neither rejected nor accepted it and that the idea of timeless eternity may be consistent with what they did accept.

This conclusion may be reinforced by a number of other considerations about the contexts and procedures of the various biblical writers, to which James Barr has drawn attention, considerations which make it hazardous to draw definite metaphysical conclusions from their writings.[4] Barr gives great prominence to the point that it is implausible to use biblical words for time as the chief or exclusive basis for the forming of a biblical doctrine of time or of anything else. Focusing upon words, and particularly upon the etymology of words, should in his view give way to the consideration of the use to which the words are put and to the force of whole contexts. However, this point, in many ways the main thesis of Barr's book, is not relevant here, for someone who wished

---

[3] For a superb philosophical survey of ancient concepts of time see Richard Sorabji, *Time, Creation and the Continuum.*

[4] *Biblical Words for Time.*

to hold that the Bible writers taught or held or implied that God was in time might well concede this point of methodology and allow Barr's claim that translation is one important way of neutralizing etymology while preserving meaning.[5]

Barr draws attention in his book to two other matters, to which he gives less prominence than to the point just mentioned, but which are of more significance to us. The first is the need for the presence in a document of what he calls 'reflective contexts' in order to determine that the expressions used are metaphysically or doctrinally significant. By a reflective context Barr means a second-order context, one in which a matter is considered in an abstract or quite general way. He claims that with the possible exception of the book of Ecclesiastes such reflective contexts are notably absent from the Bible.

The appearance of a Hebrew word for 'time' in a context of this reflective type should constitute *prima facie* grounds for supposing that this word could be used of time in general. The non-appearance of the word in such contexts does not however prove the reverse; for it may only mean that such contexts are not found in Hebrew, that is to say, that no such reflection about 'time' in general was in fact entered upon within the extant texts, and does not thereby prove that words existing for 'time' in particular senses could not be used in such contexts, or that the non-existence of a word that could be so used is a reason why such contexts are not found.[6]

What matters for the construction of a 'view' or a 'doctrine' of something as metaphysical as time is not the occurrence of certain words, but the occurrence of reflective contexts in which appropriate concepts are considered. Barr claims that there is a

very serious shortage within the Bible of the kind of *actual statement* about 'time' or 'eternity' which could form a sufficient basis for a

[5] Ibid. 115.
[6] Ibid. 98.

Christian philosophical-theological view of time. It is the lack of actual statements about what time is like, more than anything else, that has forced exegetes into trying to get a view of time out of the *words* themselves.[7]

In the Bible there are no definitions of time. In contrast to, say, Philo or Plutarch or Plotinus no biblical writer says what time is not. While there are conceptual contrasts in abundance, in for example the writings of Paul, there are no conceptual contrasts there or elsewhere about time. So it is impossible, Barr avers, to contrast Hebrew thought with Greek (and by 'Greek' is usually meant Plato). And in any case the implied contrast between two kinds of thought may be a false assumption *ab initio*. Thus.

Perhaps Philo (*op. mund* 26) was in part inspired by Greek philosophy in his interpretation here (Philo interprets Genesis as the beginning of time), but even so it is an aspect of Greek thought which seemed to him to offer a reasonable account of the text before him, and which probably seemed sound to his Jewish contemporaries.[8]

These considerations provide strong arguments for the modest conclusion that in much if not most of the Bible the contexts do not provide data from which it is possible to construct a metaphysical view about God's relation to time. To provide such a doctrine a less direct method will have to be employed.

Another kind of example may make this clearer. Did the biblical writers accept or reject a geocentric view of the universe? If it can be shown that they rejected it, then a geocentric account of the universe is inconsistent with what the biblical writers teach. If it can be shown that they accepted it, then it forms part of their teaching, or at least part of the background to their teaching. But if it can be shown that they neither accepted nor rejected it then we must conclude that with respect to whether or not the universe is

[7] Ibid. 131–2.
[8] Ibid. 75. The sentence in brackets added by P.H.

geocentric their writings leave this an open question. What this state of affairs may reflect is a phenomenon which is quite intelligible and plausible, namely that with respect to very many developed theories in the empirical sciences and in philosophy the biblical writings are underdetermined, and given that there is no evidence that the biblical writers began to discuss many of these questions this is precisely what one ought to expect. To say this is not to suppose that the biblical writers were less intelligent or sophisticated than later thinkers, only that the matter in question had never come up for explicit discussion and consideration, or that it fell outside their interests.

To illustrate this point about method further with a different theological instance we may briefly consider the procedure adopted by James Dunn in his book *Christology in the Making*. Dunn investigates the question of where if anywhere in the New Testament the writers teach a developed Christology, a doctrine according to which the earthly Jesus Christ had a heavenly existence before his birth. How far do the biblical writers develop and teach the Christian doctrine of the Incarnation in recognizable outline form?

Dunn considers the question of what evidence would or ought to satisfy an enquirer that the New Testament writers taught the pre-existence of Jesus Christ. His answer, in brief, is that only the 'became flesh' terminology of the first chapter of St John's Gospel amounts to the *teaching* of the Incarnation by a New Testament writer. 'The Logos *became* flesh—not merely entered into, clothed himself with . . . not merely appeared as . . . but became flesh. Here we have an explicit statement of *incarnation,* the first, and indeed only such statement in the New Testament.'[9] For here, though the idea of Christ's pre-existence is not stated in so many words, it is strongly implied, in the sense that these words appear logically to entail the doctrine of the Incarnation (though not

---

[9] *Christology in the Making*, 240–1.

every developed form of that doctrine) and also that the doctrine of the Incarnation logically entails John's statement.

The strength of the requirement which Dunn implies as being necessary for any New Testament writer to be said to teach the Incarnation is very striking. It is possible to think of plausible requirements of less stringency. One alternative requirement would be that a New Testament writer unambiguously suggests the doctrine, or that there is a preponderance of evidence in the New Testament in favour of it (though also some evidence against it). Yet another alternative would be an appeal to presupposition or presumption by enquiring how certain things could be said about Jesus Christ unless it was believed that he was pre-existent as God. For example, how could all things have their 'focal point' in Jesus without him being regarded as divine? How could Jesus now be Lord without being pre-existently God? How could a writer such as Paul say that all divine fullness dwells in Jesus without presupposing Jesus' Godhood and hence his pre-existence? Yet it appears that nothing less than explicit mutual logical entailment provides a satisfactory standard of evidence for Dunn.

Yet from another angle perhaps Dunn's requirements, though stringent, are not stringent enough. In coming to his conclusion that only the 'became flesh' of the New Testament expressions actually amount to a *teaching* of the Incarnation, Dunn uses a number of arguments against the evidential value of certain other New Testament expressions. Five of these arguments figure prominently in his work. The first is that an expression such as 'son of man' may not need to be taken literally but as a piece of poetic imagery or speech mannerism. The second is that in order for an idea such as that of ideal pre-existence to be properly understood it must be seen in the context of the thought-world of which it is a part, and when it is seen in this light its evidential value for the Incarnation diminishes or disappears. A third argument, already touched upon, draws attention to the lack of explicitness of the candidate statement, say the statement that

Christ is the Wisdom of God, particularly with regard to what is being denied, implicitly or explicitly, by what is asserted in that expression. A fourth argument is the adoption of an essentially reductive appeal to the origins of certain expressions such as 'wisdom' and thus a minimizing of the prima-facie force or value of the more developed expressions. The fifth is the provision of an alternative exegesis of the passage than that which has been traditionally assumed.

By at least some of these five arguments it might be possible to mount an *ad hominem* case against Dunn's conclusion that only in John 1 is anything like a doctrine of the Incarnation taught. For perhaps Dunn's arguments would exclude *any* doctrinal formulations from the New Testament. Thus he claims that another plausible candidate passage teaching the Incarnation, Colossians 1: 15, is in fact not plausible because 'embodiment' is a metaphorical expression and not to be regarded as referring to a literal embodiment. But if this is allowed, why cannot it be similarly argued that the 'became' of John's 'the word became flesh' is also a metaphorical or at least a non-literal expression, an expression not sufficiently strong to bear the metaphysical weight placed upon it? For such a statement as 'the word became flesh' is, to say the least, somewhat metaphysically opaque. And why cannot a similar argument be offered in the case of any theological formulation which appeals to the New Testament? On this view Dunn's requirement, the standard that has to be met if any New Testament text is to be regarded as teaching the Incarnation, though stringent, is not stringent enough.

Why is it not stringent enough? It is now possible to see that the issue before us is not that of providing evidence, more and better evidence, but that it is a conceptual question. For perhaps the very idea of a 'doctrinal formulation' and the question of whether some document such as the New Testament teaches a particular doctrinal formulation is not a matter of what the words and sentences of the document imply as of there being an appropriate intellectual context in which these matters are considered. The question ought then to be not, as with Dunn, is there enough evidence for the Incarnation in the New Testament, but is there evidence that the New Testament provides an appropriate intellectual context in which one might expect the doctrine of the Incarnation to be taught? The pertinence of this question can be highlighted by a comment Dunn makes on the Johannine writings. Recognizing that in these writings the divine sonship of Jesus is grounded in his pre-existence Dunn comments: 'This does not necessarily mean of course that with one bound we have reached the language and thought forms of the later creeds. We have not yet reached the concept of an ontological union between Father and Son, of a oneness of essence and substance.'[10]

What this comment fails to recognize is that concepts cannot simply be added as numbers are added, but that introducing such concepts is part and parcel of the development of a certain kind of context. Evidence for such a context would be, perhaps, the presence of a certain self-consciousness, or an appropriate level of debate, one in which certain possibilities are unambiguously excluded. The very idea of a doctrinal formulation, or at least a doctrinal formulation which involves metaphysics, is something that could not occur in a context in which there were not the conditions for such a debate. On such a view any controversy that called for the introduction of concepts such as *person, substance, unity, beginning, time,* could not be thought of as being carried on in the New Testament but had to await the importing of these concepts into the debate. And perhaps the fairest thing to conclude about the developed doctrine of the Incarnation is not that the New Testament teaches it, or that the New Testament does not teach it, but that considered as a technical theological term of art, the New Testament provides only the raw data for such a doctrine, or at most the first rough formulations of it. The very nature of any doctrine is that it

[10] Ibid. 58.

generalizes over the data, deliberately excluding certain formulations.

Where does this leave the issue of timelessness? There are two alternative ways in which the Bible might lend support to the idea of divine timelessness. The first is that the Bible teaches it. If it teaches it then the necessary scriptural warrant is provided. The second is that it does not teach it, but that it teaches many things which make the idea of timelessness a reasonable theological concept to employ, given these data, when certain controversial questions which the biblical writers did not themselves raise have arisen over the question. It will henceforth be assumed that there are biblical data of a non-technical kind which can reasonably be understood as countenancing timelessness and that a satisfactory explanation can be provided of data which appear to go the other way.

If this is the position regarding the scriptural data, that they are underdetermined when judged from a theoretical and reflective point of view, what then constitutes an appropriate context in which the question of whether or not God is timelessly eternal might be raised and the claim that he is timelessly eternal be asserted? This brings us to consider the *second* of the questions listed above, the reason or reasons for insisting that God is timelessly eternal.

In *God and Timelessness* Nelson Pike pays considerable attention to the justification of the doctrine of timelessness as he finds this set out in Anselm. Anselm argued that timelessness is among the greatness-making or perfection-making properties of God, that property which, if anything lacked it, that thing could not be a being than which no greater can be conceived; not the greatest being that there in fact is, but the greatest of all possible beings. How is this idea of a greatness-making property to be understood? The first way that Pike offers of understanding it is as a value-making property.[11] In trying to discover whether or not a property

---

[11] *God and Timelessness*, 137.

is value-making we must try to discover whether, other things being equal, a thing that has the property in question is more valuable than that thing without it, where by a 'thing' is not meant something of a particular kind or type, say a dish or a metal object, but a thing understood in a totally abstract and unqualified way. Thus suppose that we just knew that there was an object in a room, without knowing anything about what sort of an object it was. Then to suppose that the object was, say, conscious, is to suppose that it was greater, as an object, than another object that was not conscious, where by greater is meant 'better' and by 'better' is meant 'more worthy of preservation'. To suppose that God is a being which is more worthy of preservation than any possible being would be to suppose that, for example, God is a person, and that he is benevolent, merciful, and just,[12] since all these are value-making properties or characteristics the possession of which is a reason for preserving the object which has them.

So far so good. Pike then proceeds to apply this same procedure to other divine attributes such as omnipotence and immutability.[13] He allows that though a situation in which there was a powerful, benevolent individual might be a better situation than one in which there was not, because such an individual was capable of doing greater good, or of benefiting us, it is nevertheless implausible to argue that such an omnipotent individual was better *as an individual* than someone who was not powerful and benevolent. So Pike concludes that this procedure, which he regards as uncovering the essence of Anselm's justification, does not yield the traditional concept of God, as Anselm claims. Pike does not explicitly include the property of timelessness, since he regards this procedure as basically a 'practice' and one that has no serious prospect of being successful.

As part of his discussion Pike distinguishes between a *situation* in which there is a powerful and good person and a *being* who is powerful and good. He says, in effect, that the

12 Ibid. 145.
13 Ibid. 146.

fact that a situation in which there is a powerful and good person is a better situation than one in which there is not is not to say that a powerful and good person is a better being or person than one who is not. It is this contrast which repays investigation.

Pike says:

Of course, this is not to say that it might not be better (in some sense) if there existed an intelligent, benevolent, just, etc., person who is powerful rather than an intelligent, benevolent, just, etc., person who is not-powerful. Greater good would probably result in the first case than in the second. The first situation would be a better *situation* than the second. But this does not show that a being who is an intelligent, benevolent, just, etc., person would be a better *being* (or even a better person) if it were powerful rather than not-powerful. It would be better for the people of Utah if a man who is intelligent, benevolent, just, etc., were made governor of Utah rather than being allowed to function in a capacity in which he has no influence on public policy. But this does not show that the man who is intelligent, benevolent, just, etc., would be a better individual if he were made governor of Utah than he would be if he were allowed to function in a non-influential position.[14]

There are a number of ways in which one might attempt to speak of one individual as being a better being than another. The most abstract of these is the sense in which one can think of one individual apart from all other individuals, objects, and relations. But in such a situation it makes little sense to ask whether such an individual is better than another if we are not allowed to ask better *for* what, or better *than* what. The phrase 'better than' looks as though it can operate only against some scale of values, but what could these values be if the individual is unrelated to any policy or principles? How can the relative term 'better than' apply to an individual who is unrelated to any other? The difficulty of operating with 'better than' at this level of abstraction casts doubt on Pike's whole procedure and perhaps on Anselm's as well.

[14] Ibid. 146–7.

Another possible approach is to think in terms of personal development, and to ask whether a person who at a time is, say, an intelligent and powerful person, is likely at a later time to be a better person than one who at the earlier time is intelligent but less powerful. This would lead us, in turn, to ask about what the chances are of the individual, in view of his power, being perverted or corrupted in character, and whether the chances of corruption as against the chances of moral growth and maturity are greater for that individual than for an individual who is in other respects the same but who is less powerful. It is this sense that Pike appears to touch on at the end of the quotation given above. But such an investigation seems to be both impossible to carry out without knowing a lot more facts than the example provides, and also irrelevant to the question at issue, which is not how an individual will or might develop but about whether an individual is or is not a better individual if he has certain properties than if he lacks some or all of them.

There is a final sense in which it is possible for one individual to be better than another, and that is to relate the possession or absence of properties to performance, or possible performance, to the possession of certain capacities. If one grants, as Pike grants in his 'practice' argument, that benevolence, mercy, and so forth are value-making, this can only be because possession of such properties implies the possession of certain capacities. Being merciful implies the capacity of acting mercifully, and similarly with benevolence, justice, and the other properties mentioned by Pike. If the possession of such properties is not related to capacities, to the actual or possible exercise of the properties in question, then it is hard to know what ascribing or denying such properties to individuals amounts to.

If this is accepted then to say that being merciful is value-making is to say that the capacity of exercising mercy is a valuable capacity, that an individual who has that capacity is to be preferred to one who does not have it. This comparison is non-abstract to the extent that possession of the property is logically tied to certain identifiable situations which require or call for the exercise of mercy.

Given all this, it now seems·plainly false to say that an individual who is merciful, who has the capacity to exercise mercy in situations which call for it, would not be more valuable if that individual was also powerful and so would brook no opposition to the appropriate exercise of mercy. Given that mercy is a valuable capacity or disposition, being able to exercise mercy unhindered is also, so it would seem, a capacity that is valuable.

But what about timelessness? At first the suggestion that an individual who is timelessly merciful may be thought to be more valuable than an individual who was merciful but in time seems ludicrous. How can value and timelessness be connected? The brief answer is only via other concepts which only timelessness may entail, such as changelessness, the logical impossibility of growing tired or old or bored, or omniscience. Whether timelessness *is* connected with these other concepts and so with questions of value is something to be explored later.

So there is more to Pike's imaginative procedure, his rational reconstruction of what he takes to be Anselm's argument, than Pike himself reckons. This procedure can go a considerable distance in arguing that many of the classical attributes of God are value-making or great-making proper-ties. But this procedure does not go all the way, or at least I have not shown yet that it goes all the way, particularly with the crucial concept of timelessness.

What of Pike's second argument, the one to which he attaches considerably more importance? According to it God is a being than which no greater can be conceived because he is supremely worshipful.[15] Pike argues, in brief, that while this rendering of what Anselm meant or may have meant provides a number of the attributes traditionally associated with God, such as consciousness, power, and knowledge, it

---

[15] Ibid. 154.

will not yield the remaining attributes. To suppose, for example, that this procedure justifies benevolence is to forget that it is possible to worship a being who is malevolent, as in devil-worship.[16] What must be said, according to Pike, is that at best a being's benevolence provides a reason for its being worshipful, it is not logically required by worshipfulness. Could timelessness be included in this list? Pike plausibly replies that worship does not logically require timelessness[17] and professes himself unable to answer whether or not timelessness renders an object admirable, supposing admirability to be an aspect of worshipfulness. As final suggestions, Pike counters the idea that timelessness may be a holy-making feature of objects by repeating the argument about situations discussed earlier and by registering doubts about accounting for the worshipfulness of timelessness by tying it to immutability.[18]

Philosophers and theologians who have been keen to insist upon God's timelessness may have done so for two separate reasons. The first is because of what timelessness is thought to entail, because, for example, it entails immutability. Whether or not it does entail or is entailed by immutability, and what the significance of this is, will be considered later. The second reason why timelessness may be thought to be important is because it modifies the other predicates applied to God, predicates which it may not entail. Thus while *x is timeless* might entail and be entailed by *x is immutable*, *x is timeless* does not entail *x is wise*; nevertheless *x*'s timelessness may significantly modify *x*'s wisdom, not by making it less than or more than wisdom, but by saying something about how the wisdom is possessed.

Suppose, for illustration, that a certain radio signal is intermittent. We might then say that intermittence is a property of the signal, along with all its other properties, say properties of tone, or melody, or of whether it contained the sound of a human voice, and so forth. It might be that the signal is of four notes, loud and intermittent, yet its intermittence does not modify the qualities of the four notes as their loudness does; rather what its being intermittent means is that there are times when the signal is not being transmitted.

It is more appropriate to think of timelessness in this way. To say that an individual exists timelessly is to say that its properties are exemplified by that individual in a certain manner. Because the individual is timeless it is invalid to draw certain inferences about its wisdom and valid to draw certain other inferences; inferences about change, commencement, decay, growth, interruption, and the like. So that it is better to think of timelessness not as a separate attribute but as a mode of possessing attributes. It is not that God is both omniscient and timeless but that he is timelessly omniscient. And it may be that to be timelessly omniscient modifies omniscience at least to the extent of saying that there are ways of representing all that a timeless being knows which are open to those who are in time which are not open to him, and vice versa.

To the extent that these criticisms of Pike are cogent they amount to a partial endorsement of Anselm's position. But by itself such a defence hardly amounts to a justification for the introduction of timelessness in Christian theology. It will now be argued that such a justification can be found in the need to draw a proper distinction between the creator and the creature.

It is sometimes said that only a changeless being could be the cause of all things, and only a timeless being could be changeless. The cause of all things that change cannot itself change, it is said. But if this claim is not to be merely analytic there seems to be no reason why the cause of the universe should not itself change. Such a cause could not be subject to change, be *changed*, but there seems to be no reason why it could not change of its own volition. The argument that is given against this is that only particular things could change and God is not a particular thing. But this does not seem plausible. God is not a particular spatio-temporal thing, perhaps, yet he has some of the features of particular things. For instance he can be referred to by definite descriptions, and he is an agent. So this argument does not seem to be a very convincing one.[19]

Anselm considers another aspect of God's creatorhood. He claims that it is a mistake to think

that some spatial or temporal restriction confines the Creative and Supreme Substance, which must be different from, and free from, the nature and the law of all things which it created from nothing. . . . How is it not also a mark of shameless ignorance to say that space delimits the greatness (*quantitatem*)—or that time measures the duration—of the Supreme Truth, which does not at all undergo increase or decrease of spatial or temporal extension?[20]

Calvin also, in a more informal way, links timelessness with creatorhood. Commenting on Psalm 90 he writes:

God is here contrasted with created beings, who, as all know, are subject to continual changes, so that there is nothing stable under heaven. As, in a particular manner, nothing is fuller of vicissitude than human life, that men may not judge of the nature of God by their own fleeting condition, he is here placed in a state of settled and undisturbed tranquility. Thus the everlastingness of which Moses speaks is to be referred not only to the essence of God, but also to his providence, by which the governs the world. . . .[21]

Anselm again:

Nor does it (the Supreme Being) exist in the fleeting temporal present which we experience, nor did it exist in the past, nor will it exist in the future. For these are distinguishing properties of finite and mutual things; but it is neither finite nor mutable.[22]

[19] For a justification of timelessness along these lines see Brian Davies, *An Introduction to the Philosophy of Religion*, 80.

[20] Anselm, *Monologion*, in *Anselm of Canterbury*, vol. i, ed. and trans. Jasper Hopkins and Herbert Richardson, 36.

[21] John Calvin, *Commentary on the Psalms*, ad. loc. Compare Aquinas, 'God, however, brought into being both the creature and time together' (*Summa contra Gentiles*, 2. 35. 6).

[22] Anselm, *Monologion*, 38.

Of course neither Anselm nor Calvin are making the absurd claim that whatever is created has no property in common with the creator. They are saying that there are certain properties which the creator and his creatures do not and cannot have in common. Or perhaps, in view of the earlier discussion, what they are saying might be better expressed as: the properties which the creator and his creatures have in common are distinguished by their mode of possession. Can this conviction of Anselm's and Calvin's be expressed more precisely? Perhaps it can be expressed in a pair of arguments:

(1) Whatever is created is finite.
(2) Whatever is finite is mutable.
(3) Whatever is mutable is in time. Therefore,
(4) Whatever is created is in time.

and

(5) Whatever is the creator is infinite.
(6) Whatever is infinite is immutable.
(7) Whatever is immutable is outside time. Therefore,
(8) Whatever is the creator is outside time.

These arguments, which are clearly valid, have as their respective first premisses two principles drawn from Christian theology, that the creator is an infinite spirit, and that divine creation is creation *ex nihilo*. For if the creator were finite he would depend upon something else and hence would not be the creator. And if creation were not *ex nihilo* it would have to be out of existing stuff, and that stuff would be everlasting and hence the creator would not be the creator of everything.

The immutability in question might be expressed as follows. An individual is immutable in the required sense if no temporal or spatial changes apply to that thing, not even temporal or spatial 'merely Cambridge' changes.[23] A real temporal change occurs when the duration of an object is

---

[23] By a 'merely Cambridge' change is meant a change expressed by '$F(x)$' at time t true and '$F(x)$' at time t false. For discussion see Peter Geach, *God and the Soul*, 71–2.

extended, its life prolonged, just as a real spatial change occurs when an object comes into fresh spatial relations with other things. The only way in which new temporal changes occur is when one or other of the individuals in the relation begins to exist, since otherwise, given a unified spatio-temporal framework, everything that exists in that framework is in fixed temporal relations with everything else. This is one way of saying that time is uni-directional and uni-dimensional whereas space is multi-directional and dimensional. The creator is immutable to the extent that he does not have even 'merely Cambridge' temporal and spatial relations with any other subtances much less real changes. There is nothing that is at any time some distance in time from the creator or in space at any distance in space. For instance, there is no situation in which the death of Napoleon is temporally nearer, or farther, from the immutable creator, whereas the death of Napoleon is farther and farther away in time from us as each of us progresses through time. The coherence of such claims will be discussed more fully in the next chapter and subsequently.

So one justification for ascribing timelessness to God is due to the need to ascribe immutability to him. But why cannot the creator be mutable? Why is it wrong or in some respects improper to ascribe to God temporal or spatial change? Presumably because it is thought to be logically impossible for God to change in these respects and consistently be God, that is to possess those properties and fulfil those roles which according to Christians God essentially has. Whether this is so is to be explored more thoroughly in the central chapters of the book.

So timelessness can be regarded as that property or mode of possessing properties which is such that it will ensure that property of immutability that is necessary for explicating the creator–creature distinction as this is understood in Christian theology.

Earlier the question was raised of whether the idea of divine timelessness was to be found in Scripture, and whether, if it could not be, or if it is doubtful whether or not it could be, there was any justification for introducing it. Might not introducing it not clarify biblical thought but actually succeed in imputing to God properties or modes of possessing properties which the Bible expressly excludes? The present discussion of the justification of timelessness and of the alleged connection between immutability and timelessness enables us to gain a different perspective on this earlier discussion.

The introduction of timelessness offers a metaphysical underpinning for God's functioning as the biblical God. Earlier, in discussing Pike's comments on Anselm, a mild protest was made at the excessive level of abstraction at which the justification of timelessness was conducted, at the way in which Pike (and Anselm?) thought it proper to discuss certain properties in abstraction from other properties and to ask, *in vacuo*, whether these properties were perfection-making or greatness-making or worshipful properties. There is, not surprisingly, great difficulty in providing a convincing or sensible answer to this question, given its level of abstraction.

The language of Scripture about God is far from abstract. According to the Bible God creates, judges, delivers, and redeems; he speaks, sustains, predicts, and assures. And the question may reasonably be asked: what has to be true for it to be possible for an individual to do all these things? What mode of existence must an individual have who is able to do all these things? This question moves the discussion away from the abstract consideration of perfection or worshipfulness to the consideration of a God who (Christians believe) has acted in certain definite ways, and has promised to act in still other ways. Supposing that all such scriptural assertions about God are, when properly interpreted, true, or that they are prima facie true, the question arises as to how, from a conceptual and metaphysical point of view, they can all be true together.

The outline answer to this question is: only a God who is

immutable in a particularly strong sense can (logically) perform all that Scripture claims that God performs, and a God can only be immutable in this strong sense if he exists timelessly. So if these scriptural claims are true God exists timelessly. It is the coherence of this metaphysical underpinning which is defended in what follows.

Such a proposal has one final advantage. It enables us effectively to sever Christian theological construction from the bugbear of discussing whether a certain concept used in such construction work is or is not a concept derived from Greek philosophy. On the proposal sketched above it does not matter where the concept comes from. What does matter is not the genetic question but the adequacy question.[24] Even if it is granted that the idea of timelessness is pure Greek invention what matters is whether the thought that God is timeless is a necessary truth-condition of all else that Christians want to say of God, which is certainly not a Greek invention. Thus it no more matters whether timelessness is a concept introduced by the Greeks than it matters (for the viability or otherwise of the idea) that the concept of a shepherd is the product of a pastoral society.

[24] In *The Divine Trinity*, David Brown makes a similar methodological claim, denying the view that unless the biblical writers believed themselves to be teaching the Trinity they could not have been.

2
What is Divine Eternity?

T H E rationale for introducing the possibility that God exists in a timeless eternity lies in the fact that this supposition will enable more sense to be made of what would otherwise be difficult, and so to vindicate an unattenuated Christian theism. It is agreed that the idea of timeless eternity is obscure and not fully graspable, but there is nothing novel in the introduction of a concept such as *electron* or *virus* to make sense of data otherwise unaccountable. Yet it would not be appropriate to introduce the idea of timeless eternity, or more precisely of God's timeless eternity, if that idea is not so much obscure as downright incoherent. For if it is incoherent then although numbers and propositions may be timelessly eternal, God could not be.

This chapter addresses the question of the coherence of the idea of God's timeless eternity.

There is no better place to begin than the celebrated account by Boethius:

That God is eternal, then, is the common judgment of all who live by reason. Let us therefore consider what eternity is, for this makes plain to us both the divine nature and knowledge. Eternity, then, is the complete possession all at once of illimitable life. . . . Therefore, whatever includes and possesses the whole fullness of illimitable life at once and is such that nothing future is absent from it and nothing past has flowed away, this is rightly judged to be eternal, and of this it is necessary both that being in full possession of itself it be always present to itself and that it have the infinity of mobile time present to it.[1]

To say that God is eternal is thus to say that he is not in time.

    [1] Quoted by E. Stump and N. Kretzmann, 'Eternity', *J. of Philosophy* (1981), 430.

There is for him no past and no future. It makes no sense to ask how long God has existed, or to divide up his life into periods of time. He possesses the whole of his life at once: it is not lived successively.

Prima facie, a timelessly eternal God, an individual, has some relations with individuals who are in time. It is the fact of these positive relations which generates the charge that the idea of divine timeless eternity is immediately incoherent. This problem does not arise for other entities that philosophers have sometimes regarded as timeless, such as propositions and numbers, because they are incapable of entering into relations with individuals such as you and me. Propositions can be thought about and argued over, but they cannot think or argue. The only relations (and changes) that they are capable of are, in Geach's terminology, 'merely Cambridge' relations and changes. They can be thought about and so they can 'change' only by now being thought about, and now ignored.

But things are different with an allegedly timeless being such as God, who has intelligence and will. He can not only be thought about, he can think, and the relations into which he enters with his creation appear to be real relations, even though they cannot issue in any changes in God, since (by definition) God is timeless and changeless. The exploration of this asymmetry between the *relata* of the real relations between God and his creatures—they change but he cannot—will be undertaken later. It is sufficient for the present to note that conceptual problems about God's timelessness cannot be sloughed off by saying that God is like a proposition or a number in being timeless.

More than this, not only does God enter into relations with things in time but we must also suppose that he has some concept of time. For instance, he knows what it means for *A* to exist in time, or for it to occur before *B* and *C*. This much seems to be implicit in the idea of creation. To suppose otherwise would lead to insuperable difficulties. It would be to suppose that God created the universe having features which are likewise timeless, and this would mean that God was incapable of creating anything which changes.

It is more debatable whether having this concept of time, the idea of objects existing in a temporal sequence, God also has the concept of temporal indexicals such as 'yesterday', 'ago', 'now', and 'then'. If he is not in time himself these expressions cannot apply to him; *a fortiori* he cannot apply them to himself. But may not God have the idea of a person who understands that, say, his birthday was so many days ago? Does it follow that if God knows what it is like to have had a birthday ten days ago he must be in time? This does not seem plausible. A bachelor may know what it is like to be married. Is this only because bachelors could be married? But even if an understanding of what is involved in individuals in time applying temporal indexicals to themselves is denied to God this may not matter very much because it has been plausibly argued that the use of such indexicals depends on there being a non-indexical concept of time for their proper employment.[2]

Nor is God having the idea of creatures in time at odds with the idea of divine simplicity. This book does not offer a defence of divine simplicity, nor an attack upon it. What divine simplicity means is that God is incapable of being divided into parts, either temporal or spatial, and that though the sense of his various attributes is different, 'God is wise' meaning something different from 'God is good', the reference of these predicates is the same, the one supreme moral nature. While God's being in time rules out this simplicity, God's timeless eternity is a necessary condition of it. But proponents of divine simplicity do not extend that doctrine to the intentional objects of God's mind. The doctrine of divine simplicity is not logically inconsistent with the idea that there is at least one thing which God has created and knows.

So it is quite consistent with the idea of divine timeless

---

[2] See e.g. D. H. Mellor, *Real Time*, ch. 2.

eternity (at least that version of it that will be defended here) that God has the concept of time, and that God has the concept of a multiplicity of individual beings in time even though it is more problematic (though not particularly worrying) whether God has the mastery of temporal indexicals which intelligent individuals in time may employ. We may say, then, that God knows (timelessly) the whole temporal series in rather the way in which for us certain things are known at a glance or in a flash of insight or intuition in which the active recalling of memories or the anticipation of the future plays no part. We may say, then, that God knows *at a glance* the whole of his temporally ordered creation in rather the way in which a crossword clue may be solved in a flash.

Where, then, is the conceptual problem? It may be stated as follows. 'But, on St. Thomas' view, my typing of this paper is simultaneous with the whole of eternity. Again, on this view, the great fire of Rome is simultaneous with the whole of eternity. Therefore, while I type these very words, Nero fiddles heartlessly on.'[3] and further:

The inner incoherence can be seen as follows. God's timelessness is said to consist in his existing at all moments of human time— simultaneously. Thus he is said to be simultaneously present at (and a witness of) what I did yesterday, what I am doing today, and what I will do tomorrow. But if $t1$ is simultaneous with $t2$ and $t2$ with $t3$, then $t1$ is simultaneous with $t3$. So if the instant at which God knows these things were simultaneous with both yesterday, today and tomorrow, then these days would be simultaneous with each other. So yesterday would be the same day as today and as tomorrow—which is clearly nonsense.[4]

As indeed it is.

How can this 'inner incoherence' as Swinburne calls it, be met? The obvious way to avoid it is by placing restrictions upon the idea of simultaneity so that it is not transitive in

[3] Anthony Kenny, *The God of the Philosophers*, 38–9.
[4] Swinburne, *Coherence of Theism*, 220–1.

certain contexts. But there may be another way of meeting the difficulty. Why cannot the use of simultaneity in expressing the relation between the timeless God and individuals in time be abandoned altogether? For the concept of simultaneity is obviously one which implies time. If *A* and *B* are simultaneous they exist or occur at the same time. But God is time*less*. Suppose that there exists (timelessly) a set of propositions expressing the history of some event which is of the form '*A* at *t1* and then *B* at *t2*'. The occurrence of *A* is at a different time from the occurrence of *B*. Why should the question of what the temporal relation is between such a set of propositions and what they say about *A* and *B* ever be raised? It could be raised about the inscribing of the sentences, which is an event, but surely not about the inscription with a fixed meaning? Call the inscription a record; why does it make any sense to ask whether the record is *simultaneous* with the occurrence of *A* or *B*, and if so whether *A* and *B* must be simultaneous, thus reducing the idea of a timeless record of the events to absurdity? Swinburne objects to timeless eternity because he takes God's timelessness to 'consist in his existing at all moments of human time—simultaneously'.[5] But it is far from clear that this follows from Boethius' account, or from any account of timelessness that is attractive. Why cannot divine timelessness consist in a manner of existence which sustains no temporal relations with human time? If God timelessly exists he is neither earlier nor later nor simultaneous with any event of time. He exists time*less*ly.

One objection to this is that it might be supposed that it makes impossible *any* relation between God existing timelessly and his temporal creation. But why? Let us suppose that in creation God brings into being (timelessly) the whole temporal matrix. He knows (timelessly) all about it. In his mind all events are brought together, but they are not brought together at a time, but timelessly. God is time-free.

[5] Ibid. 220.

It is worth looking at a line of thought about timeless eternity which has effectively ruled this out. In their paper on eternity Stump and Kretzmann say:

Although the stipulation that an eternal entity completely possesses its life all at once entails that it is not part of any sequence, it does not rule out the attribution of presentness or simultaneity to the life and relationships of such an entity, nor should it. Insofar as an entity *is*, or *has* life, completely or otherwise, it is appropriate to say that it has present existence in some sense of 'present'; and unless its life consists in only one event or it is impossible to relate an event in its life to any temporal entity or event, we need to be able to consider an eternal entity or event as one of the *relata* in a simultaneity relationship.[6]

This seems to be a very strange line of argumentation. For on the one hand it is averred that the individual who has eternal life is not a part of any sequence; this obviously follows. It is also quite acceptable to say that such a timeless individual has present existence in some sense of 'present', for the same may be said about a number or proposition. But then follow two claims which are much harder to accept.

The first of these supposes that the life of a timeless individual may not consist of only one event. But how could the life of a timeless being *not* consist of only one event, whether by an 'event' one means something that is simple, like the falling of a leaf, or an event that has complex elements, like the Battle of Waterloo? Surely the life of a timeless being must consist of only one event,[7] however ramified the consequences of that event may be in created time. Because for it to consist of more than one event these events would have to be temporally ordered, and this would mean that the supposedly timeless existence of God was in fact a temporally ordered life, albeit a temporal ordering in 'super-time'. So it is hard to see how Stump and Kretzmann

---

[6] 'Eternity', 434.

[7] It could be argued that neither an ontology of events nor of substances is applicable to a timeless being, but even if this is so, it would be of no help to Stump and Kretzmann.

can use this consideration as an argument justifying the introduction of the simultaneity relation in connection with timelessness, for that seems to be equivalent to the abandoning of timelessness *stricto sensu*.

The second argument is that the only way in which the life of a timeless being can be related to a temporal sequence is by means of a simultaneity relationship. Otherwise, Stump and Kretzmann say, 'it is impossible to relate an event in its life to any temporal entity or event'. But is this so? Suppose we say 'God (timelessly) knows that Helm is typing on Thursday 19 November 1987'. The question is, granted that there is a sense of 'present' in which God's knowledge is present as I am typing, is God's knowing really simultaneous with my typing? Why should it be? Why is this particular way of thinking inevitable, and not a trap? Suppose it is denied that God's knowledge is simultaneous with my typing, why should it follow from this that God cannot know that I am typing? What is the argument? Of course the proposition has to be present to the mind of God, that is, God has to know it, but something being present to his mind has not to be confused with God being temporally present with anything.

So the force of the Stump and Kretzmann argument here is not clear, and it seems sufficient simply to deny what they allege and to wait for an argument to be produced to support it. The other matter, the sense in which (despite what has just been said) it may be acceptable to say that God's knowing is present will be discussed in due course.

But let us suppose that for some reason not yet uncovered it is impossible to refrain from allowing, as part of an explication of divine timelessness, that God's timeless life is in some sense simultaneous with the events of our lives, that God's life is simultaneous with my typing today. The problem now is, how can the *reductio* proposed by Kenny and Swinburne be avoided? One way, hinted at already in the above quotation from Stump and Kretzmann, is to distinguish between different kinds of simultaneity—divine simultaneity and human simultaneity, for example. A number of analogies come to mind which indicate that this is quite plausible. Stump and Kretzmann themselves mention different temporal frameworks. From the standpoint of someone watching a train pass lightning may strike it simultaneously at front and rear whereas from the standpoint of someone in the train—supposing that it is moving very fast—the lightning is not simultaneous. Thus to ask whether the flashes of lightning are simultaneous is to ask an insufficiently precise question. The question should be: from *A*'s standpoint are the lightning flashes simultaneous? A similar analogy can be constructed using the distinction between author's time and character's time. A question about when a certain event recorded in a novel happens could be a question about the writing of the event, a question as to when, in the author's life, he came to write down that event, or it could be a question about when in the novel the event occurs. It would not follow that two events that occur simultaneously in the novel were written simultaneously, or conceived simultaneously. And it would not follow that two events in the novel which occur one after the other occurred one after the other in the author's writing. In novel-time, they may be generations apart, but simultaneous in author-time. Thus there is no one, straightforward, unambiguous answer to the question, 'are the two events simultaneous or not?'.

These analogies are imperfect. What they show is that it is sometimes necessary to indulge in talk of different frameworks of reference, different standpoints. The analogies are no more than this, because although it is possible to distinguish the framework of the author from the framework of the character in the play the author still employs time in constructing his novel just as the novel has a temporal sequence in which the events in it unfold. In other words, the analogies indicate how it is possible and natural to talk of two different times, but not how it is possible to talk of the relation between timelessness and time, the timelessness of God's eternity and the time of his creation. The analogies do show, incidentally, how it is possible for an author to have a relation to his work without there being any need, *pace* Stump and Kretzmann, to introduce simultaneity talk. The author is the author of the whole, but it does not make sense to go on to ask whether his writing the play or novel is simultaneous with any of the events in the work. His writing, being in time, is simultaneous with what he writes, but the act of writing is not simultaneous with any of the events that occur in the work, not even if the author writes himself into the novel.

So illustrations such as the author-novel relation, and that provided by different physical frameworks, only serve as analogies and do not suffice to remove the *reductio* charge against the idea of timeless eternity. Although the events in the author's life are not simultaneous with any of the events in the written work, both the life and the narrative of the work are in time, whereas what is needed is an analogy or model in which one of the *relata* is timeless. Nevertheless, as Stump and Kretzmann stress, an analogy is no more than this.

What of their own proposals for avoiding the *reductio*? These involve the introduction of what they call ET-simultaneity, 'a species of simultaneity that can obtain between what is eternal and what is temporal'.[8] ET-simultaneity is characterized as follows:

(ET) for every x and for every y (where 'x' and 'y' range over entities and events), x and y are ET-simultaneous if:

  (i) either x is eternal and y is temporal, or vice versa; and

  (ii) for some observer, A, in the unique eternal frame, x and y are both present—i.e., either x is eternally present and y is observed as temporally present, or vice versa; and

  (iii) for some observer, B, in one of the infinitely many temporal reference frames, x and y are both present—i.e. either x is observed as eternally present and y is temporally present, or vice versa.[9]

---

[8] 'Eternity', 436.
[9] Ibid. 439.

According to Stump and Kretzmann it follows from this definition that any temporal event is ET-simultaneous with any eternal event and vice versa, where the events in question are observed as present by some appropriately placed temporal or eternal observer.

What is crucial about the notion of ET-simultaneity is that according to Stump and Kretzmann it is not transitive. Thus if x is ET-simultaneous with y, and y is ET-simultaneous with z, it does not follow that x is ET-simultaneous with z. This is because the notion of ET-simultaneity only applies or obtains within appropriate frames of reference—there must be an appropriately placed observer. That is, it is crucial to this account that ET-simultaneity applies not to pairs of events but to pairs of events observed either from an eternal standpoint, or from a temporal standpoint, one of the pairs of which is eternal, the other of which is temporal. So that x and y can only be ET-simultaneous by being observed as such by an appropriate observer; hence no event, *qua* event, is ET-simultaneous with any other event.

Nevertheless, although it avoids the *reductio* of the idea of timeless eternity by making the relevant relation not transitive, it does so at a price. It carries difficulties with it that are sufficient to cast doubt on their procedure and to incline us to the alternative account proposed earlier, the account according to which timelessness is time-freeness, and in which nothing time-free is simultaneous in any sense with anything which occurs in time.

What are the difficulties? There is one central obscurity in Stump and Kretzmann's account connected with the idea of an eternal observer observing an event as temporally present, and the corresponding idea of a temporal observer observing an event as eternally present.[10] What could these expressions mean? According to Stump and Kretzmann what they mean is that to an eternal being two temporal events, say Nixon's becoming president and Nixon's dying, are present. Whereas

[10] See Paul Fitzgerald, 'Stump and Kretzmann on Time and Eternity', *J. of Philosophy* (1985).

it is now true that Nixon is alive, and it will be true at some later time that he is dead, to an eternal being Nixon is both alive and dead. But this

cannot be taken to mean that the temporal entity Nixon exists in eternity, where he is simultaneously alive and dead, but rather something more nearly like this. One and the same eternal present is ET-simultaneous with Nixon's being alive and is also ET-simultaneous with Nixon's dying; so Nixon's life is ET-simultaneous with and hence present to an eternal entity, and Nixon's death is ET-simultaneous with and hence present to an eternal entity, although Nixon's life and Nixon's death are themselves neither eternal nor simultaneous.[11]

While this explanation removes the obscurity it does so by merely relocating it. For the solution proposed by Stump and Kretzmann is a purely formal affair. Crucial to it, as we have seen, is the introduction of ET-simultaneity; but while the device of ET-simultaneity 'solves' the alleged *reductio* over timeless eternity, it does so simply by stipulating that the *reductio* will not be allowed rather than by offering an explanation of why it cannot or need not follow. The 'solution' to the problem is found simply by rewording the problem with the help of the device of ET-simultaneity. ET-simultaneity has no independent merit or use, nothing is illuminated or explained by it. Its sole purpose is to avoid the alleged *reductio*, which it does.

For the problem is, how can something which is an event in time be wholly present 'to an eternal entity'? The answer given is that it is ET-wholly present. But this answer is wholly obscure. It is not wholly present as two exactly simultaneous temporal events are wholly present to each other, but wholly present in the sense in which what is eternally existing is wholly present to what is temporally existing. But how can an eternal entity be aware of a temporal entity as present, as Stump and Kretzmann's definition requires? What sort of presentness is the eternal presentness of a temporal entity? And what sort of presentness is it that can have wholly present to it the occurring of two temporally distinct events? Further, it is hard to see how for a temporal observer, two events one of which is temporal and the other eternal can fail to exist at one and the same time in that given observer's temporal reference frame. Surely any event that occurs in a temporal observer's temporal framework is itself temporal?

The introduction of ET-simultaneity, with its attendant difficulties, may only have been possible because Stump and Kretzmann have assumed eternal existence to have (some of the) features of temporal duration, with the idea of an ordered sequence with differently enduring individuals occupying different positions along it.[12] On this view timeless eternity is super-time. The reason for saying that the authors must make such an assumption is because only thus can one make sense of what is crucial to their account, namely an eternal observer observing a temporal event. Put differently, it is only by supposing that eternity has the character of an (endless) duration that there can be an eternal event to be a *relatum* on the eternal side of the ET-simultaneity relation. And at times the authors explicitly commit themselves to the view that eternity has features of a temporal duration.

The eternal, pastless, futureless present is not instantaneous but extended, because eternity entails duration. The temporal present is a durationless instant, a present that cannot be extended conceptually without falling apart entirely into past and future intervals. The eternal present, on the other hand, is by definition an infinitely extended, pastless, futureless duration.[13]

Paul Fitzgerald explicates E-duration in terms of three notions which he regards as revealing the (partial) incoherence of the idea.[14] In the first place he claims that E-duration

[12] Fitzgerald, 'Stump and Kretzmann', 262–3.
[13] 'Eternity', 435.
[14] 'Stump and Kretzmann', 262–3.

is incompatible with divine simplicity (even though he himself does not favour divine simplicity). Stump and Kretzmann claim that E-duration is compatible with it. Even if we suppose that it is, and that divine simplicity ought to be defended, it is certainly not the only view of eternity which is compatible with it, since non-durational views of eternity are equally compatible with it.

Secondly, Fitzgerald claims that events can have a different location in E-duration, but Stump and Kretzmann take the opposite view. In their view everything that has E-duration exists 'all at once', occupying the whole of it. This may be granted, but the consequence of granting it is an attenuation of the claim that timeless eternity is a *bona fide* case of duration. It is a whole that cannot have parts, but what kind of duration is that?

Finally, Fitzgerald claims that any duration (including E-duration) is potentially divisible. Once again Stump and Kretzmann deny this, and this eats away further at the meaning of 'duration'. Yet Stump and Kretzmann claim that denying successiveness to E-duration does not mean abandoning it in favour of non-durational accounts.[15]

But if E-duration is qualified in these ways—if there is a duration which has no successiveness and no divisibility—and yet duration is still affirmed, does this not amount simply to saying that the mode of divine eternity is durational, and nothing more? What is the value of introducing a concept and then so paring it away that hardly anything is left? Indeed, what is left except the bare claim?

What is the philosophical point of claiming, as Stump and Kretzmann do, that E-duration is genuinely durational, that eternity is not to be compared to an unextended point, but that nevertheless eternal duration does not have succession?[16] What is it about eternity that requires its explication in terms of E-duration and not in non-durational terms?

---

[15] 'Atemporal Duration: A Reply to Fitzgerald', *J. of Philosophy* (1987), 219.
[16] 'Eternity', 434.

What is at stake here? In their answer to this question, in reply to Fitzgerald, Stump and Kretzmann claim that eternity is the foundation of temporal existence, and that time-boundedness cannot be a perfect being's mode of existence.[17] This can be readily granted; but why does it follow that in order for this contrast between eternal perfection and temporal imperfection to be maintained a perfect being has to have duration at all, even if it is a temporal duration that is not even conceptually divisible? The answer may be that E-duration is needed because it implies a limitlessness in a way that the idea of eternity does not.

But instantaneousness is not the only alternative, and certainly it is as bad an alternative as E-duration since, if words mean anything, both notions are as time-infected as each other. Rather it is preferable that timeless eternity be explained in terms of time-freeness, where the only questions of simultaneity and non-simultaneity are *quoad nos*, and from which both the notions of duration and instantaneousness are banished.

If ordinary temporal simultaneity generates a *reductio* of the idea of timeless eternity, and the introduction of ET-simultaneity carries with it the difficulties touched upon above, then it is reasonable to conclude that it makes no sense to speak strictly and philosophically of God's eternal existence as being either at the same time as or at a different time from the existence of some temporal event or state. God's eternal existence has no temporal relations whatever to any particular thing which he creates. This does not mean that there are no relations at all between the eternal God and his creation, only no temporal relations. There is, for example, the relation of knowledge. God knows his creatures. This knowledge is time-free; it is not, for example, foreknowledge, or memory, nor is it contemporaneous knowledge. It is knowledge about which it makes no sense to ask how long the knower has known, or when he came to

---

[17] 'Atemporal Duration: A Reply to Fitzgerald', 218.

know. Thus to attempt to raise, in a strict and philosophical manner, questions about the simultaneity and non-simultaneity of the divine will and human wills (for example) is to be guilty of a category mistake. It is like asking for the physical dimensions of a thought. The eternally timeless God is not the sort of individual that can have temporal relations with anything distinct from him. Thus to suppose that what God perfectly knows is (in some philosophically significant sense) temporally present to him is to suppose what is both otiose and misleading. The creation is not temporally present to God in his knowing it, nor is it distant. God knows, and that is all.

What then are we to say about the theologians' talk of foreknowledge, of an eternal duration, of the claim that God knows now, that God remembers, and the like? Following Fitzgerald it is plausible to suppose that such expressions are the proper and inevitable expressions of someone in time who wishes to speak of his relation to a timeless being. It makes sense to say that God endures all through my life and the history of the universe, but this does not mean that God has the property of eternal duration, or duration of some other kind. Rather it means that as regards individuals in time it makes no sense to say, at any time in their lives, that God does not exist. But to license such expressions is not to imply that God exists in time. A full examination of the idea of foreknowledge in this light will be undertaken in Chapter 6 in connection with the idea of foreknowledge and human freedom.

So far in this chapter an account of timelessness has been offered which consists largely of *ad hominem* rebuttals and qualifications of others' strictures on the concept. But there is a more positive argument that can be offered. It might be argued that if God's existence in time requires the occurrence of time before the creation of the universe then this would, by a *reductio*, lead to an overturning of the idea that God is in time. For the idea that God exists in an infinitely backward extending time runs up against the idea of an actual infinite.[18] For such a prospect requires that an infinite number of events must have elapsed before the present moment could arrive. And since it is impossible for an infinite number of events to have elapsed, and yet the present moment has arrived, the series of events cannot be infinite. Therefore, either there was a time when God began to exist, which is impossible, or God exists timelessly. Therefore, God exists timelessly.

To this argument the following reply might be made. Those who argue for God's existence in time before the creation of the universe require only that the time before the creation is undifferentiated. Thus there is a difference between the claim that infinite time existed before the creation and the claim that an infinite series of events existed before the creation. And it is only the second claim that generates problems over the actual infinite.[19]

But this reply overlooks the fact that one of the prime reasons for maintaining that God is in time is that only such a conception makes it possible to suppose that God has life. A timelessly existing God or, presumably, a God who existed in undifferentiated time, time without events, would be, in Swinburne's words, 'a very lifeless thing'.[20] The full implications of what such divine life in undifferentiated time means are not clear, but presumably one thing that it must mean is that there is a succession of thoughts in the divine mind, a mental life. But if this is so then time could not be undifferentiated before the creation but would be marked by a series of mental events in the divine mind. But then if so either God exists in a timeless eternity or he exists in time with a 'life' which is differentiated by events. But this latter idea is ruled out by the arguments for the

[18] For a defence of this impossibility see Pamela M. Huby, 'Kant or Cantor? That the Universe, if Real, must be finite in both Space and Time', *Philosophy* (1971), and William Lane Craig, *The Kalam Cosmological Argument*. For a thorough discussion of these issues see Sorabji, *Time, Creation and the Continuum*.

[19] This distinction is drawn by Craig, *The Kalam Cosmological Argument*, 172 n. 170.

[20] *Coherence of Theism*, 214.

impossibility of an actual infinite. Therefore God exists in a timeless eternity.

This chapter began with Boethius' well-known definition of timeless eternity as 'the complete possession all at once of illimitable life'. An attempt has been made to defend this idea against the obvious *reductio* which would make it immediately or directly incoherent, by in effect arguing that divine timeless eternity is not to be understood as involving duration of any kind. Hence God, considered as timeless, cannot have temporal relations with any of his creation. He is time-less in the sense of being time-free. This at once provides an answer to the *reductio* brought by philosophers such as Kenny and Swinburne by denying that what any of us is now doing is taking place at the same time as anything God is doing, and by denying also that there is a relation of E-simultaneity, as defined by Stump and Kretzmann. Whether, if this is sufficient to rebut the charge of incoherence, divine timeless eternity can also be satisfactorily defended against less direct objections is the subject of the next chapters.

Is this conclusion incompatible with anything that Boethius says about eternity in his celebrated definition with which this chapter began? It is clearly consistent with the idea of divine life, that is, with the idea of God as the creator and sustainer of all that is. Boethius says that this life, in God, is illimitable, and this means not, as Stump and Kretzmann suggest, eternal duration, but a property modifying the other attributes of God—his power, goodness, wisdom, knowledge, and so forth. Each of these attributes is illimitable. Boethius, in the passage in which the definition occurs, seems to be contrasting the possession all at once of illimitable life and the possession in temporal sequence or series of illimitable life: 'Whatever includes and possesses the whole fullness of illimitable life at once and is such that nothing future is absent from it and nothing past has flowed on, this is rightly judged to be eternal'.[21] So what Boethius appears to

---

[21] Cited by Stump and Kretzmann, 'Eternity', 430.

be saying is that nothing in time can be illimitable in character. Hence this aspect of Boethius' definition has nothing to do with duration, and his definition does not require the introduction of the idea of eternal duration at any point. But of course the main thrust of this discussion has been not to make a proposal that Boethius could defend but to make one that is of more general appeal.

3
Indexicals and Spacelessness

IN 'The Formalities of Omniscience'[1] A. N. Prior claimed that an expression such as ('It is raining now' uttered on Monday 23 July 1984 is not equivalent in meaning to 'It is raining on Monday 23 July 1984', and that an omniscient being who knew that it was raining on a certain date would not necessarily know that it is raining *now*. Indeed, if the omniscient being were timeless, he would necessarily not know that it was raining now, since, being timeless, he could not be temporally present on the occasion on which it is raining. Clearly what this argument sets out to show is that there are severe difficulties over the idea of an omniscient being who is timeless. If God is omniscient, and what Prior says is correct, then God cannot be timeless.)

Prior's argument has those who defend it[2] as well as those who attack it.[3] This chapter is not a further direct contribution to that debate. Rather, it argues in a more oblique fashion that the considerations, such as that used by Prior, that are used to cast doubt upon the idea of divine timelessness, have parallels that cast equal doubt upon the idea of divine spacelessness. Perhaps it is a consequence of Prior's argument that if God is in time then he is also in space. If the idea of God being in space is unacceptable, this is a reason for rejecting Prior's argument and for providing an alternative account of divine omniscience. One reason for

---

[1] *Philosophy* (1962), reprinted in *Papers on Time and Tense.*

[2] Norman Kretzmann, 'Omniscience and Immutability', *J. of Philosophy* (1966); Nicholas Wolterstorff, 'God Everlasting', in C. J. Orlebeke and L. B. Smedes (eds.), *God and the Good.*

[3] H.-N. Castaneda, 'Omniscience and Indexical Reference', *J. of Philosophy* (1967); Pike, *God and Timelessness*, ch. 5; Swinburne, *Coherence of Theism*, ch. 10; Murray MacBeath, 'Mellor's Emeritus Headache', *Ratio* (1983); D. H. Mellor, 'MacBeath's Soluble Aspirin', *Ratio* (1983).

thinking that the idea of God being in space is unacceptable is that such a god would be finite, or at least the arguments used to show that he is in space would show that he is in space finitely or boundedly, and so is finite. So anyone who wishes to maintain that God is infinite, as traditional theists do, will either have to find other arguments than the argument from indexicals for the view that God is in time (and such arguments will be considered in due course) or opt for divine timelessness.

In brief, it will be argued in this chapter that one consequence of God being in time is that God is finite because there is a relevantly parallel argument for God being in space which carries this consequence.

In a particularly clear version of the argument from indexicals Nicholas Wolterstorff argues that to replace the present tense of a verb by a tense-indifferent use of the same verb together with a designator of time is to construct a wholly new proposition. That is, while from

(1) The kettle is boiling,

we can infer

(2) The kettle is boiling at present,

from

(3) The kettle boils on 19 January

we cannot infer (2): (1) conveys something that (3) does not convey, namely the presentness of the kettle's boiling. Without the ability to distinguish between the presentness, pastness, and futurity of facts we would not know where we are in the sequence of events. The significant fact about propositions like (1) is that they can only be known to be true when they are true.

The application of this argument to the idea of timeless knowledge is quickly made. Take God's knowledge of the fact that the kettle is boiling. He cannot know this until it is true, and so God's coming to know that the kettle is boiling is synchronous with the onset of the kettle's boiling:

But every temporal event has (by definition) either a beginning or an ending. So every case of knowing about some temporal event that it is occurring itself either begins or ends (or both). Hence the act of knowing about *e* that it is occurring is infected by the temporality of *e*. So also, the act of knowing about *e* that it *was* occurring, and the act of knowing about *e* that it *will be* occurring, are infected by the temporality of *e*.[4]

So if God were timelessly eternal there are matters that he could never know, nor remember, nor plan. Hence the character of God, particularly the God of Christian theism who judges and redeems, is radically compromised.

As was noted earlier some writers, for example Nelson Pike, have rejected this type of argument. They claim that it rests on a confusion between an utterance and a proposition, and that though God could not know that the kettle is boiling he could know the proposition expressed by 'the kettle is boiling'. This response may, by itself, be sufficient to rebut Prior's argument, at least for those who accept that there are propositions. However for the purposes of this chapter it will be assumed that there is a distinction of meaning between (2) and (3), and in particular that (3) could be known when (2) was not known.

A precisely parallel argument can be constructed for space.[5] It is of course not an accident that ways of constructing future and past tenses of verbs are well-entrenched in a natural language such as English while there are no 'tenses' for expression distance in space. The reason for this has something to do with the fact that time is only one-dimensional whereas space concerns not only distance but direction. However vague a thing it is to say, 'he will be

---

[4] Wolterstorff, 'God Everlasting', 198. See also id., 'Can Ontology do without Events?', in Ernest Sosa (ed.), *Essays on the Philosophy of R. M. Chisholm*.

[5] In view of the general strategy of this chapter it is interesting to note that in the *City of God* Augustine draws parallels of a similar kind between temporal and spatial indexicals in order to make the point that to ask why God has created the universe *now* (for those who, unlike Augustine, believe in infinite time) prompts the question, Why has God created the universe *here*? (for those who believe in infinite space). (*City of God*, XI. v.)

coming' it is precise to the extent of fixing his coming in the future, whereas to say, 'he is there' is hopelessly vague until accompanied by gestures or directions of other kinds.

Still, the fact that there are no 'space tenses' as there are 'time tenses' need not worry us. The argument can proceed without them. While from

(4) The kettle is boiling here,

we can infer

(5) The kettle is boiling at this place, (that is where I am or we are),

we cannot infer (5) from

(6) The kettle is boiling in the Old Kent Road.

For (5) conveys something that (6) does not convey, namely the fact that the kettle is boiling at the place where the utterer of the statement happens to be. Further, if all we had to use in expressing the places at which events took place were proper names or certain definite descriptions for places (those that made no use of indexicals for space) then we would never know where we were in relation to the total array of places.

Let us suppose that God knows that the kettle is boiling here. But he cannot know this except where it is true. He cannot know this until he occupies a place in the Old Kent Road near to where the kettle is boiling in the Old Kent Road. So God cannot know that the kettle is boiling here until he arrives at or near the place where the kettle is boiling. That is, God's coming to know that the kettle is boiling here cannot occur until he arrives at the Old Kent Road.

So if God is spacelessly present in his creation there are matters that he cannot know. Just as Christian thought portrays God as knowing *when* things take place so he is portrayed as knowing *where* they take place. Accordingly if the earlier argument establishes the presence of God in time this argument establishes the presence of God in space.

Wolterstorff also argues that if God were timelessly eternal he could not be the object of any human act whatever, since to suppose that he could would be to suppose that God changed, changed from not being referred to, or worshipped, by Smith to being referred to or worshipped by Smith. This argument can be rebutted by using the distinction noted earlier between different kinds of change, between 'real' and 'merely Cambridge' changes. However, the distinction between a 'real' and a 'merely Cambridge' change is a difficult one to express exactly. If for that reason we were to suppose that Wolterstorff's argument cannot be rebutted by employing the distinction, then the parallel argument with regard to space would be: if God were spaceless no human being would be able to move, for to move is to establish new spatial relations between the mover and God, and so to involve God in change.

Although it was noted earlier that Swinburne rejects the argument from indexicals he does employ another argument, referred to briefly in Chapter 2, to show the incoherence of the idea of God being timeless which has certain features in common with the argument from indexicals. It makes no use of the supposition that a timeless individual knows about events in a temporal sequence, but otherwise similar sorts of considerations apply. Let us call this sub-argument of the argument from indexicals the argument from simultaneity. It can be stated as follows:

(7) God exists timelessly.

(8) God exists simultaneously at all moments of human time (from (7).)

(9) God is simultaneously present at what I did yesterday, am doing today, and will do tomorrow.

(10) If time t_1 is simultaneous with time t_2, and t_2 is simultaneous with t_3, then t_1 is simultaneous with t_3.

(11) If God is simultaneously present at what I did yesterday and am doing today then yesterday and today are simultaneous (from (9) and (10)).

(12) But the idea that yesterday and today are simultaneous is absurd.

(13) Therefore (7) is incoherent.[6]

---

[6] Swinburne, *Coherence of Theism*, 220–1.

As previously, in Wolterstorff's argument, we shall assume the soundness of this argument. But a precisely parallel argument can be constructed to show the incoherence of the idea of God's spacelessness, as follows:

(14) God is spaceless.
(15) God is wholly spatially present at different places.
(16) God is wholly spatially present at what I am doing here and you are doing there.
(17) If an individual *A* is wholly spatially present with another individual *B*, and *A* is wholly spatially present with a third individual *C* then *B* is wholly spatially present with *C*.
(18) Thus if God is wholly spatially present at what I am doing here and you are doing there then where you are and where I am are the same place.
(19) But the idea that this place and that place are the same place is absurd.
(20) Therefore (14) is incoherent.

So if the timeless existence of God is incoherent then so is the spaceless existence of God. It ought to be stressed that in these arguments it has not been assumed, nor argued, that space and time are in all respects analogous, but that they are analogous in those respects that are relevant for the propounding of these arguments. The exact extent to which time can be regarded as similar to space is a matter of controversy into which there is no need to venture.[7] But we can see that Wolterstorff is mistaken when he writes:

In contemporary Western philosophy the phenomenon of temporal modality has been pervasively neglected or ignored in favour of the phenomena of temporal order-relationships, temporal location, and temporal duration. Thus time has been 'spatialised'. For though space provides us with close analogues to

---

[7] See e.g. G. Schlesinger, 'The Similarities Between Space and Time', *Mind* (1975), and the literature there cited; also Paul Helm, 'Time and Place for God', *Sophia* (Oct. 1985).

all three of these latter phenomena, it provides us with no analogue whatever to the past/present/future distinction.[8]

This is not so. There is some analogue of the distinctions between past, present, and future provided by the spatial distinctions between here and there, and before and behind. There are spatial modalities just as there are temporal modalities. Suppose that two spatial operators 'It is the case that here' (*H*) and 'It is the case that there' (*TH*) are introduced. The verb 'to be' in these operators is of course to be understood tense-indifferently. Then 'The kettle is boiling here' comes to be *H* (The kettle is boiling), 'It is raining here and it is snowing there' comes to be *H* (It is raining) and *TH* (It is snowing). This is pretty unilluminating stuff by comparison with Prior's *Past, Present and Future* (I doubt very much that there is a book waiting to be written entitled *Here, There and Everywhere*). But all that this shows is that the modalities of time are philosophically more interesting than the modalities of place.

Let us now consider another argument against divine timelessness, what might be called the argument from personality. This is offered in William Kneale's paper 'Time and Eternity in Theology',[9] in which, alluding to the famous definition of eternity by Boethius as 'the complete possession of eternal life at once', Kneale confesses 'I can attach no meaning to the word "life" unless I am allowed to suppose that what has life acts. . . . life must at least involve some incidents in time and if, like Boethius, we suppose the life in question to be intelligent, then it must involve also awareness of the passage of time.'[10]

This argument is taken up and embellished by J. R. Lucas in *A Treatise on Time and Space* in which he says that 'To say that God is outside time, as many theologians do, is to deny, in effect, that God is a person'.[11] According to Lucas, since

---

[8] 'God Everlasting', 188.
[9] *Proc. of the Aristotelian Soc.* (1960–1).
[10] Ibid. 99.
[11] *Time and Space*, 300.

minds are necessarily in time but only contingently in space it is reasonable to suppose that everything that exists is present to God spacelessly, but not timelessly.[12] The argument from personality is connected with the argument from indexicals in the following way. The argument from personality, if it is regarded as sound, provides a reason for treating the argument from indexicals as relevant to the issue of God's timelessness, since otherwise it could be argued that the indexical argument is beside the point because God only needs to know the truth of tense-indifferent expressions. The reason why it is thought that God needs to know more than the truth of tense-indifferent expressions is that it is claimed that he observes and initiates changes in the universe. That is, he is a person.

Kneale claims that to act purposefully is to act with thought of what will come about after the beginning of the action, and that therefore Boethius' definition of eternity as 'the complete possession of eternal life all at once' is a contradiction in terms. But though this consideration is relevant to timelessness as such, to whether or not there could be a timeless conscious agent, it is not quite what is relevant to the question of whether or not God is timeless. For the question here is not whether

(a) Whatever has life must have an awareness of time,

but whether

(b) Whatever consciously brings about changes in the states of things in time must have an awareness of being in time,

and if (b) whether

(c) Whatever consciously brings about changes in the states of things in space must have an awareness of being in space.

So in saying that the agent in question must have an

---

[12] *Time and Space*, 304.

awareness of time Kneale seems to mean more than that the agent must have the concept of time. It obviously does not follow that if one has the concept of something temporal or spatial that one is at that time or that place. It is possible for a person to have the concept of being somewhere else than the place where he is at present, but it would be absurd to suppose that one had to be somewhere other than where one was at present in order to have this concept.

In a similar way Lucas's claim that minds are necessarily in time but only contingently in space does not meet the case in hand because the question is not whether God is a mind, and therefore possibly in time but not in space, but whether God knows and acts within a spatial universe. Lucas has to show not merely that minds are contingently in space, and that therefore it is possible that God is spaceless, but that minds that bring about changes in the states of things in space are possibly not in space themselves. But let us look at his argument more closely.

(21) I cannot conceive of a mind being conscious of something about whom the question 'When?' does not arise.

(22) There are many states of consciousness for which the question 'Where?' does not arise.

(23) Therefore, minds are contingently in space, necessarily in time.

A number of questions arise about this argument. (21) is unclear, in at least two respects. If it is a statement about the contents of minds then it is obviously false. There are many objects of consciousness for which the question 'When?' does not make sense. If a person is conscious of the proposition that seven and five make twelve it makes no sense to ask when seven and five first made twelve, so by (21) Lucas must mean something like

(21*a*) I cannot conceive of a mind being conscious of something about which the question 'When did you first conceive of that thing?' does not arise.

'Does not arise' here presumably means 'is not capable of being given a positive answer, i.e. a named date'. If so then (21a) would rule out not only the idea of an eternal, timeless mind, but also a sempiternal mind as well. For it is possible that there should be a sempiternal being that had a belief that it never acquired, that is a being such that it had existed for all time and there was no time at which it failed to have the belief. In which case the question 'When did you first have that belief?' would not arise. But perhaps 'Always' would be a satisfactory answer to that question. If so (21a) can be accepted. What has to be compared to it for the purpose of considering Lucas's argument is not (22) but (22a).

(22a) I can conceive of a mind being conscious of something about which the question 'Where did you conceive of that thing?' does not arise.

Let us take it that (23) follows from (21a) and (22a). It follows then that it is possible that there is a mind which is not in space. But what precisely does this mean? And, more particularly, what does it mean to say that God is spaceless?

To say that a mind exists that is not in space may mean that the mind does not occupy any area of space. Presumably it means at least that. Does it also mean that there is no point of space at which the mind exists? If so, this seems to amount either to the view that such a mind exists nowhere, or that it exists everywhere. The second possibility seems absurd, except perhaps in the case of God, and we shall look at that possibility in a moment. But with regard to the first possibility it is hardly intelligible to suppose that there is a mind that is conscious of things happening in space and yet is nowhere. But perhaps the supposition is that there could only be a spaceless mind if there was no space. It is not clear whether this is intelligible or not, or how to decide the question.

Some of the things that Lucas means by saying that God is spaceless are (a) that God possesses all space, (b) that nothing can be distant or remote from God, and (c) that God's relation to space is non-token-reflexive.[13] Let us examine (b): (b) cannot mean that nothing is spatially more distant from God than another thing. For if neither of two things in a given direction is more distant than the other from an individual then they are equidistant from that individual in that direction. So that if nothing in a given direction is more distant from God than anything else in that direction then everything in that direction is in the same place. But perhaps what Lucas means is that nothing is either distant or near as far as God is concerned.

Further, either (a)–(c) are true of every mind that is spaceless or they are not. If they are true of only some spaceless minds then the negations of (a)–(c) are presumably true of the rest. If they are true then for a mind that is spaceless everything in a given direction is in the same place. If they are not true then for a mind that is spaceless some things are more spatially distant than others. If it is only in the case of God that an individual can be spacelessly present to the whole of space, whereas in the case of minds other than God spacelessness is possible only if there is no space to be located in, then it seems that 'spaceless' does not mean quite the same when applied to God and when applied to other minds.

Even if it is possible to sort out all these points and to answer them satisfactorily, there is still the earlier problem of what to say about the claim that God, who brings about changes in space, is not himself in any spatial relations to the changes in space, i.e. in the states of individuals in space, that he brings about. The chief problem here is: if God is not in spatial relations with the individuals in space whom he affects how does he know where to bring about the changes? If God wishes to bring about certain changes in the Red Sea, how does he know where the Red Sea is? Two answers seem possible. Perhaps he knows where the Red Sea is just as we generally know without observation what the positions of our limbs are. Alternatively, perhaps he knows by means of

---

[13] *Time and Space*, 304–5.

using proper names and non-indexical definite descriptions. Perhaps so. But it will not have escaped attention that parallel answers are also open to the advocate of God's eternal timelessness.

What has been argued so far is that two sorts of argument against the timelessness of God—the argument from indexicals, and the argument from personality—are also arguments against the spacelessness of God. If the conclusion of these arguments is that God is in time then, *pari passu*, God is in space. This conclusion might well be welcomed by someone who claims that God is in time, even though, as we have seen, it is not welcome to everyone who makes this claim. To see whether it ought to be welcome it is worth exploring some of the consequences of saying that God is in space.

One thing that God's being in space seems to mean is that God has some spatial perspective, as he has some temporal perspective if he is in time. Let us consider the biblical story about Elijah, (1 Kings 20: 9). Elijah flees and Gods finds him. He says to Elijah, 'What doest thou here, Elijah?' Taken literally and in accordance with the conclusions of the previous arguments, what God says is, 'What are you doing where I am, Elijah?' From the idea that God must have some spatial perspective it does not follow that he has only one spatial perspective at once. Yet we must not be misled by the analogy of a person in a control room watching a series of television screens relaying pictures from differently positioned cameras. The cameras each have a different spatial perspective, but the person in the control room has one perspective. To have more than one perspective in the sense that interests us the object must have more than one position at once, and in effect be a scattered object.

A second thing that God's being in space seems to mean is that God cannot be wholly present at two or more separated places at once. It seems to be a conceptual truth about any individual in space that it cannot be wholly present in two places at once.

A third thing that it means is that if God is capable of being at two places at once, then God is spatially divisible. For if God can be at two places at once, though not wholly at two places at once, then it would seem to follow that he can only be in two or more places at once by having a part of him in one place and a part of him in each of the other places where he is. Hence it seems to follow that God has parts, proper parts that is, and is not simple, as has traditionally been thought.

But the main difficulty with supposing that God is an individual in space, at least on the reasons considered earlier, can be expressed as follows. Suppose God says,

(24) Elijah is here.

Suppose further the truth of the doctrine we might call the omnispatiality or spacefulness of God, the doctrine that at any time God occupies (in some sense) all the spaces in the universe that there are. It follows from

(25) God is omnispatial,

that

(26) Of every space at a given time God can truly say both 'I am here' and 'I am there'.

With respect to any particular place, say Carmel, God can say 'I am here' and also, since he is omnispatial, he can say with respect to Gilead, 'I am there'. But given the truth of God's utterance of (24), (26) contradicts it, for by (26) God can also say, with respect to the place where Elijah is,

(27) Elijah is there.

Given the truth of God's utterance of (24), God's utterance of (27) cannot be true since an individual who is here cannot be there. What might be true is not the utterance (27) but

(28) I am where Elijah regards as there,

or

(29) I am at the place which is there for Elijah.

But both (28) and (29) mean something different from (27). So God cannot occupy all space. If God can assert (24) then (25) must be false.

The basic point can be expressed as follows. Either the 'heres' and 'theres' of the argument are ordinary spatial indexicals, in which case God is bounded in space, for on the ordinary meaning of these expressions 'I am here and I am there' is a self-contradiction except perhaps where the 'here' and 'there' refer to places where parts of one's body are. Alternatively the 'heres' and 'theres' are peculiar and extraordinary 'heres' and 'theres' according to which it is consistent to assert 'I am both here and there'. But in this case the way in which God is in space differs from the way in which other individuals are in space.

Perhaps the matter can be put more simply, as follows. Suppose that God knows that Elijah is here. If he knows that Elijah is here then he also knows that Elijah is not there. If he knows that Elijah is not there he knows that Elijah is not at a certain place distant from both Elijah and himself. If he knows that Elijah is not at a certain place distant from himself then there is such a place distant from him. If there is a place distant from him then he is bounded by space, and if he is bounded by space then he is finite.

In Chapter 8 of *God and Timelessness*, Nelson Pike considers the question of whether or not the timeless eternity of God is entailed by the Anselmian claim that God is a being than which no greater can be conceived. He concludes that it is not entailed by it, and thus that the doctrine of God's timeless eternity is not something that is required by theism.[14] But it has now been argued that the arguments currently used to establish that God is in time are strictly parallel to arguments that would establish that God is in space. Moreover, if God is in space in the sense that he can properly use ordinary spatial indexicals then he is enclosed by space. There is here a reason for thinking that such a God is a being than which a greater *can* be conceived, namely a being that is not bounded by space but who is otherwise as similar as can be to the God who is in space. Hence an infinite God must

---

[14] Pike, *God and Timelessness*, 161 ff.

be spaceless. And if we come to this conclusion on the basis of arguments about space then there is no good reason to withhold the conclusion that God is outside time, since the arguments that establish the one are strictly parallel to the arguments that establish the other.

Thus theism seems to require that God be spaceless. The spacelessness of God in turn involves denying the soundness of the sorts of arguments considered earlier. If these arguments are unsound there is no reason why the parallel arguments about the timeless eternity of God ought not to be judged unsound. Or at least a reason must be given why the parallel does not hold. Failing the provision of such a reason we can say that even if Pike is correct in his claim that theism does not directly require divine timeless eternity, it indirectly requires it.

In saying that we ought to conclude that if God exists he is outside space and time it is not being claimed that the meaning of such a proposition is clear. Perhaps the best way to grasp what it means, or to try to grasp what it means, is to use models or analogies. And then again, perhaps not. All that is being claimed is that the spacelessness of God seems to be a requirement of traditional theism and hence that the timelessness of God is.

4

Eternity and Personality

THE argument of the previous chapter drew certain parallels between time and space in order to cast doubt on the idea that God is in time. That argument is only of *ad hominem* effectiveness as a defence of divine timelessness for it is only cogent against anyone who is alarmed by the thought that God is in space. For anyone who is happy with such a thought all that the argument does is to elucidate certain points of resemblance between time and space.

In the course of this argument a side-long glance was taken at another argument against divine timelessness which I called the argument from personality. In order to confront the case against timelessness more directly it is now necessary to look at the argument from personality in a less oblique fashion.

It is alleged by a number of philosophers that nothing that exists timelessly could be a person—a timeless being could not act, intend, or remember, for example, and such capabilities are necessary for being a person. Robert C. Coburn is typical of philosophers who make this point.

Surely it is a necessary condition of anything's being a person that it should be capable (logically) of, among other things, doing at least some of the following: remembering, anticipating, reflecting, deliberating, deciding, intending, and acting intentionally. To see that this is so one need but ask oneself whether anything which necessarily lacked all of the capacities noted would, under any conceivable circumstances, count as a person. But now an eternal being would necessarily lack all of these capacities inasmuch as their exercise by a being clearly requires that the being exist in time. After all, reflection and deliberation takes time; deciding typically occurs at some time—and in any case it always makes sense to ask, 'When did you (he, they, etc) decide?'; remembering is impossible unless the being doing the remembering has a past;

and so on. Hence, no eternal being, it would seem, could be a person.[1]

Richard Swinburne makes the same point:

If God had thus fixed his intentions 'from all eternity' he would be a very lifeless thing; not a person who reacts to men with sympathy or anger, pardoning and chastening because he chooses to there and then. . . . if God did not change at all, he could not think now of this, now of that. His thoughts would be one thought which lasted for ever.[2]

Standing behind these philosophers is the figure of Hume:

For though it be allowed, that the Deity possesses attributes, of which we have no comprehension; yet ought we never to ascribe to him any attributes which are absolutely incompatible with that intelligent nature, essential to him. A mind, whose acts and sentiments and ideas are not distinct and successive; one, that is wholly simple, and wholly immutable; is a mind, which has no thought, no reason, no will, no sentiment, no love, no hatred; or in a word, is no mind at all.[3]

The concept of a person is a philosophical minefield. It is claimed that embodiment is necessary for being a person, and this is also denied. It is claimed, and denied, that only language-users are persons, that only individuals in community are persons, and that only individuals who are capable of being conscious are persons. It is claimed, and denied, that the notion of a person is an ethical notion. Coupled with these disagreements is the difference in meaning between 'person', 'personality', and 'mind'. In view of these divergencies it would be extremely hazardous to attempt to offer one knockdown argument for the conclusion that the idea of a

[1] Robert C. Coburn, 'Professor Malcolm on God', *Australasian J. of Philosophy* (1963), 155.
[2] *Coherence of Theism*, 214. Other contemporary philosophers taking a similar view are Kneale and Lucas.
[3] David Hume, 'Dialogues Concerning Natural Religion', in *Hume on Religion*, ed. R. Wollheim, 133.

timeless person or personality is coherent. Moreover, to show that there is a sense in which the idea of a timeless person is coherent would not be very powerful if it is conceded that there are numerous other senses in which it is not coherent, especially if these other senses contain the most important or central cases.

How, then, are we to proceed? There seems to be no alternative but to consider the specific arguments that have in fact been levelled against the idea of a timeless person and to attempt to refute them, or at least to cast doubt upon them. Such a procedure is inherently unsatisfactory since what it can at the best provide is not a proof of the coherence of the idea of a timeless person but the absence of a disproof. In this situation there is no guarantee that other arguments against its coherence can not and will not be devised. But this rather unsatisfactory state of affairs often occurs in philosophy.

It is not necessary to spend much time contending against Swinburne's claim that a timeless person would be 'lifeless', since at one level such a charge is beside the point, while at another level it is question-begging. A timeless person would certainly not be lifeless in the way in which a beached jellyfish is lifeless. It is not a deficiency that a timeless person would lack physical life since by definition such a person would not be physical. Whether such a person would be lifeless in some further sense is precisely the question to be discussed.

So in this chapter we shall first consider what seem to be the three main and most-cited arguments against timelessness—the arguments from *memory*, from *purpose*, and from *knowledge*, and then consider the argument from *agency*.

The argument from memory can be stated briefly, as follows. It is essential to being a person that one remembers or has memories. But remembering is something that is possible only for an individual in time, since what is remembered is by definition past. Therefore persons are necessarily in time. Nothing that is a person exists out of time. Furthermore, Nelson Pike says that not only does remembering require location in time, it also requires temporal duration.[4] 'To remember is to think about something after one has experienced it or learned about it. Thus, if one is to remember something, one must have position in time. A timeless individual could not remember.'[5] Even if it is supposed that remembering does not take any time, the individual who remembers would have to be in time, since an individual can remember only what he has experienced or learned in the past or about the past, and thus he must have a past. So a timeless individual could not engage in certain kinds of activity essential to being a person, and hence could not be one.

There are two possible replies to this argument. The first is to say that remembering is not something which requires or takes up time. Remembering is knowing something about the past, and to remember p might be analysed as: knowing that p and having not forgotten that p. In the case of a timeless being, perhaps this could be amended as: a timeless being remembers p when he knows p and it is impossible for him to forget p. What such an individual knows and what he remembers would be logically equivalent, and the question of whether such an individual remembers (as against whether he knows) would arise only when prompted by a certain kind of question, such as, 'Could a timeless being forget?' 'No, he remembers everything he knows.'

If this is coupled with the idea that for a timeless being what is known is not learned, i.e. is not the result of some time-taking process but is 'innate', then it appears that a timeless being remembers in the sense that he can forget nothing he knows, and what he knows he knows 'innately', and not as the result of a process of learning.

So even if a timeless being could not remember in any way which involves temporal processes there is a timeless

---

[4] Pike, *God and Timelessness*, 123. Pike himself does not conclude from the fact that an individual cannot remember that he is not a person. For Pike what is central to the concept of a person is not mental activity but knowledge. This claim will be considered shortly.

[5] Ibid. 122.

analogue of 'remember' which preserves the point of us saying that such an individual remembers. Though a timeless being does not remember in the sense of call to mind or retain for a time what he has learned in the past, or learned about his own past, he nevertheless may be said to know and to not forget. But more than this, such a being cannot forget, for to be able to forget is to be able to obliterate from one's mind, or to allow to go from one's mind, or to fail to prevent going from one's mind, something that one knows. And such a state of affairs would be a *happening*, which a timeless being could not undergo or undertake. Incidentally, such a result would suit a theist admirably, in that it offers support to a strong notion of omniscience. [Furthermore it allows a particular understanding to the notion of omniscience. An omniscient being is not to be thought of as a superior elephant, an individual with total recall, but as one of whom it makes no sense to say he forgets, because forgetting is something which only an individual in time can do. This is not to say that timeless remembering entails omniscience, only that it is consistent with a strong view of omniscience, for on our reading if p is known by a timeless being it is not possible for p to be forgotten.]

But is there reason to think that such a being, an individual who could not forget, and who in this sense remembered, could not be a person? In trying to answer this question we seem to be cast back upon our manifold and conflicting intuitions about what a person essentially is. Yet matters may not be quite as bad as that. For although everyone is forgetful it is hard to see that forgetting things, whether this is regarded as an ability or as a defect, is essential to being a person. Suppose a person with a total recall. Nothing that he knows he forgets, but he remembers everything at will. Would this extraordinary capacity render him in some way not a person? Surely not. For, Freudian speculations apart, we regard forgetfulness as something to be avoided. To suppose that an individual who could avoid forgetting things was not a person is rather like supposing that an individual who, by taking a drug, could avoid physical tiredness, did not have a body.

But what about the supposition of an individual who could not forget? Such an individual would be not only unfailingly correct in his rememberings—nothing that he knew he ever lost—but would also be necessarily correct—nothing that he knew he ever could forget. This would certainly be extraordinary. But why should it be thought that if an individual had this extraordinary power he could not be a person? Who says, and by what argument? Surely in such an eventuality as this the onus is firmly on the shoulders of those who would claim that necessary non-forgetfulness rules out being a person to provide an argument for this conclusion.

It is worth emphasizing that in attempting to provide an analogue for 'remember' in the case of a timeless individual no appeal is being made to vagueness or to metaphor, but rather an attempt has been made to set out the meaning of such a verb for a timeless individual in literal terms, using, in particular, the concepts of knowledge, of forgetfulness, and of necessity.

A further argument is that an eternal individual could not have purposes or act purposefully, for to act with purpose or intentionally requires that the individual who so acts occupies a position in time. Intention or purpose is conceptually linked to the intender's or purposer's future. As William Kneale puts it, to act purposefully 'is to act with thought of what will come about after the beginning of the action'.[6]

Here we seem to have two separate arguments conflated, or rather one argument that is based upon a premiss which is accepted without argument. The unargued-for premiss is that an eternal being acts, and that actions have beginnings and endings. The argument is that to act with purpose is to have regard to what happens after the beginning of the action. What is questionable about this overall argument is

---

[6] 'Time and Eternity in Theology', *Proc. of the Aristotelian Soc.* (1960–1), 99.

not the point about purposiveness, which seems correct, but the assumption that an eternal being acts. If one acts in a sense of 'act' which requires an action to have a beginning then *a fortiori* to act purposefully is to act with regard to what happens after the beginning of the action. But if acts have beginnings, then an eternal individual cannot act, and the point about purposes is irrelevant. Yet if an eternal being cannot act is not this, to say the least, rather inhibiting?

This conclusion would be too hasty. It does not follow from the claim that an eternal being does not purposefully initiate actions that such a being does not have purposes. He may have timeless purposes, purposes which are brought about in time, that is, in the temporal order of his creation. These effects, it may be supposed, come about as a result of the eternal being's purposes, but they do not come about after those eternal purposes, nor are they contemporaneous with them. The distinction between the eternal purposes and their effects is not a temporal distinction in the sense that certain actions occur after the formulation of the intention or purpose, but the distinction is a logical one. The purpose is not identical with the effect, and the effect comes about as a result of the purpose. The effect may be a physical change, but the purpose is not physical and is timeless. One way to think about this relationship is to think of contemporaneous causation, for instance whistling, though of course in the case of the eternal being the effects of his purposes are not strictly contemporaneous with those purposes. It is misleading to think in these terms, as was seen earlier when the coherence of timeless existence was discussed.

So, in spite of what Nelson Pike claims,[7] in order to have purposes an individual does not have to have position in time, it is rather that the purposes have to take effect in time. And perhaps not even this. For perhaps an eternal being has eternal purposes that have no culmination or fulfilment in time but only in eternity. Perhaps, for example, one of the purposes of

---

[7] *God and Timelessness*, 122.

such an eternal being is to glorify himself. A timeless being is, or could be, essentially purposive, eternally purposing to exemplify certain ideals.

To illustrate the possibility of an eternal being having purposes which take effect in time, compare the disposition of a substance, or the standing orders of a legislature, which may mould or modify the occurrence of certain events while themselves remaining unchanged. Such a substance, or system of standing orders, is in time, and the changes effected are not changes initiated by the substance or by the legislature. Nevertheless the comparison may be a useful one in that the substance or the system of standing orders is responsible for changing without themselves being changed, and this is a necessary condition of the existence of an eternal purpose.

Thus, to have a completed eternal purpose is to have (tenseless) a purpose that is completed relative to some other event or action in time. Thus a timeless God's eternal purpose that it will rain today is accomplished by its raining today. His eternal purpose is specifiable as: 'That it rain on 24 July 1987'.

Pike claims that even if both the arguments from personality which have been considered survive criticism and a timeless being could have no memory or purposes, yet if a timeless being could be shown to be omniscient it would have to be conceded that such a being was a person. Omniscience is sufficient for personhood. (Even if this is granted, it might nevertheless be counter-argued that an omniscient but purposeless timeless being could not be God. Hence the need to consider seriously the argument about purposes.) Pike says:

If a timeless individual could have knowledge—at least if it could have unlimited knowledge—then we could at least conceive of the case in which a timeless individual would have to be counted as a person. This is true if it is also true that a timeless individual could not deliberate, anticipate or remember.[8]

[8] Ibid. 125.

But Pike claims that such a timeless individual could not be omniscient. And the reasons he gives for this are that a timeless individual cannot meet any of the conditions under which we could say that an individual knew something or other. A timeless being could not communicate anything to us by speaking or in any other way provide any reason for us to believe that he is omniscent. He, in general, could not give us any evidence for the idea that he is omniscient, and therefore could not be. And if there is nothing he knows he could not be a person. 'It would appear that the kinds of things one must do before we would have warrant for saying that he knows or believes something are not the kinds of things that could be done by an incorporeal being.'[9] *A fortiori*, they could not be done by a timeless being, since a timeless being is essentially incorporeal. Further, even if we suppose that this argument is deficient in that a timeless being may produce or bring about certain data which would warrant belief in its omniscience, in fact a timeless being could not bring about such circumstances. Indeed a timeless being could bring about nothing at all.[10]

Let us first look at the claim about omniscience and then turn attention to the idea of power or agency, the alleged impotence of a timeless individual.

There is a basic confusion here. Pike argues that a timeless being could not act in the various ways usually required of someone who would qualify as knowing, believing, or being aware of something.[11] The confusion is between those conditions which are necessary for p being true, and the conditions necessary for someone or other being warranted in believing that p is true. For it to be possible for there to be a timeless, omniscient individual it is necessary to specify what omniscience is, and to rebut any arguments to the effect that a timeless being could not be omniscient. We might, as a first attempt at specifying what omniscience is, say that an

---

[9] Ibid. 126.
[10] Ibid. 127.
[11] Ibid.

individual is omniscient if that individual knows all true propositions and has no false beliefs, that is, does not believe any proposition to be true which is not true. (Some of the alleged difficulties with this definition of omniscience will be considered in the next chapter. It is reasonable to postpone them because none of Pike's points depends upon this aspect of the matter.) Could an individual who is timeless know all true propositions and hold no false beliefs? Why not? Pike offers no argument against such a possibility. Instead what he does offer is an argument against the following proposition: 'If we could have no warrant for believing *p* then *p* could not be true.' If we could not ourselves be convinced, upon evidence, that a timeless being is omniscient, then according to Pike the very idea of a timeless, omniscient being is not possible. But it would certainly be strange to suppose that there could be no evidence of any kind for a timeless, omniscient being. Perhaps such knowledge as there is is of a kind that only the timeless being himself could have, in the way in which there are certain kinds of evidence available only to human beings, and not to non-human animals.

Someone who argues as Pike does could be maintaining the stronger thesis that 'if we could have no warrant for *p* then *p* is cognitively meaningless'. But to maintain such a view would be to become embroiled in the tentacles of logical positivism. And Pike certainly does not go that far, for he explicitly draws back from the idea that it is meaningless to speak of a timeless being as having knowledge or as being aware of something.[12]

Alternatively, Pike could be hinting that there is something very like a category mistake involved in supposing that a timeless being could be omniscient or have cognitive states of any kind. He seems to hint at this in calling for a way of understanding what the difference would be between a case of timelessness that does not have knowledge (such as the number two) and one that does. Why could not the number

---

[12] Ibid.

two have knowledge? Because it is not the sort of thing that can have knowledge. While granting this, why should it not be granted that there could be a timeless being of a different sort than the number two that *can* have knowledge?

Pike's objection here might be developed as follows. Suppose we grant, for the sake of argument, that knowledge is to be defined as justified, true belief. For any individual, including a timeless individual, to know, it follows that he must have a belief. But how could it be established that a timeless being has a belief? He could not tell us, or show us or otherwise indicate to us that he has a belief, for all these are ways of providing information which require the provider of the information to be in time. What then would the claim that he does—or for that matter that he does not—have the belief amount to? At this point, perhaps, the argument collapses into another one which we are shortly to consider, for it is now seen to be crucially based not on the concept of knowledge as such, but on the ability or inability of a timeless individual to do certain things, such as convey or communicate beliefs to us—his alleged impotence.

Before considering this argument, however, there are two more arguments regarding knowledge which ought to be discussed. It might be claimed that the only way in which a timeless being, or a being of any kind, can have knowledge is either by being given it, or by acquiring it for himself. But, it may be said, a timeless being cannot be given knowledge, since he would not have the requisite sensory faculties to understand what was allegedly communicated to him. And further, he could not acquire knowledge for himself since, again, he would have no sense organs which would enable him to learn.

To the claim that a timeless being could not gain knowledge by being given it, it may be replied that a timeless being could know and understand provided that he had an appropriate conceptual scheme in terms of which to understand what was said to him. And to the more general objection that such a being could not acquire knowledge for himself there are two possible answers. The first is that a timeless being may be the causal source of contingent truth, as he would be if he were the creator of the universe. The second is that such a being may not have to learn in order to know—he may just know, in a way which is akin to human 'innate' knowledge.[13]

It is possible to reverse the argument that we have been considering by saying that far from omniscience being inconsistent with a timeless being, omniscience is inconsistent with temporal being. Some philosophers who, like Pike, suppose that God is in time, suppose that he has to respond to and react to new circumstances as they arise.[14] Such a being, in time, knows now what he would do if A were to do X or what he would do if A were to do Y, but he does not now know which alternative A will choose.

Pike's case against the idea of a timeless being knowing anything, and particularly against the idea of him being omniscient, boils down to an objection that a timeless being could not be a (certain sort of) agent, for according to Pike there are no means open to a timeless being to convey to us what he knows, no 'way of understanding what the difference would be between a timeless being that does *not* have knowledge (e.g. the number two) and a timeless being that does have knowledge'.[15] And so Pike claims that 'a timeless individual could not *produce*, *create*, or *bring about* an object, circumstance, or state of affairs'.[16] From this it follows that a timeless being could not be omnipotent or potent to any degree and that we could have no reason for thinking that a timeless individual is omniscient, nor even that he has knowledge which falls short of omniscience, and hence no reason for thinking that a timeless individual is a person. As far as it is possible to tell Pike offers one argument

[13] On this possibility see Kenny, *God of the Philosophers*, 32–3.
[14] Keith Ward, *Rational Theology and the Creativity of God*. Swinburne, *Coherence of Theism*, 177.
[15] *God and Timelessness*, 127.
[16] Ibid. 110.

for this conclusion, namely that if it is supposed that a timeless being should produce *A* occurring at a particular time, it follows that such a timeless being would have to be in time and hence could not be timelessly eternal after all.

> The point seems to be that if God were to create or produce an object having position in time, God's creative activity would then have to have occurred at some specific time. The claim that God *timelessly* produced a temporal object (such as the mountain) is absurd.[17]

This is Schleiermacher's view, according to Pike, a view which he substantially endorses.

One argument used to support this contention is that causes precede their effects in time. Even if this is not always the case, and examples of contemporaneous causation can be given, this hardly meets the point, since as noted earlier contemporaneousness is in any case a temporal relation.

Pike concludes from this that God can produce nothing whatever, and that because a timeless being cannot produce anything, such a being cannot produce everything that there is. But we shall now attempt to argue the precise opposite. It is because a timeless God can produce everything there is that it makes sense to say that he can produce particular items.

Whereas particular items, such as the felling of a tree, occur in time, it makes sense to think that the universe as a whole does not exist in time, and that to suppose otherwise betokens a confusion. Although one can ask about what happened before one was born, and receive an answer, and ask about what happened before Oliver Cromwell was born, and receive an answer, it makes no sense to suppose that one can ask what happened before the universe existed, and hope to get an answer which specifies some other event or events. There comes a point when such questions are logically odd, inappropriate because although the question can be framed there could not be an answer to it. Such logical inappropriateness in this case signals the limit, or one of the limits, of the

---

[17] Ibid. 105.

universe. A timeless being may not act within the universe, yet it makes sense to say that such a being produces (tenseless) the universe. The production of the universe is thus not the production of some event or complex of events in time; it is the production of the whole material universe, time included.

But does not the idea of God timelessly 'producing' the universe involve a contradiction, for is not such a production a change? It is a change, but not a change *in time*, nor is it a change in the mind of the timeless individual since to choose to produce the universe does not imply changing one's mind. Rather it is the free determination of the mind to bring about what is chosen.[18]

But what, positively, does such a use of 'produce' signify? To say that a timeless being produces (timelessly) the universe is to say at least the following things:

(i) that the universe is logically contingent and would not have come into being if God had not willed so;
(ii) the universe has temporal development.

It is the fact of the universe's temporal development or change which *is* the divine sustaining of the universe. Thus to say that a timeless being produces the universe is to say not that some event occurred before (in a temporal sense) the existence of the universe, but that the timeless being produces (tenseless) all that is, and that but for that tenseless production there would not be the universe. These elucidatory assertions are not intended even as a beginning of a proof of the truth of such, for perhaps there is no proof of them. They are rather to provide part of what such a claim means.

If this makes sense, then we can say, by extension, that God has produced every event that the universe contains. But what is not a part of this claim and what is (following Pike) possibly incoherent, is the idea that God produces every

---

[18] See R. L. Sturch, 'The Problem of the Divine Eternity', *Religious Studies* (1974).

event separately, by a separate exercise of agency. It would be fallacious to argue:

> God produces (tenseless) the whole universe.
> The universe contains events occurring in a temporal sequence.
> Therefore, God produces events in a temporal sequence.

But it would be equally uncalled-for to argue:

> The universe contains events occurring in a temporal sequence.
> God is timeless.
> Therefore, God cannot produce such events.

This is fallacious, because it may be that how a timeless being produces events in time is by timelessly producing the whole temporal order.

It may be objected that it is begging an important question (though one that is incidental to the present discussion) to say that the way in which a timeless being produces things is by timelessly producing the whole order in which these events occur, since it may be that there are changes within the temporal order which the timeless being does not produce. He does not produce, it might be said, that I eat lunch, for this is something I do. This objection could be accommodated by allowing that what God produces timelessly is not the whole temporal order including everything in it, but the whole temporal order with such powers, including my own powers, as will causally ensure my eating lunch. And similarly with acts which are morally evil, which God (granted his impeccable moral character) could not himself perpetrate. In these cases what he timelessly ensures, or, on a more libertarian view, timelessly makes possible at a time, is the occurrence of some event. These matters will be taken up in more detail later. The chief positive point that it is necessary to make here, against Pike but with his help, is that it is not incoherent to suppose that a timeless being such as God might timelessly produce the whole temporal order, or such aspects of that order as the timeless being is directly responsible for.[19]

And for such a timeless God to sustain the universe over a period of time, say from Monday to Friday, is simply for God timelessly to decree that the universe created has duration for that period. 'Sustain' here does not mean, as it does for some theists,[20] 'create anew', nor does it mean to extend what is in existence at a time by a new act at that time (for that would reintroduce the idea of God being in time), it means rather that God has timelessly decreed that the universe shall develop, unfold, or continue at least until *now*, this stage in its development, the stage it has reached, say by 1988. Or, alternatively, that God has timelessly decreed that the universe has a 1988 stage. Whether it will continue to develop and whether God has decreed timelessly a post-1988 stage is presumably not something that can be determined a priori, but must wait upon experience.

Perhaps this is what Augustine means when in his *Confessions* he writes of the universe being created by God not *in* time, but *with* time.

Furthermore, although you are before time, it is not in time that you precede it. If this were so, you would not be before all time. It is in eternity, which is supreme over time because it is a never-ending present, that you are at once before all past time and after all future time. . . . Your today is eternity. And this is how the Son, to whom you said *I have begotten you this day*, was begotten co-eternal

---

[19] This distinction is a standard one for Catholic and Calvinist alike. 'Nothing, therefore, prevents our saying that God's action existed from all eternity, whereas its effect was not present from eternity, but existed at that time when, from all eternity, He ordained it.' Aquinas, *Summa contra Gentiles*, 2. 35. 3. 'The decree itself was eternal and immutable, but the thing decreed was temporary and mutable. As a decree from eternity doth not make the thing decreed to be eternal, so neither doth the immutability of the decree render the thing so decreed to be immutable.' Stephen Charnocke, *Discourses upon the Existence and Attributes of God* (1682), 207. For an extension of this distinction to cover the sense in which a timeless God may be said to answer petitionary prayer, see Paul Helm, 'Omnipotence and Change', *Philosophy* (1976).

[20] e.g. Descartes, *Meditations* III, and Jonathan Edwards, *The Great Christian Doctrine of Original Sin* (1757), ch. 4, sect. 3.

with yourself. You made all time; you are before all time; and the 'time', if such we may call it, when there was no time was not time at all. . . . It is therefore, true to say that when you had not made anything, there was no time, because time itself was of your making.[21]

To some, the idea of a unitary eternal divine decree by which all that God produces in time he decrees to produce may conjure up the spectre of Leibnizianism or of monisms of an even more rigid, monocausal kind. It may suggest the doctrine of internal relations, of world-bound individuals and the like. But such fears are without foundation, as will be seen in the later discussion of divine freedom. Such a view as we have been sketching is compatible with Leibnizianism, just as it is compatible with an ontology which distinguishes between individual essential and individual accidental properties, and a Hume-like ontology of radical causal contingency.

Earlier in the chapter I deliberately avoided the prospect of arguing that a timeless God could be a person on the grounds that there are in fact numerous different concepts referred to by the word 'person'. We have opted, instead, for the task of considering arguments levelled against the idea of a timeless person and of attempting to refute each of these. But what has emerged from this defence is that it is consistent to ascribe to a timeless God powers which we normally say that only persons have even though such powers are not what all persons have.

Thus it is coherent to say that God timelessly knows that *p*, and that he timelessly desires (provided that such desires do not imply the cravings of a physical organism); and also, as we have just seen, it is coherent to say that he acts. While such powers are not perhaps sufficient for personhood they are certainly necessary, and in the absence of any compelling argument to the contrary they at least permit the view that a timeless person is possible, and *a fortiori* that possibly God exists timelessly.[22]

---

[21] *Confessions*, XI. 13–14, trans. R. S. Pine-Coffin, p. 263.
[22] For a defence of God's personhood along these lines see William E. Mann, 'Simplicity and Immutability in God', *International Philosophical Quarterly* (1983).

5
Eternity, Immutability, and Omniscience

In this chapter I shall first deploy and consider two arguments in favour of the logical consistency of the idea of God being both timelessly eternal and omniscient, then discuss the idea of divine immutability. On occasion divine eternity has been said to entail immutability, and sometimes immutability has been said to entail eternity. It has been claimed that divine eternity reduces to divine immutability, and that divine omniscience and immutability are incompatible.[1] All these claims will be discussed.

There are two principal arguments against divine omniscience which have implications for divine timeless eternity. The first, which we can call *the metaphysical doctrine*, is the claim that until a human being has freely chosen to perform some action *A* not even an omniscient being can know that *A* is to be performed. God cannot know the future since there is no future to know until that future has been rendered 'present in its causes' by the irrevocable decisions of free human agents.[2] But this is not so much a rebuttal of omniscience as a restriction of it; not even God can know what is not knowable, and until a free individual has chosen to act there is nothing for God to know, for it is not knowable that the individual will choose to act. It is a question whether an eternal omniscient being could exist given a universe in which there were individuals who are free in this sense, since

---

[1] For these positions see Ward, *Rational Theology*, ch. 7; Kenny, *God of the Philosophers*, 40, and Pike, *God and Timelessness*, ch. 3.

[2] Prior, 'The Formalities of Omniscience', 38. Divine omniscience is fully discussed in Jonathan L. Kvanvig, *The Possibility of an All-knowing God*. In ch. 5 Kvanvig provides a limited defence of the compatibility of timelessness, omniscience, and immutability.

such a universe seems to require that anyone, including God, who would know all about it, would have to undergo real change, and such change is incompatible with timeless eternity. God would have to change to come to know what any free agent has decided. If so, then God could not eternally know what such a free creature will do.

This more radical objection to omniscience will be postponed until later. The present chapter is concerned with an argument against omniscience of a different type, but one which also depends upon the fact that the universe changes. This argument has taken two forms in the literature, which can be called the *argument from indexicals* and the *argument from immutability*, respectively.

The argument against omniscience from indexicals can be expressed in the following way:

(1) An eternal God is not subject to change.
(2) An eternal God knows everything.
(3) A being that knows everything always knows what time it is.
(4) A being that always knows what time it is is necessarily subject to change.
(5) Therefore an eternal God is subject to change.
(6) Therefore an eternal God is not an eternal God.
(7) Therefore there is no eternal God.[3]

Whatever the merits of the argument it shows how closely the concepts of eternity, omniscience, and change are logically intertwined.

The crucial step in the argument is obviously (3), for if it is true that there is at least one thing which an eternal being cannot know then such a being cannot be omniscient and if omniscience is essential to God, no timelessly eternal being, whatever his other powers, can be God. But is the argument sound and convincing? We shall consider two counter-arguments to it, the first a *reductio ad absurdum* of it.

If one can only know now precisely what is happening

---

[3] This argument has been adapted from Stump and Kretzmann 'Eternity', 455.

now, then presumably the same principle applies to God's knowledge of what is happening here, as we saw when considering the idea of divine spacelessness. But as we also saw this *reductio* is perhaps not too serious for the defender of the view that God is in time, since such a person may be prepared to settle for God's existence in space as well. Yet it would involve certain other rather serious consequences, consequences which could be pressed to the point of incoherence. For if God has to be here to know what is going on here, then perhaps he cannot also be there as well.

But the *reductio* can be pressed further, in a different direction. If one can only know now precisely what is happening now, then, by the same token, one can only know precisely what is happening to *me* if one is *me*.[4] For on the view of omniscience being considered, just as God, to be omniscient, has to know not only what is happening on 30 July 1987, but also (supposing 30 July 1987 to be the present moment) what is happening *now*, so God, to be omniscient, has to know not only that Helm is married, but also to know the truth of the statement (uttered by Helm), 'I am married'. For as there are certain times (and places) which an omniscient being must be at if he is to know certain statements to be true, so there are certain people he must be if he is to know certain statements about those people. He can know, while not being Helm, that Helm is married, but he cannot know the truth of 'I am married' as uttered by me. He cannot know what it is to be me married, unless he is me.

But surely this is an absurd result. If an omniscient being has to be me now in order to know the truth of the true utterance 'I am married' and if he has to be you now in order to know the truth of your utterance 'I am married', then he has to be both me now and you now. But it follows, from the principle of the transitivity of identity, that I now am identical with you now, since some omniscient being is now

[4] See John Perry, 'The Problem of the Essential Indexical', *Nous* (1979). The argument being considered is given in Kretzmann, 'Omniscience and Immutability'.

identical with us both. Hence we are both identical with each other and with God, that is, we both are God. It would seem, from this, that the *reductio* could only be avoided at the price of some version of pantheism or panpsychism, views which are at odds with classical Judeo-Christian theism.

It might be replied to this argument that God, if he exists in time, might know what it is like to be married without being married, and without being me married, but that he could not even know what it is like to be in time if he is eternal. Even if this last point is correct, it will not suffice as a rebuttal of the *reductio*, for what God needs to know if he is to retain his omniscience is the precise truth, *as I express it*, when I now say 'I am married' or otherwise correctly represent to myself the fact of being married. It is reasonable to conclude that this requirement for omniscience is too strong, or alternatively that omniscience is unstatable in any plausible form.

In *The God of the Philosophers*, Anthony Kenny deploys a similar though not identical argument to the one just considered. Kenny claims that 'Today is Friday' (uttered on Friday) and 'Yesterday was Friday' (uttered on Saturday) do not express the same items of knowledge because 'what I am glad about when I am glad that today is Friday is not at all necessarily the same thing as what I am glad about when I am glad yesterday was Friday'.[5] What Kenny says here is correct, but as expressed it reveals no difficulties for omniscience and indexicals. For the true comparison to be drawn is between 'I am glad that today is Friday' uttered on Friday and 'I was glad (yesterday) that yesterday was Friday' uttered on Saturday, and these two utterances do express the same fact.

But do they? If for the moment we waive further discussion of the argument just considered, can omniscience be salvaged by employing the technical notion of a proposition? If so, we can then say that even though two reports of knowledge were phenomeno-logically distinct, as

---

[5] *God of the Philosophers*, 46. Cf. Prior, 'Formalities of Omniscience'.

'I am glad that today is Friday' uttered on Friday and 'I was glad (yesterday) that yesterday was Friday' (uttered on Saturday), the two utterances are cognitively equivalent, they both express the same fact. If so, then omniscience could be defined as 'the knowledge of all facts and the absence of belief in any falsehoods'.

But can such an equivalence be made out? In particular, can utterances containing temporal indexicals such as 'now' and tensed verbs be given equivalents in which there are no temporal indexicals and no tensed verbs?

Answering this question satisfactorily clearly depends upon what counts as two or more expressions being or expressing the same proposition. Let us begin by considering one or two possible answers to this problem.[6] One possible criterion is in terms of propositional attitudes: *a* and *b* both express the same proposition if it is impossible to believe *a* and not to believe *b*, or vice versa. The basic problem with such a criterion is that for it to operate in the case of a timeless God such a God must be able to adopt a propositional attitude to, to believe, temporal indexical expressions, when manifestly this is impossible. Any occurrence of a temporal indexical such as 'now', 'then', or 'already' in an expression, cannot be used by a timeless God to refer to any time or times in his history, since a timelessly eternal God does not have a history. So this criterion is hardly satisfactory.

Alternatively, one might simply hold that every temporal-indexical expression has a non-indexical equivalent, and that it is sufficient for an omniscient, timelessly eternal God to believe all such non-indexical equivalents that are true, and none that are false. God would know that what some time-bound individual said was true by knowing its timeless equivalent. But even God would presumably need to know which two were equivalent, and to know this he would have to know, that is properly to express, the indexical. Yet

---

[6] Criteria for propositional identity are discussed in Richard M. Gale, 'Omniscience–Immutability Arguments', *American Philosophical Quarterly* (Oct. 1986).

perhaps not. Perhaps God can go beyond identifying Smith's indexical utterance as 'What Smith said on such and such an occasion' to actually knowing what he said, his utterance, to knowing that there is a non-indexical equivalent to what he said, and to knowing what that non-indexical equivalent actually is.

So while the first criterion is unsatisfactory it is not altogether clear that the second is, and there is a third possibility: that two expressions are identical if they have the same truth value in every possible world. If this criterion is applied only to contingent propositions, since necessary truths and falsehoods obviously fail to meet it, then a sentence such as 'It is raining now' uttered by A on 30 July 1987 has the same truth-conditions as the sentence 'It is raining on 30 July 1987', and so expresses the same proposition. So a timeless God knows that it is raining now if he knows its dated equivalent.

But failing the cogency of any of these suggestions it is open to a defender of the idea of divine timelessness to retreat to what Gale calls 'co-reporting': for every tokening of 'It is raining now' there is an equivalent of the form: that it is raining at t_1.[7] The objection to this is that it only allows for second-class omniscience. But what is wrong with second-class omniscience? Gale argues that it has an insuperable difficulty; it leads to a paradox of perfection in that an absolutely perfect being lacks items of knowledge, the knowledge that it is raining now, for example, which non-perfect beings may possess. But even if such a being knew the truth of all temporal indexicals at the times when they were true he would know nothing timelessly. So while an omniscient being in time would know more than a timeless omniscient being he would also know less.

Let us consider these points further, first by looking again at our illustrative discussion of non-temporal indexicals, and then by discussing omniscience once again.

[7] Ibid. 325.

I know that I am married. But the only person who is able truly to represent to himself the fact that he is married to one particular individual is me. Does this mean that I know facts that no other individual knows or could know, and therefore know facts that an ostensibly omniscient being does not know? In a sense, yes. But is this sense merely trivial? Consider that an omniscient being, while not knowing that he is married to some particular person, indeed necessarily not knowing this, will nevertheless know the following facts:

   (i) Helm exists;
  (ii) Helm is married to some particular person;
 (iii) Helm can truly represent (ii) to himself by the utterance 'I am married to . . .'; and
 (iv) On (say) Thursday 3 September 1987 Helm truly represents (ii) to himself by the utterance 'I am married to . . .'.

Furthermore, while the truth of Helm's utterance or thought 'I am married to . . .' entails (i)–(iv), these same conditions also entail Helm's uttering 'I am married'. So that an omniscient being, if it is plausibly supposed that he knows the truth of (i)–(iv) knows what entails Helm uttering the truth 'I am married' or representing to himself that true thought. What the omniscient being lacks is the ability himself truly to utter 'I am married', in the very same sense in which Helm can utter 'I am married'. But this is an 'inability' of a curious kind. For if the omniscient being were to lose this 'inability', or to have it removed, it would follow that he would cease to be the individual he is, and become someone else.

It is a conceptual truth about individuals that they are distinct from all other individuals. And one way of expressing this distinctness in individuals who have the gift of thought and speech about themselves of an indexical kind is to refer to themselves indexically. It is hardly therefore a deficiency in an individual that he cannot refer to *others* in the indexical mode which he can necessarily employ only of himself, any more than it is a deficiency in such an individual that he does not know what it is like to be a stone or a five-barred gate or any other object which necessarily does not have such powers of indexical self-reference.

Let us compare the situation just discussed with the expression 'It is raining now'. It is correctly said that a timelessly eternal God cannot know that it is raining now, supposing this to be true. But in a situation in which someone truly utters 'It is raining now' on say 30 July 1987, a timeless omniscient individual can know the following:

(i) It is raining on 30 July 1987.
(ii) Someone living on 30 July 1987 can, and does, utter the true expression 'It is raining now'.

If the timelessly eternal omniscient individual knows all facts then his knowing that it is raining on 30 July 1987 entails that it is raining now for anyone who exists on 30 July 1987, and vice versa. That is, for an omniscient individual these states of affairs are mutually entailing. For the person in question this is not so, of course. Helm may believe that it is raining now without believing it is raining on 30 July 1987, because he may not know what the correct date is, and he may know that it is raining on 30 July 1987, without knowing that it is raining now, 30 July 1987, because someone may reliably tell him that it is raining on that date, and he not know that that date is now. By contrast, an omniscient, eternal being can believe that it is raining on 30 July 1987. He cannot believe that it is raining now, but he can believe that it is raining now for Helm.

This argument is a version of one reproduced in the literature about omniscience and immutability, in which it is claimed[8] that the same item of knowledge can be variously expressed, in different propositions.

Besides the difficulty of supposing that a God who is

---

[8] See e.g. Castaneda, 'Omniscience and Indexical Reference'; Swinburne, 203–9; Kenny, *God of the Philosophers*, ch. 4. For further discussion of Castaneda, see Gale, 'Omniscience–Immutability Arguments', 328–32.

eternal is also omniscient it may also be argued that it is equally difficult to suppose that a God who is in time can be omniscient. For, it may be said, if God is in time, existing at *t2* when *t2* is now, then he cannot now know precisely what was taking place at *t1* since there are facts about *t1* which he cannot know now. And if there are facts which God cannot know now then God is not omniscient now. Hence no God who is in time can be omniscient.

Suppose that it is raining at *t1*. Then God, at *t1*, can know the truth of the utterance 'It is raining now' but at *t2*, which is later than *t1*, he cannot know the truth of the utterance. Hence there are matters which God knew before which he does not know now, and vice versa, and so he is less than omniscient. So, on this argument, there are facts about his past which God does not now know because there are facts about a time which can only be known at that time. So there are facts which God keeps on learning and unlearning. While God on 25 September no longer knows that 24 September is now, and so unlearns it, he comes to learn that 25 September is now. Stephen Davis seems to commit himself to this view and it appears to be inconsistent with the view that God is omniscient.[9]

One straightforward way to deal with this problem is to say that certain facts are no longer facts. 'It is now raining' uttered on 24 September no longer expresses a fact once that date slips into the past. It is a fact that it *was* raining on 24 September, but that it *is* raining on 24 September is a different fact from the fact that it *was* raining then. But this argument rests upon a very narrow view of what a fact is. As we saw, it is sometimes said that two expressions express the same fact if one of those expressions can be believed without the other being believed. But the present argument rests upon an even stricter criterion of what counts as a different fact. Two expressions express the same fact, on this view,

---

[9] *Logic and the Nature of God*, 34: '*B* does not report the same fact on June 17 when *B* says "Yesterday it was 16 June", as *A* does on 16 June when *A* says "Today is 16 June".'

only if the fact is expressed by two (or more) token indexical utterances of the same type.

A preferable way of handling the same difficulty is to adopt a different criterion of what is to count as a fact, such as the one already discussed, which allows that the same facts can be expressed using different expressions. If one says that what counts as sameness of fact is sameness of truth-conditions, then 'It is raining now' uttered on 24 September and 'It was raining then' (uttered on the 25th) have the same truth-conditions, namely that it is raining on 24 September. What an omniscient God knows about what happened in the past remains the same, though the past continues to enter into new relations as God's progress through time continues, and his mode of expressing what he knows correspondingly varies.

This saves God's omniscience even supposing that God is in time, though even in these circumstances God does not know at a time all the facts about a time in the past since that time is continually entering into new relations with new facts previously unknown to God (if there is human free will in an agent-causal or libertarian sense). But this solution to divine omniscience takes away any supposed advantages there might be in thinking of God as being in time, for as we have seen it is also open to someone who holds that God is timelessly eternal.

Returning to the argument set out at the beginning of this chapter let us reconsider

(3) A being that knows everything always knows what time it is.

We may suppose that the first 'knows' that occurs in (3) is present-tensed, but if so (3) will not do as a statement of timeless knowledge. So we must amend the proposition taking the 'knows' to be tenseless. The proposition now becomes

(3a) A being that knows (tenselessly) everything always knows what time it is.

Perhaps this does not satisfactorily meet the objection that an omniscient being would not know what the time is *at*. As Norman Kretzmann put it such a God would know only 'the entire scheme of contingent events from beginning to end at once, and not *at what stage of realization* that scheme now is'.[10] A possible reply to this claim is that it is based upon an inadequate understanding of what eternity is. Eternity is such that the whole of eternity is eternally simultaneous with the actual occurrence of every event in time. 'The only way in which an eternal entity can be aware of any temporal event is to be aware of it as it is actually happening. And from the eternal viewpoint every temporal event is actually happening.'[11] So eternity is eternally simultaneous with every successive now, and so an eternal being experiences every now—and every then—as present. Earlier we noted certain difficulties in formulating a coherent account of timeless eternity in this way, but let us waive these for present purposes.

While this reply is consistent with the concept of a timelessly eternal being, and brings out clearly that the simultaneity in question is not a tensed simultaneity, it still does not go all the way to meet the objection, and perhaps it does not do as much as Stump and Kretzmann believe that it does. Take the claim that an eternal being cannot be aware of any temporal event as it happens. This claim does not leave itself open to the objection that it makes all temporal events simultaneous with each other (since the eternal being is simultaneous with each of them) because the notion of simultaneity used to elucidate that claim is that of eternal-simultaneity, a simultaneity which cannot bear any relations of tense to any periods of time.

But if so, it is hard to see how the claim that an eternal being is aware of any temporal event 'as it is actually

---

[10] 'Omniscience and Immutability', 414 (italic in the original).
[11] Stump and Kretzmann, 'Eternity', 457.

happening' is going to satisfy the objector, since the 'actually' here is—and must be—not the temporal 'actually' on which the objection is based but the eternal 'actually'. For the eternal being the happening cannot take time. The eternal being cannot know, say, that 2 May is present, 1 May is past, and 3 May still future. For not only does he eternally experience today as now, he eternally experiences yesterday as now, and tomorrow as now as well. ('From the eternal viewpoint every temporal event is actually happening'.)

To see the basic unsatisfactoriness of this proposal, let us revert to the analogy of knowing that one is married. Stump and Kretzmann's proposal is as though someone had proposed that an omniscient individual knows not only that Helm is married but also that he knows that I am married as I do. Yet he does not know this because he is me, nor does he know that Jones is married as he does because he is Jones. Rather he knows these things because he is both me and Jones. To transpose what Stump and Kretzmann say: 'The only way in which an omniscient entity can be aware of any personal state (let my awareness of the fact that I am married be my awareness of a personal state) is to be aware of it as actually personal.' But the omniscient being is not me in the way in which I am me, for in the way in which I am me I am distinct from everyone else. Rather, the omniscient being 'is me' in a way in which I am *not* me, in a way which is compatible with him also being Jones (in a way in which Jones is not Jones).

Perhaps this is a possible state of affairs. It is certainly not my purpose in considering it to argue that it is not. But possible or not it can hardly be thought to meet the basic issue, which is that an omniscient being cannot know that I am married in precisely the way in which I know I am married, or that an eternal being cannot know in precisely the same way as I do that 30 July is now. And since ways of knowing facts are themselves facts, there are facts that a timeless being does not know, and hence such a being cannot be omniscient.

The argument from indexicals against the idea of omniscience has some force against anyone who claims that omniscience and timelessness are compatible properties of an individual, yet the view that God is in time my find itself in a set of parallel difficulties. But we have seen, in considering the argument from indexicals, that this objection is not as powerful as it may have seemed at first. For though there are ways in which an eternal being cannot represent certain facts to himself he can still know those facts, or at least he knows facts that entail the facts that he cannot represent to himself, and he knows that this entailment holds. And this is sufficient for omniscience. It is satisfactory, in other words, simply to deny that certain ways of representing facts are themselves additional facts of any great significance for the understanding of omniscience.

In considering the problems of formulating an adequate concept of God it would not be surprising if it were necessary to balance one set of considerations against another. So, in the case of divine omniscience, if it is granted that there are expressions of propositions which a timeless omniscient being could not use, this must be balanced against the fact that a timeless omniscient being knows the future, our future, something which other accounts of divine omniscience find difficulty in accommodating, as we shall see.

The argument against divine eternity just considered has also been used as an argument against divine immutability, the immutability of God who is in time. Frequently in the literature a connection is claimed between eternity and immutability—a connection perhaps borne out by the result just noted—and equally frequently such a claim is modified or denied.

It is possible to think of divine immutability in two ways, or as having two strengths. To say that God is immutable may refer to his essential character, or it may refer to any predicate that is true of God. And the immutability may be

logical, or it may have some weaker force.[12] This gives four
possibilities:

(a) God is immutable if in fact his character never changes;
(b) God is immutable if his character could not change;
(c) God is immutable if in fact nothing about him
     changes;
(d) God is immutable if nothing about him could change.

For someone who is immutable in sense (a) there is a
character trait (or a set of these) such that it is psychologically
or morally impossible for him to change that trait. He is
immutably generous, say, because on any occasions on which
generosity is called for, and he has something to be generous
with, he is uniformly generous. According to sense (b) a
person is immutable if there is a character trait or set of traits
such that if he lacked that trait or that set he could not be the
individual he is. If he is such that he could not be the person he
is unless he were generous, then he is essentially and
immutably generous.

For sense (c) a person is immutable if as a matter of fact
there is no respect in which he changes, where by 'change' is
not meant 'merely Cambridge' change. And for sense (d),
the strongest sense, a person is immutable if there is no respect
in which he could really change; if he were to undergo real
change in any respect whatsoever then he would cease to
exist.

How do these four senses apply to the concept of God?
Swinburne suggests that one of the reasons that theologians
and philosophers have had for thinking that God is timeless is

---

[12] There is some confusion in Swinburne's account of immutability. On the
one hand he distinguishes between God not changing in character, and God not
changing at all, and he labels the latter the 'stronger' sense (*Coherence of Theism*,
212). Later (214) he calls the doctrine that God cannot logically change (as
opposed to the doctrine that God does not in fact change), the 'stronger sense'. Yet
clearly there are two different issues—the question whether the immutability if
factual or logical, and the question of whether or not immutability covers all
predicates or only 'character' predicates. For a defence of divine immutability see
Mann, 'Simplicity and Immutability in God'.

'that it would provide backing for and explanation of the doctrine of God's total immutability'.[13] More precisely, timelessness would entail total immutability and total immutability would entail timelessness. If this mutual entailment could be established then it would provide another reason for arguing that God is timelessly eternal, for only such a God could be immutable.

But this is to anticipate. Let us look first at how the four senses of 'immutable' which have been distinguished apply to the concept of God. There are difficulties in supposing that senses (*a*) and (*b*) could apply to God. If God is immutable in sense (*a*), then it would be possible for many other individuals than God to be immutable. Someone who is incorrigibly and uniformly brave or stupid would be immutable in exactly the same sense in which God is immutable if God is immutable in sense (*b*), and this is obviously unsatisfactory. If God were immutable in sense (*c*) while the last objection would be ruled out, it would follow that there is a possible world in which whoever is in fact, that is, in the actual world immutable is not immutable in that world.[14] But this is clearly inappropriate in the case of God. For what is usually understood by divine immutability is not merely that God is in fact unchanging but that he could not change.

We are thus left with sense (*d*), which we might dub 'essential total changelessness'. I shall now argue that divine immutability in this sense entails eternity.[15] Pike regards this as plausible, given certain assumptions to be examined shortly, and Swinburne denies it only because he is working with a sense of 'immutable' weaker than our sense, and because he is already, in his discussion of divine immutability, making the assumption that God is in time.[16]

---

[13] *Coherence of Theism*, 218.

[14] For further discussion on this sense, see the exchange between Vincent Brummer and myself in *Religious Studies* (1984), and T. V. Morris, 'Properties, Modalities and God', *Philosophical Review* (Jan. 1984).

[15] In this endeavour I am not alone. Thomas Aquinas and Augustine do the same. (See Pike, *God and Timelessness*, 41.)

[16] Swinburne, *Coherence of Theism*, 214.

So does divine immutability (in sense (*d*)) entail eternity? (The question of whether divine eternity entails immutability is less central, because divine immutability is not what is in dispute, and the fact, if it is a fact, that eternity entails immutability provides no reason for concluding that God's existence is eternal.) In his discussion of this issue Pike calls into question Thomas Aquinas's argument[17] and provides one of his own. His own argument is one that, according to Pike, rests on a number of questionable assumptions[18] and eventually he opts for a weaker sense of immutability for God.[19] The assumptions that Pike regards as questionable concern 'sufficient conditions for certain *possibilities*'.[20] The two assumptions are:

(i) If a given individual has location in time it would be consistent to say that that individual persists for more than one moment.

(ii) If it is consistent to say that a given individual persists for more than one moment in time, it is consistent (though, again, it might be false) to say that that individual undergoes change.[21]

Clearly these assumptions, or some such assumptions, are required in order to be able to dispute the claim that being in time is consistent with immutability in sense (*d*) above.

The plausibility of the first assumption can be strengthened by the thought that it is actually true. For there are individuals who exist in time for more than a moment. In these cases, temporal location is a sufficient condition not for the possibility of persistence but for the actuality of persistence. That is, the fact that there are individuals in time which persist for more than a moment shows that this is possible. But is it possible for all individuals in time? Perhaps

[17] Pike, *God and Timelessness*, 42.
[18] Ibid. 50–1, 165.
[19] Ibid. 178.
[20] Ibid. 43.
[21] Ibid. 43.

there are individuals which are not only momentary, but essentially momentary. Perhaps a flash of light could not last for more than a moment, but has only one temporal part. But even if this is so it will not have relevance to the case of God, for it is agreed on all hands that God, if he exists, either exists eternally or for a temporal duration which is longer than a moment.

What about the second assumption, which is clearly the more important of the two? Does anything that exists for more than a moment have the possibility of changing? If so, then nothing in time is immutable in sense (*d*). This assumption of Pike's might be questioned by considering, with Swinburne, that 'a totally immutable thing could just go on existing for ever without being timeless—especially if other things, such as the universe, changed, while the immutable thing continued changeless'.[22] What Swinburne claims, plausibly enough, is that something could exist in time and not change, i.e. not really change. But this plausible suggestion does not meet Pike's point for it does not challenge Pike's second assumption, which is not the denial that something could persist through time and not change, but the denial that something could persist through time and not possibly change. What Swinburne would have to show, to meet Pike's point, is not that such a persisting thing *does* not change, but that it *could* not change.

Furthermore, while what Swinburne says may be logically possible in the case of an 'immutable thing', supposing that this thing is not a part of the universe, it is less clear that it could be true of God. For while an immutable thing might go on existing for ever, such a thing could not be God because God has in fact acted in the creation of the universe

[22] *Coherence of Theism*, 219. Peter Geach holds that although God is in time he does not have a successive mental life nor does he enter into real relations with his creation. God does not really change, for to suppose that he does makes it impossible to think of God as the cause of the world. Geach rejects the idea of God's timelessness because of its inherent difficulties, not because of any alleged advantages that follow from God being in time. See 'Causality and Creation', in *God and the Soul*, and 'God's Relation to the World' in *Logic Matters*.

and presumably still acts to sustain it moment by moment. Furthermore, according to Swinburne, one reason for supposing that God is in time is that it enables us to think of him as having a rich, successive mental life, a life of intentions and purposes, and for him to witness the fulfilment and frustration of his plans. Thus an immutable thing which existed alongside a changing universe, and which only changed by continually entering into new relations with the changing universe, could hardly be God, at least not the God of classical theism. A God who acts, but who is immutable in sense (*d*), must be timelessly eternal, since any action in time (as opposed to an action the effect of which is in time) presupposes a time before the act, and a time when the act is completed, and thus presupposes real change, which rules out immutability in sense (*d*). Not only is it true that such a God may change, he must change. So immutable (in sense (*d*)) agency does appear to entail the eternity of the agent. Hence while some individual's immutability may not entail timeless eternity, considered in the abstract, yet *God's* immutability would appear to.

But why is it of importance to stress God's total immutability? Would it not be sufficient to maintain that God is immutable in character, that he will not become either morally better or morally worse, and that he is not subject to fits, passions, or moods? Though the distinction between total immutability and immutability in character may seem to be of the merest academic interest, issues of considerable importance quickly intrude, as we shall now see.

In a classic discussion of God in Chapter Eighteen of the *Monologion* Anselm provides three arguments for the conclusion that divine immutability entails timelessness. Keith Ward has argued not against this entailment but against the cogency of the reasons given for immutability. Against Anselm's argument that God cannot be changed by anything other than himself, Ward replies that 'God could freely create beings which are themselves free, in being self-determining, within the limits set by him. If this is conceivable, then even

God cannot know in advance how they will choose, since the choice is undetermined.[23] When such choices have been made God will know something which he could not know before.

Whether God could know beforehand the choices of agents which have the liberty of indifference or agent-caused freedom is a vexed and controversial matter, and later on I shall argue that there is reason to think that he cannot. For the moment I shall anticipate the conclusion of this discussion and agree with Ward. So Ward argues:

(1) It is possible for God to create free creatures.
(2) If God does create free creatures he will not know in advance what they will do.
(3) God will know what they do when they have done it.
(4) So God comes to know things of which he previously was ignorant.
(5) Therefore God changes.
(6) Therefore God is not immutable.

But by itself this is not a very powerful argument against divine immutability, for it is open to the defender of divine timelessness to deny (1). For if God is timeless then it is not possible for him to do anything that requires that he change over time. What Ward's argument does show, however, is that if God can be changed in the sense that he learns things then he is in time, and if there are people with the liberty of indifference or agent-causal freedom and this is incompatible with the timelessly eternal knowledge of what they will do, then God changes in coming to learn what they do. But as an argument against immutability it is stalemated, since the defender of divine timelessness is naturally enough not going to allow that God could do anything which required that he be not timeless.

But Ward's argument is of value in that it provides further evidence for the fact that the concepts of divine full immutability and eternity are connected in that no individual

[23] *Rational Theology*, 51.

creator or knower in time could be immutable in sense (*d*). Furthermore the argument shows that the concepts of omniscience and immutability are also connected, not by the already discussed argument from indexicals, but from the considerations about creaturely freedom. For if there are creatures with the power of indifferent or agent-causal freedom then the exercise of their choice will change God by increasing his knowledge. God will know more after his free creatures have acted than he did before. The existence of such creatures would be sufficient to deny to God both omniscience and changelessness. Further aspects of this matter will be considered later when we discuss two different concepts of foreknowledge, the concept of foreknowledge which depends upon what is going to happen (foreknowledge in which God learns) and foreknowledge which does not depend upon what is going to happen, but which is a sufficient condition for what is known happening (foreknowledge in which God does not learn). But for the moment one can concur wholeheartedly with Ward when he writes (assuming the existence of creatures with agent-causal freedom or the liberty of indifference, what Ward calls 'real freedom') that:

It is useless to say, with Boethius, that God knows free acts non-temporally. For, given real freedom, God cannot complete his act of creation until he knows all the differences that the acts of creatures make to the initial conditions of various time segments. One has a picture of God seeing all the choices of creatures, and then determining the whole world to take account of them, by a non-temporal act. But this picture is incoherent.[24]

Ward's second argument against the need to ascribe immutability in the strong sense to God is that though random change in God would be a defect, 'creative spontaneity', akin to human artistic creativity, would not be.[25] Such spontaneity would make God capable of thinking

---

[24] Ibid. 152.
[25] Ibid. 152.

of some possibility at some time which he had not anticipated thinking of at some earlier time. Here once again we can notice a strong relation between changelessness and omniscience, since if God comes to know of certain possibilities which he did not know of previously, he could not previously have been omniscient.[26]

This argument does not show, any more than the previous one did, that God is immutable in the strong sense but not timeless, but rather that God is mutable and therefore in time. It is an argument for the conceptual connection between mutability and being in time (and, by implication, for the conceptual connection of immutability (in sense (*d*)) and timelessness). But it is not an argument for the superiority of one of these pairs of concepts over the other in developing a coherent concept of God.

The problem with this second argument of Ward's is not one of showing it to be formally invalid but of evaluating the debate in more general terms. Ward suggests that a God who is the creator would be imaginatively spontaneous in ways that not even God himself could anticipate, and this entails God being in time. So God is called 'creator' by analogy with human artistic creation. Such appeals to analogy are difficult to weigh up, because it is not clear which elements of the comparison to allow and which not. But suppose that it is argued that the element of spontaneous creativity ought to be retained in our understanding of God. By what argument can such a conclusion be reached? How does one decide on general grounds without appeal to divine revelation, say, that a God whose creativity is exercised through creative spontaneity is superior (or better, or truer) than one whose creativity is exercised by an eternal fiat *ex nihilo*?

Ward's third argument is a response to the Anselmian claim that God cannot change himself[27] because to do so God would have to precede himself, and this is incoherent. He argues that the intelligibility of the universe can be

---

[26] Ibid. 154.
[27] Ibid. 157.

grounded in God in a way that does not require his full changelessness; God need be changeless only in the sense that he is the only creator, and his creativity is exercised spontaneously.

But this argument raises general issues (for example, about intelligibility) which go beyond the issue of timelessness. And certainly Ward is not arguing here that immutability *per se* does not entail timelessness.

It is time to draw a philosophical moral from this discussion. What I have shown is that the claim that God exists in timeless eternity enables one to trade off one particular mode of divine knowledge, a mode which requires the use of temporal indexical expressions, for an enlargement of the range of God's knowledge, a range which encompasses God's knowledge of the future, that which is future to those who are in time. And as trading away a particular mode of knowledge does not decrease God's knowledge in any material respect, and enlarging the range of God's knowledge increases it, and as God is by definition omniscient, the trade-off is worth making.

We have also seen that there is a conceptual connection between divine immutability and divine eternity in that an individual who is immutable in the strong sense must be eternal, and vice versa. It follows in turn that divine timeless eternity is the conceptual link between immutability (in the strong sense) and omniscience. Only a timeless God can be both strongly immutable and omniscient.

6

Timelessness and Foreknowledge

THIS chapter and the next are concerned with different sets of arguments about the alleged incompatibility between divine foreknowledge and human freedom, according to which God's knowledge of human actions is inconsistent with those actions being performed freely, performed in a way that is incompatible with causal determinism. In the present chapter we shall examine Boethius' claim, and one modern reconstruction of it, that divine timelessness holds the key to the reconciliation of the two, because foreknowledge is not, in God's case, foreknowledge at all. I shall argue that this claim fails. We shall then go on to look at the legitimacy of talking of divine foreknowledge where God is timeless and rebut the presumption that such talk has metaphysical implications. The inevitability of such talk leads to some general remarks about the semantics of all our talk of a timeless, eternal God.

Then, in the following chapter, we shall consider whether the prospect of reconciling divine foreknowledge and human freedom fares any better on the assumption that God is in time.

One of the alleged consequences of Boethius' classic definition of God's timeless eternity, and one strong reason for some philosophers and theologians maintaining divine timelessness, is that it provides a way of reconciling divine foreknowledge and human freedom. We shall look, in the first instance, at the criticisms which have been made of the coherence of Boethius' account, and then at the problem of timelessness and foreknowledge itself. In his definition of eternity as 'the endless and perfect possession of life all at once'[1] Boethius is followed by Anselm, Augustine, Aquinas, and many another.[2] While one reason for predicating

---

[1] *The Consolation of Philosophy*, v. 6.
[2] Anselm, *Proslogion*, ch. 24; Augustine, *Confessions*, XI. 11, *City of God*, XI. xxi.

timeless eternity of God is that it allegedly provides an argument for the logical compatibility of divine foreknowledge and human freedom,[3] it is interesting that neither Anselm nor Augustine appears to use divine eternity in this way, though Boethius and Aquinas do. In deploying the notion of divine eternity in this way Boethius uses the following simile.

Since the state of God is ever that of eternal presence, His knowledge, too, transcends all temporal change and abides in the immediacy of His presence. It embraces all the infinite recesses of past and future and views them in the immediacy of its knowing as though they are happening in the present. If you wish to consider, then, the foreknowledge or prevision by which He discovers all things, it will be more correct to think of it not as a kind of foreknowledge of the future, but as the knowledge of a never ending presence. So that it is better called providence or 'looking forth' than prevision or 'seeing beforehand'. For it is far removed from matters below and looks forth at all things as though from a lofty peak above them.[4]

On this simile Martha Kneale has commented:

Presumably what he means is that the man on the top of the mountain can see the bends and ups and downs of a road all at once whereas the traveller on the road sees only a limited stretch at a given time. But when we come to think it out, the simile does not help. The spectator on high sees the road all at once but he does not see the traveller in all positions at once. This would be a contradiction. His perceptions must be as successive as the positions themselves.[5]

---

[3] e.g. Swinburne, *Coherence of Theism*, 216.

[4] *Consolation of Philosophy*, v. 6.

[5] Martha Kneale, 'Eternity and Sempiternity', *Proc. of the Aristotelian Soc.* (1968–9), 227. Perhaps Mrs Kneale is taking Boethius' simile too literally, in assuming that God's knowledge is gained by perception and also that God, the spectator, must be in time. All that the simile is intended to convey is that a hilltop spectator is aware at once of all the features that a traveller down below can only encounter successively. On this point see E. J. Khamara, 'Eternity and Omniscience', *Philosophical Quarterly* (1974).

But perhaps the validity of this comment depends upon taking Boethius, in his definition and his simile, to be understanding the divine life *all at once* as a temporal all at once, thus in effect contradicting himself, saying that God's eternity is a kind of compressed time. By contrast in their 'Eternity' article Stump and Kretzmann indicate that they understand Boethius' argument as follows:

It is impossible that any event occur later than an eternal entity's present state of awareness, since every temporal event is ET-simultaneous with that state, and so an eternal entity cannot *fore*know anything. Instead, such an entity considered as omniscient knows—is aware of—all temporal events, including those which are future with respect to our current temporal viewpoint; but, because the times at which those future events will be present events are ET-simultaneous with the whole of eternity, an omniscient eternal entity is aware of them as they are present.[6]

So Stump and Kretzmann claim that all contingent events are ET-simultaneous with God's eternally present state of awareness. In an earlier discussion I have already claimed that the use of ET-simultaneity is *ad hoc* and unilluminating. 'ET-simultaneity' is a device introduced to permit certain inferences and to prevent other inferences, particularly any which make use of the transitivity of simultaneity, but which is otherwise unilluminating. ET-simultaneity has no independent merit, for it does not explain anything which is otherwise mysterious. So while such an understanding of Boethius is formally consistent it does not actually advance understanding.

So prima facie the logical incompatibility between divine foreknowledge and human freedom remains. For if God knew yesterday that Jones will perform a particular action at some time in the future then God's knowledge is past. Being

---

[6] 'Eternity', 453–4.

past it is unchangeable, and so necessary. If God knew yesterday what will happen, then it cannot now be the case, or any time in the future be the case, that he did *not* know yesterday what will happen. Nothing can happen to make him not know. But if a proposition *p* is necessary and *p* entails *q*, then *q* is necessary. (That is, $[Np. N(p \supset q)] \supset Nq$.) So the action in question, being foreknown by God, is necessary, and so not free. For if we were to suppose that Jones were free, he would have the power to change the past. God's foreknowledge of Jones's action 'secures' its performance. Even if this conclusion is disputed, on the grounds that one of the premises of the argument, that God has foreknowledge of human actions, is false, because God is timeless, the problem is not really solved. For this 'solution' proceeds not by demonstrating the logical compatibility of divine fore-knowledge and human freedom but by claiming that there is no divine foreknowledge in the first place.

So the conclusion we are faced with is that appealing to divine timelessness does not solve the problem of divine foreknowledge and human freedom. I accept this conclusion. Divine foreknowledge *is* logically incompatible with human (indeterministic) freedom.

Yet it could be said that, at the very least, the appeal to divine timelessness does modify the problem to the extent of ruling out of order any argument based upon divine *fore*knowledge. Nevertheless, talk of divine foreknowledge is still inevitable, and points to more general features of the semantics of our talk about a timeless God. For what I wish to claim is that in such talk the concept of foreknowledge applies not to a timeless knower's knowledge of certain events or actions, but to a temporal agent's recognition of timeless knowledge under certain temporal circumstances.

What is it that the timeless foreknowledge is before? It cannot be before anything for the timeless knower, for for him there is no temporal before or after, since he occupies no position in time. Thus for a timeless foreknower the statement (*a*) I foreknow that *A*,

where *A* is some event or action in a temporal 'stream', is necessarily false, since for it to be true *A* would have to stand in some temporal relation to the foreknower, which is impossible if the foreknower is timeless. However, though (*a*) is necessarily false, it does not follow that

(*b*) He foreknows that *A*

is necessarily false, where 'He' refers to the timeless knower, and where (*b*) is uttered by a temporal individual. In the same way, although temporal individuals can say that God, if he exists, has existed a day longer today than yesterday, God could not say this. This is a parallel to the fact that while the utterance 'I am not talking now' is necessarily false, 'He is not talking now' can be true, even though 'I' and 'He' refer to the same person. For 'I am not talking now' to be true the speaker would not have to be uttering anything and *a fortiori* not uttering the words 'I am not talking now', and likewise for 'I foreknow that *A*' to be true the speaker would have to be in time, but if he were he could not be timeless.

But if (*b*) is not necessarily false, what does it mean, and under what conditions would it be true? (*b*) might be paraphrased as:

(i) At a time before this time (the time of (i)'s utterance) the statement '*T* timelessly knows *A*' (where *T* refers to the timeless knower, and *A* is an event future to the time of the statement's utterance) is true.

Or, more neatly

(ii) Before *t* (where *t* is the present) the statement that *T* knows (timelessly) that *A* was true.

Where *T* is a timeless knower, it will follow that (i) and (ii) refer not simply to a particular time before the statement's utterance, but to any time before that time. What (i) and (ii) imply is that if anyone had asked yesterday, or at any time before the present, whether *T* timelessly knew *A* the answer would have been 'Yes'. But what would the point be of asking whether T timelessly knew A? If T is a timeless knower would it not be obvious that he timelessly knew A yesterday? What do (i) or (ii) say that the unvarnished 'T timelessly knows A' does not?

One thing that 'T foreknows A' implies that 'T timelessly knows A' does not is that A is an event. For suppose that A were the proposition *Red is a colour*, then it would be absurd to say that T foreknows that red is a colour, just as it would be absurd to say of a temporal individual that that individual foreknows that red is a colour. Knows before what? There can only be foreknowledge of things that happen. So whereas in 'T timelessly knows A' A could be an event, in 'T foreknows A' A must be an event; (i) and (ii) indicate this in a way in which 'T timelessly knows A' cannot.

A further way of making this point is to say that for T to know the future timelessly is for T to know an event future to some individual in time, and for T to know all about the future is for T to know all events future to some individual in time.

None of this implies the propriety of saying that all events are present, even eternally present, to such an omniscient, timeless knower. This way of talking is perfectly in order if all that is meant by it is that the knower knows all events, and knows them without having come to know them. But it generates unnecessary difficulties (perhaps encouraged by analogies drawn from hill-tops) to say that all events are present or eternally present to a timeless knower. He knows them not presently, but timelessly.

In a similar way, as was pointed out in earlier discussion, it will not do to claim that for a timeless knower every event is simultaneous with every other event. For simultaneity is a temporal relation, or can be. But why should the advocate of timelessness be drawn here, and say anything?[7] Otherwise, as we saw in Chapter 2, he appears to be committed to the view that there are two orders of time, the ordinary

---

[7] On this point, see Martha Kneale, 'Eternity and Sempiternity', 227.

unfolding of events for temporal agents and knowers, and one moment of super-time into which every event is compressed, for a tenseless knower. Instead of such nonsense why not say that the timeless knower knows timelessly, and leave it at that?

I suggest therefore that it makes sense to speak of a timeless knower's foreknowledge of events where the notion of foreknowledge expresses a temporal knower's belief or recognition that certain events were known timelessly before this time. But to say this is not to claim that the timeless knower's knowledge is analogical or anthropomorphic. It is literally knowledge, and it is literally foreknowledge, but it is not foreknowledge for the timeless knower.

If it is proper to speak of God's knowledge in this timeless way, then from the point in time of the temporal agent God knows beforehand. If he knows beforehand that p then it was true yesterday that God knows that p. But this knowledge is past, and hence unchangeable, and so necessary. What it entails, the action that is foreknown, is likewise necessary. Hence there cannot be free will, even if God's knowledge of human actions is timeless.

It is plausible to suppose that what is past is, in a certain sense, fixed, that it is impossible now to do anything to make the past different. The past is not logically necessary, but accidentally necessary. Plantinga attempts to clarify the sense in which it is and is not possible to change the past as follows: x is accidentally necessary if there is no basic action which I can now perform to change x.[8] So, accepting this, is what God believed yesterday about what I will do tomorrow accidentally necessary on this view? According to Plantinga, no, since I could by how I choose to act tomorrow change God's belief about me.

This raises the following problem: in discussing the relationship of divine foreknowledge to human freedom do we use as a premiss the accidental necessity of God's belief or

---

[8] 'On Ockham's Way Out', *Faith and Philosophy* (1986), 252–3.

the basic power to act and so to change any such belief? To answer this question it is necessary to know what individuals have power over and what not. That is, we need to clarify the intuitive distinction between 'hard' and 'soft' facts. This is an extremely difficult undertaking as is seen from various recent attempts, each of which has problems.[9]

Some of these problems will be examined in Chapter 8. For the moment, let us suppose that such difficulties can be overcome, and consider the question which lies behind them. In the controversy over divine foreknowledge and human freedom, which has explanatory priority, God's believings or what he believes? Those, such as Pike, who argue for the incompatibility of divine omniscience and indeterministic human freedom affirm the former. Given that God believes that certain things will happen how can they not happen? Those, such as Plantinga, who argue for the compatibility of divine omniscience and human freedom, stress the latter. Given that a person has the power to do A or to do not-A as he chooses, and that he chooses to do A, then God, since he is omniscient, must have believed that he would do A.

According to Kvanvig,[10] the incompatibilist is stuck because he cannot provide an argument from God's believings to the content of the beliefs. But neither can one provide an argument in the opposite direction. Perhaps the resolution of this *impasse* revolves around the degree to which God's believing can be modelled on ours.

However this may be, given the *impasse*, the argument from the necessity of the past, and hence the necessity of God's knowledge yesterday of what I shall do tomorrow, is entitled to be taken seriously.

To this line of argument it is possible to imagine Boethius (and Stump and Kretzmann) replying that whatever may be true of individuals in time, what 'It was true yesterday that God (timelessly) knows that p' cannot mean is that God's

---

[9] See ibid. 251 ff., Kvanvig, *The Possibility of an All-knowing God*, 102 ff., and John Martin Fischer, 'Freedom and Foreknowledge', *Philosophical Review* (1983).
[10] *The Possibility of an All-knowing God*, 109–10.

knowing is past (as opposed to present and future), any more than 'It will be true tomorrow that God (timelessly) knows that p' can mean that it is not true today, and that before tomorrow arrives God will have made up his mind. So whatever 'It was true yesterday that God (timelessly) knows that p' means it does not mean that God's knowledge is past, and so necessary.

There is the following reply to this argument. In the question 'What does God timelessly know now?', the 'now' may be regarded as providing an indexical reference to the questioner,[11] and not to God. If so, it will not follow that the verb in the question, 'know', is tensed. In such a question, the verb may or may not be tensed, depending upon the exact case. And so the question 'What does God (timelessly) know now?', is equivalent to 'What does God (timelessly) know at the time this utterance is being made?' The question is about what an individual who is in time judges at a particular time that God knows (timelessly). For a believer in timeless divine omniscience the answer to this rather bizarre question is that God may be said now to know timelessly exactly what he may be said at any other time to know timelessly. Thus to say that God may be said now to know timelessly that p is not to say that God, considered as a timeless knower, also exists sempiternally. Here we are arguing against Mrs Kneale's claim that timeless objects are also sempiternal objects.[12] Her grounds for this claim are that to say of an object that it is timeless is simply another way of saying that it is pointless to ask, for example, about its temporal origin. But though it is pointless to ask what the temporal origin of an object is it may nevertheless be true to say that it has no temporal origin.

[11] For this suggestion, see A. N. Prior 'Now', *Nous* (1968). To say that God timelessly knows now does not entail that what he knows is likewise indexed. What God timelessly knows are truths which are not exclusively about either our future or our present or our past even though we might express them as such. This matter will be discussed more fully in Chapter 8.

[12] 'Eternity and Sempiternity', 230–1.

Mrs Kneale is correct in saying that an utterance can be a pointless thing to say and yet still be true. But it appears to be a mistake to say that claiming that *A* is timeless is simply another way of claiming that it is pointless to ask such questions as 'When did *A* begin to exist?' For it is pointless to ask such questions of, for example, an indestructible substance but indestructible substances are not timeless.[13] In any case it seems odd to say that timeless objects are also sempiternal in rather the same way that it seems odd to say that because something such as a mental happening is spaceless it is present throughout space. Just as '*A* is spaceless' is not logically equivalent to '*A* is present throughout space' so '*A* is timeless' is not logically equivalent to 'A is present at all times'.

Mrs Kneale's further claim is that necessity entails sempiternity in the sense that God's necessary existence entails his sempiternal existence. She uses the following argument:

(1) God is a necessary being (assumption).
(2) Suppose that God is not sempiternal.
(3) If God is not sempiternal then there is a time when God does not exist.
(4) If (3), then possibly God does not exist.
(5) Thus God necessarily exists, and it is possible he does not exist (from (1) and (4)).
(6) Therefore, necessity entails sempiternity.[14]

But why should we suppose that (3) follows from (2)? For (1) and (2) are compatible with

(7) There is no time.

If so, then (2) does not entail (3). And if (3) does not follow from (2) then (4) does not follow, and the *reductio* fails.

It might be objected that (7), although possibly true, is certainly false. But it is not clear that one can appeal to

[13] Mrs Kneale makes this point herself and suggests that it may provide a *reductio* of her notion of timelessness (ibid. 231).
[14] Ibid. 231–2.

logically contingent propositions, however certain, to rebut the argument. (1), (2), and (7) are logically consistent. Hence even if (7) is in fact false its possible truth shows that (3) does not follow from (2). And if (3) does not follow from (2) then the fact that God is not sempiternal (supposing God to be a necessary being) does not entail a contradiction. Given that there is time, at any time '*T* exists timelessly' (where *T* is a timeless object) will be true. But where there is no time, there is no entailment. So there is a notion distinct from sempiternity, distinct in the sense that it does not entail it, namely timelessness.

And so while it is pointless to ask 'What does God timelessly know now?', pointless in the sense that there could be no different answer to this question than to the question 'What did God timelessly know then?', there is nevertheless a true answer to the question, namely that God timelessly knows now (if he is omniscient) all true propositions, and believes no false propositions. And so the assertion 'It was true yesterday that God knows (timelessly) that *p*' makes perfect sense.

Suppose that a small boy asks 'Was it true yesterday that $2 \times 2 = 4$?' The answer is most certainly yes. For since $2 \times 2 = 4$ is necessarily true, it was true yesterday that $2 \times 2 = 4$ and it will be true tomorrow, and for any other time that you wish to name, that $2 \times 2 = 4$.

If such assertions are meaningful, even though they have a rather low pragmatic value, then it makes sense to suppose that it was true yesterday that God knows what I will do tomorrow. And if so then God's knowledge is past, past for certain individuals in time, and so necessary for them.

There is a further argument for the incompatibility of divine foreknowledge and human freedom which rests upon considerations about time and timelessness which might be deployed at this point. If God's knowledge of our future is timeless then it is necessary not merely because it was true yesterday, but in a further sense, namely that nothing can happen, now or at any time, to alter God's cognitive state, since to alter God's cognitive state by bringing it about that he knows that *p* is false and not true would be to make God undergo real change. But God cannot undergo real change if he is timeless. So that if God timelessly knows that I am going to mow my lawn tomorrow then I cannot be in a position not to mow my lawn tomorrow, since to do so would be to bring it about that God changed, and God cannot change if he is timeless. Given a timeless being, whatever that being knows he unchangeably knows. The stock of propositions which he knows cannot be augmented or diminished or changed in any way.

This argument is rather different from one deployed by Pike, which depends on God's omniscience being essential to him. For that argument is compatible with God being in time, the key claim of the argument being that whatever is omniscient is necessarily or essentially so, and hence that any attempt to falsify one of an omniscient God's beliefs must fail.[15]

The necessity of God's knowledge is not, on the argument now being put forward, ensured by the pastness of the knowledge in question, nor by such knowledge being had essentially by the knower, but by its being held timelessly and so unchangeably. The cogency of this argument will be discussed further in Chapter 8.

We can conclude therefore that despite what seems to have been Boethius' original motivation for giving prominence to the idea of divine eternity, ascribing timeless eternity to an omniscient God does not succeed in reconciling divine omniscience and human freedom, but that this does not matter.

The usefulness of ascribing time (and place) to a timeless and spaceless God reveals a general point about the semantics of our talk of God. The inevitability of such talk reflects the inevitable fact that we ourselves who speak about God are in space and time, but it does not reflect a parallel fact that God is

---

[15] Pike, *God and Timelessness*, 55, 58.

in space and time. Both these facts are worth consideration. The inevitability of we ourselves being in time and space stands in need of no philosophical defence, being so obvious, but the inevitability is not that supposed by Kant, which carries with it the epistemological consequence that we can only think of God (for instance) in the categories of space and time, and that all else in theology is the postulation of the pure practical reason. Nor does the inevitability of such talk imply that God is in time any more than our talk about the sun commits us to geocentrism. The geocentrism is not a physical, scientific geocentrism, it is indexical. Such indexical talk of God is indulged in not because of its pragmatic value, not at least in any unadorned sense of 'pragmatic', but because of the religious need or desire to respond to God. To contemplate God, merely, does not require such resources of thought or language.

Such claims can be supported by two arguments. The first, direct, argument for such a conclusion is the claims that have been made for the intelligibility of divine timelessness, in many places including this book. The extent to which divine timelessness can be articulated and defended against objections is both evidence for its intelligibility and also provides a refutation of Kant's claim that intellectual attempts to transcend time and space generate antimonies.

The second argument is less direct. The fact that our talk of God is primarily tensed and spatialized does not itself prove that God is in space and time because, in pursuit of certain ends such talk can, like other sorts of talk, be revised. Just as a tree can be thought of as made up of a collection of objects which we cannot observe without thereby making reference to the tree as a palpable physical object impossible, so the God to whom we refer as acting in time and space in fulfilment of his own purposes and in reaction to human needs can be thought of, albeit with difficulty, as transcending space and time. The difficulty is real enough, but it need be no more intellectually embarrassing than is talk of unobservable electrons. In religion and theology, as in other sophisticated ways of thought, abstract and theoretical reflection can go hand in hand with more concrete and practical modes of thought and speech.[16]

A more theocentric point of view than most of us habitually adopt in thinking about God would allow us to think of God accommodating himself to human time-bound and space-bound modes of thought, as he must be thought by all theists (or at least by all theists who recognize a divine revelation) to accommodate himself to human powers of visual or other imagery in the use of what are traditionally called anthropomorphisms.[17]

The argument of this chapter has rested on the assumption that what is past is in some sense necessary. What has happened cannot now not have happened; it is fixed, over and done with. This assumption will be discussed more fully in Chapter 8 when we consider theological determinism or (as it is rather misleadingly put) theological fatalism.

What I have tried to argue, in this chapter and the one before it, is that it is possible to show that a timelessly eternal God is omniscient, that he knows all about the pasts, presents, and futures of those in time, but that timelessness does not provide the way of effecting a reconciliation between divine foreknowledge and human freedom. In the next chapter it will be argued that the prospects for omniscience, and for such a reconciliation, are made no brighter on the assumption that God is in time.

---

[16] For an interesting development of these ideas, to which I am indebted, see Bruce Aune, *Metaphysics*, 124 ff.

[17] Not surprisingly, perhaps, such a motif is prominent in the thought of John Calvin. On this, see F. L. Battles, 'God was Accommodating himself to Human Capacity', *Interpretation* (1977).

7

Omniscience and the Future

IN a previous chapter we explored the logical consequences that follow for an account of omniscience if it is supposed that God is timeless. We noted that there has to be a trade-off of God's timelessness against the mode of God's knowledge. Although nothing that happens escapes God yet there are certain ways of knowing what happens, time-bound ways, which are not open to such a God.

But does the idea of God being in time fare any better? Can a more plausible account of omniscience be given on such an assumption?

One main reason that certain philosophers have for maintaining that God is in time is that only so is it possible to think of God reacting to human choices. The idea of a responsive divine life, and of divine and human freedom, are closely intertwined in their thinking, and perhaps entail each other. While a Boethius may argue that God's timelessness is formally consistent with human freedom (though we have seen reason to doubt this) even so such timelessness does not do justice, in the eyes of such philosophers, to the idea of the life of God, to his spontaneous creativity. It is only if God has a future which is unknown to him that he can genuinely react to the unfolding events of that future. And God can only have a future which is unknown to him if either he has chosen not to know the future, or if there are metaphysical reasons, due to his own and human freedom, for denying that the future, or much of the future, is knowable in advance.

Swinburne takes the view that there are propositions about the future which now have a determinate truth value but which God, who exists in time, cannot know. This requires some modification of the concept of omniscience.

A person *P* is omniscient at a time *t* if and only if he knows of every true proposition about *t* or an earlier time that it is true *and* also he knows of every true proposition about a time later than *t*, such that what it reports is physically necessitated by some cause at *t* or earlier, that it is true. On this understanding of omniscience, *P* is omniscient if he knows about everything except those future states and their consequences which are not physically necessitated by anything in the past; and if he knows that he does not know about those future states. If there is any future state which is not physically necessitated by goings-on in the past or present, then, of logical necessity, no person can know now that it will happen—without the possibility of error.[1]

So there is no need, in Swinburne's view, to be driven to the doctrine of divine timeless eternity in order to avoid a clash between divine omniscience and human freedom. Instead, one limits the notion of omniscience in the interests of both divine and human freedom.

Keith Ward takes a similar view.

It is a coherent supposition that, where *p* is an event future in time relative to *t*, and where its actualization depends to some extent upon the free choice of some creature at *t*, no being before *t* could know that *p* will be true. For some *p*, if *p*, then *x* will not know that *p*, under certain conditions (namely, at and before *t*). This is true even of a maximally knowing being, though, naturally, such a being will know *p* as actual, as soon as its actualization is effected; and it may know that *p* will be actual, as soon as its actualization has been determined for certain. An omniscient being, if it is temporal, can know for certain whatever in the future it determines, to the extent that it determines it, but not absolutely everything. If this is a limit on omniscience, it is logically unavoidable for any temporal being.[2]

Swinburne claims that propositions about the future have a truth-value, including propositions which depend for their truth on either free divine or free human choices, but that there are logical limits to supposing that an omniscient being can know the future. There are only logical limits to

[1] Swinburne, *Coherence of Theism*, 175–6.
[2] Ward, *Rational Theology*, 130–1.

omniscience in the case of those propositions which are not know*able*. He claims that omniscience is limited by what is knowable and also that what God will freely choose to do, what he will choose to do some time in the future, is not knowable to him.[3] What God will freely choose to do has a determinate truth-value, it is timelessly true or false, but even a God who is omniscient cannot know it, because he has yet to decide what to do and by definition a person who has yet to decide what to do cannot know what he will do before he has decided. So the picture Swinburne presents is of a God in time, having created people with free will in time, and while the future of the universe has a definite truth-value now, neither God nor free human beings can now know what the truth-value is because neither can now know what the outcome of their free decisions will be.

Put rather differently, Swinburne's objection to God knowing the future free actions of human beings is based upon certain logical limits to knowledge. It is a thesis about God's knowledge, and says that knowledge of what people will in future freely do is logically impossible. God can *truly believe* what people will freely do, since it is possible to have beliefs about the future, and for those beliefs to be true, according to Swinburne, but he cannot *know* what people will freely do. No true beliefs about the future free actions of people can be infallibly justified, and such infallible justification is required for God. God does know many other truths about the future. So there are truths about the future which you and I can fallibly know which an infallible, omniscient God cannot know, according to Swinburne. So it follows that a fallible and ignorant person may know things that an infallible, omniscient being does not and cannot know.[4]

[3] *Coherence of Theism*, 176. Compare D. M. Mackay, 'On the Logical Indeterminacy of a Free Choice', *Mind* (1960), who argues that even if there is a true specification of the outcome of a free choice, knowable in advance, the free agent in question would not be correct to accept it.

[4] These points are discussed thoroughly by Kvanvig, *Possibility of an All-knowing God*, 14–22.

It is possible to distinguish between two degrees of ignorance. According to the first degree, while an omniscient, free individual will not know the outcome of the decisions of his free creatures until they are taken, nor his own reactions to them, he will know the truth of all counterfactual propositions of the form:

If Jones were to do *A* I would do *B*.

According to the second degree of ignorance, an omniscient being would not even know the truth of such counterfactuals, but only of counterfactuals of the form:

If Jones were to do *A* I do not know what I would do.

It would appear to be stretching the idea of divine freedom to breaking point to suppose that God has no idea what he will do when the free individuals he has created act in some definite way in the future. For one thing, to suppose that God does not know what he going to do about such situations before they require action would reflect not only on his knowledge, his self-knowledge, but upon his wisdom. We may suppose, therefore, that an omniscient God is restricted only to ignorance of the first degree by the as yet unmade free decisions of his creatures.

If this is so then the crucial element in Swinburne's account of omniscience is not divine freedom, but human freedom. What attenuates omniscience, and requires Swinburne's definition of omniscience, is human freedom. For there are other future situations contemplated by God, and to be resolved by him, which do not involve the free choices of his creatures. For example, God might contemplate the possible growth of a seed, and decide whether or not to germinate it. But to suppose that God does not know what he is going to do to resolve different possible futures of such a purely naturalistic kind would reflect adversely upon his wisdom.

The divine freedom, as Swinburne conceives it, presupposes that God is in time since it makes essential reference to the future, God's future, and thus cannot be used as an argument for God being in time without begging the question. It is true that Swinburne does not use this as an argument for God being in time but relies upon other arguments.[5] But if these arguments fail, or are unpersuasive, then the appeal to divine freedom to establish God's being in time is unacceptable because it begs the question.

So it emerges that one important reason for maintaining that God is in time is that this alone provides scope for human indeterministic freedom. Such a claim might appear surprising to someone who has been taught to think that one reason for holding to divine timelessness is that *it* provides the best prospect of providing for human freedom in theism. But it is a strange and little-noticed feature of Boethius' argument that human actions which are ostensibly responses to divine action, and vice versa, are left totally out of account.

In turn, the reason for maintaining human freedom in a causally indeterministic sense is the belief that such freedom alone preserves human responsibility. But it may be possible to argue that the incompatibility of divine foreknowledge and human indeterministic or agent-causal freedom does not carry the catastrophic consequences for human responsibility and accountability that is often assumed. If so, then the concept of divine timeless omniscience could be retained in its unattenuated sense. We shall consider such a position in Chapter 9.

But God's knowledge of the future can be restricted on other grounds. The question can be raised as to whether there is a future for anyone, including God. If not, then not even an omniscient God can know the future until it is present, and thus is no longer the future. If there are events and states such that it has not always been the case that they would come to pass then it was not knowable, before such events and states were 'present in their causes', that they would come to pass, and *a fortiori* God could not know that they would come to pass.

This is A. N. Prior's view. It is sometimes expressed as the

---

[5] *Coherence of Theism*, ch. 12.

thesis that the future is indeterminate. That is: 'Nothing can be said to be truly "going to happen" (*futurum*) until it is so "present in its causes" as to be beyond stopping; until that happens, neither "It will be the case that *p*" nor "It will be the case that not *p*" is strictly speaking true.'[6] Prior holds that such propositions are not yet either true or false. He does not mean to deny that no proposition can be both true and false (the 'Law of Excluded Middle') but to deny that every proposition must be either true or false (the 'Law of Bivalence').[7]

Geach also argues[8] that the idea of a determinate future is a dangerous piece of mythology. There is no future now to be known, by God or by anyone else, but only knowledge of the tendencies of what presently exists. But even supposing that what Geach says is correct it has little or nothing to do with determinateness unless it can be shown or assumed that the present tendencies of things are also indeterminate.

It is possible to distinguish five main arguments offered by Geach for the conclusion that the future is non-determinate. None of these seems to be decisive on the question.

In the first place Geach claims that the fact that not everything that was going to happen eventually did happen can only be true if the future is non-determinate. That is:

(1) Some things happen that were not going to happen

entails

---

[6] Prior, 'The Formalities of Omniscience', in *Time and Tense*, 38.

[7] Prior's thesis regarding the future and the non-identifiability of future individuals is a particular application of a more general thesis, namely that singular propositions, propositions directly about particular individuals, are ontologically dependent upon the existence of contingent objects. There cannot be the property of *being identical with Nero*, unless *Nero exists*; so one cannot identify Nero unless Nero exists or has existed, because, it is thought, there is nothing identical with Nero unless *Nero exists*. This more general view is discussed critically by Alvin Plantinga in 'On Existentialism', *Philosophical Studies* (1983), 1–20.

[8] 'The Future', *New Blackfriars* (1973). These views have been incorporated in *Providence and Evil*, ch. 3 'Omniscience and the Future'.

(2) The occurrence of those things is not determined before they happen.

It is true that it is commonly said that things that were going to happen do not happen. But what does it mean? It may mean

(1*a*) Some things happen that (for all we know) were not going to happen.

But Geach clearly means to assert something stronger than this, for there is not the shadow of a reason to suppose that (1*a*) entails (2). Perhaps what Geach has in mind is the following:

(1*b*) Some things happen that, but for certain free choices, were not going to happen.

But this clearly requires a separate thesis about free will. Geach claims, on the basis of (1), that the future is indeterminate. But it could well be argued that if (1) is true then (3) follows:

(3) Whatever failed to happen was not going to happen otherwise it would have happened.

It is impossible to conclude from the use of such expressions as 'not everything that was going to happen eventually did happen' that the future is indeterminate, for it is equally possible to argue that whatever happened was going to happen. So the first argument is indecisive.

Secondly, Geach has argued[9] that events represented by noun phrases such as 'Queen Anne's death' can be replaced by a clause linking a name to some part of a verb. Thus 'Queen Anne's death is past' becomes 'Queen Anne has died'.[10] The logically perspicuous way of presenting time order is by sentences whose clauses report (and do not name) events. In space, individual objects (represented by names) are related, as in 'John is further away than Peter', but temporal relations

[9] 'Some Problems about Time', *Logic Matters*, 302–18.
[10] Cf. Prior, 'Formalities of Omniscience', 1–2.

do not relate individuals in a parallel way. Geach's view becomes even clearer in the case of verbs such as 'avoid', which can be verbs of time or space. In

(*a*) Smith avoided Jones,

there is a nameable individual avoided by Smith. It makes sense to ask who Smith avoided. But in

(*b*) Smith avoided a nasty accident,

it is claimed that it makes no sense to ask which accident Smith avoided, if this is a request for an actual accident, though the accident could be specified counterfactually as 'the accident that would have occurred between the 8.30 a.m. train and Smith's car had he failed to restart it on the level crossing'. Such sentences as (*b*) are not to be understood as expressing a relation between a person and a (nameable) event but as

(*c*) That so-and-so should happen was avoided by Smith.

According to Geach there is no event standing in the wings of time ready and waiting to happen, or not happen, or existing in the deep freeze of a frozen future, ready to be presently thawed into life. A non-event is not a peculiar kind of event, like a happy event or a momentous event. It is no event at all. To prevent an event is to exclude what was going to happen from the universe. What is true of 'avoid' is also true of other verbs such as 'prevent', 'call off', and 'abandon'. Geach claims that the proper use of such verbs can only be understood in terms of what is going to happen. If the accident was prevented or avoided this is because it was about to occur. But such reasoning is not obviously sound.[11]

Two views need separating here; the thesis that the future already exists, and the thesis that what will happen is already

---

[11] It is thoroughly discussed, and rejected, by Kvanvig, *Possibility of an All-knowing God*, 5–13. Kvanvig argues that the notion of prevention can be understood purely in terms of the truth-values of propositions about the future.

determinate.[12] These are logically distinct propositions. Geach's strictures on treating the future as consisting of nameable events apply to the first thesis but it is hard to see that they apply to the second also. It is possible to make statements about what will happen but this does not mean that what will happen is already happening any more than to say that what is past is fixed entails that the past continues to exist, that the Battle of Waterloo is still being fought. The future does not consist of events which are already occurring, but of sets of propositions which, because they are true, entail the happening of certain events. But these events are not occurring yet. The propositions are true now, but what the propositions are about has not yet occurred.

Not to insist on the distinctness of these two theses would be to allow possible counter-examples to Geach's point about the unnameability of the future. Take, for instance, the following example:

(*d*) The theatre company cancelled the performance.

In this case it makes perfect sense to ask what performance, and to be told that it is the Tuesday matinée that is being referred to. But the fact that the cancelled performance can be referred to by a definite description in this way would only be troublesome given the truth of the first thesis, for it might appear that because the cancelled performance can be described, it exists, and that all such describable performances exist before they take place. But if the first thesis is denied what (*d*) means is that the theatre company will not give the

---

[12] In his *Confessions* Augustine says: 'By whatever mysterious means it may be that the future is foreseen, it is only possible to see something which exists; and whatever exists is not future but present. So when we speak of foreseeing the future, we do not see things which are not yet in being, that is, things which are future, but it may be that we see their causes or signs, which are already in being. In this way they are not future but present to the eye of the beholder, and by means of them the mind can form a concept of things which are still future and thus is able to predict them. These concepts already exist, and by seeing them present in their minds people are able to foretell the actual facts which they represent' (XI. 18). Here Augustine is denying that the future already exists, but affirms that it is possible that what will happen is already determinate.

matinée performance arranged for Tuesday, and this is quite compatible with the second thesis.

It is important to appreciate that Geach's arguments about the future not being nameable only apply to the restricted class of verbs, such as 'prevent', 'call off', 'cancel', and 'avoid', the grammatical objects of which are non-occurrences. As Geach puts it, such verbs do not assert 'real relations' between individuals.[13]

This is shown by the fact that human agency affects what happens in other ways than by calling things off, or preventing them. For example, human acts can speed up or delay events. Events can be brought forward, or put back. The opening of the Channel Tunnel can be brought forward, and my trip to London can be put back. Why in such cases may we not speak of a relation between an agent and a nameable event?

Geach's argument might be fatal to the fatalist (the question of fatalism is taken up in the next chapter) but it is hard to see why it should be conclusive against all forms of belief in a determinate future. He may be correct that thinking of the future as existing off-stage until brought on-stage (or kept forever existing off-stage) helps to foster the idea of a determinate future, but this idea does not seem to require such a dubious picture.

Furthermore, such a rephrasing as Geach's still permits us to say that what is prevented was going to happen but did not happen.[14] It is this expression that the real argument is about. If the accident was avoided or prevented then the believer in the determinate future can say, with Geach, that there was no accident, but that this was because there never was to have been one. If accidents exist, then, by definition, they happen. But this particular accident never existed. To know what is going to happen is not to see the series of future events already existing; it is to know that certain events are going to come to pass.

---

[13] 'Causality and Creation', in *God and the Soul*, 83.
[14] 'The Future', 211.

Taking a phrase out of the *Westminster Confession of Faith* the theist who is also a believer in the indeterminate future might still say that God has ordained 'whatsoever comes to pass'. In Geach's idiom this reads: that so-and-so happens is due to God's ordination. More generally, anything that happens is fore-ordained by God. So far as I can see, in this paraphrase there is not a trace of the ethereal future against which Geach rightly protests.

We may conclude therefore that Geach's second argument adds nothing to the first and that the first is by no means conclusive against the notion of a determinate future.

In the third place Geach interprets the saying 'Whatever will be, will be' not as a tautology, but as false, being equivalent to 'Whatever at some time was to be, will at some future time be'.[15] But this distinction between earlier and later times need not disturb the believer in a determinate future, as Geach's own example shows. He says:

> If it is true at some later time that Johnny will die of polio, then nobody ever was able at some earlier time to bring it about Johnny was not going to die of polio. And this of course we do not believe: Johnny could have been preserved by a suitable injection, but his foolish parents neglected the precaution.[16]

A believer in a determinate future might ask: how could Johnny have been preserved from death by polio by a suitable injection if it is true that at some later time he will die of polio? He can accept Geach's rephrasing of the slogan 'Whatever at some past time was to be, will at some future time be', but for him it is not a tautology, much less false, but it is a causally necessary or rationally necessary truth.

The fourth argument provided by Geach claims that prevention presupposes the idea of what was—in a non-fatalistic sense—going to happen. But this is false, or at least not necessarily true. What prevention presupposes is the efficacy of causal processes, including human agency. As we have noted, far from it being the case that a believer in a determinate future has to dispute the existence of such processes he needs them for his account. Thus, when something is prevented what is prevented is precisely the outworking of certain causal processes. That is, the *ceteris paribus* clauses which normally hold, and in virtue of which the causal processes continue, do not hold when something is prevented from happening. As a consequence, what happens is that the causal processes are inhibited. If a parked car was going to roll away down the hill but is prevented from doing so by the quick thinking of a passing pedestrian what this means is that the causal processes normally operative in the case of cars on inclines were, on this occasion, inhibited, and certain events prevented.

The existence of such causal processes also provides a justification for saying that such and such a thing has become impossible. If it takes forty-five minutes to travel to Liverpool then by 9.00 a.m. it has become impossible, that is, causally or physically impossible, to get to Liverpool by 9.30 a.m.

Finally, Geach claims, as support for his view, the fact that a bet placed binds no one to pay up until the race has been won. 'Even if there were a determinate result in advance and we had a man who saw it, we'd not go by what definitely will happen but only by what has happened.'[17] This is disputable. When a bet is paid depends upon convention. The convention of paying after the result is very strong because there is no reliable (much less infallible) prophesying of the outcome of race-meetings and general elections. But if, as Geach imagines, someone did have the power to forecast races infallibly then it is quite conceivable that winnings would change hands before the race was won, just as in a different world from the present one it is conceivable that people would settle their grocery bills before picking up the groceries. Though one ought not rashly to conclude from the

[17] Ibid. 212.

possibility of such a custom that the race need never be run, nor the groceries picked up, nor that, in a situation in which someone has an infallible 'vision' of winners the institution of betting will long continue. Thus none of the five arguments seems very strong. We can conclude that Geach has not by them established the indeterminancy of the future. There may be other, more effective arguments. But until these are deployed there is no reason to depart from the view that the future is determinate.

To these detailed arguments against Geach's specific claims about the non-reality of the future a more general argument can be added. Central to Geach's argument is a thesis about the limitations of reference, that no one can successfully refer to the future (where it is not already 'present in its causes') for the simple reason that there is, at present, nothing to be referred to. To this it may be replied that the reason why such a future reference is not possible is not because it is metaphysically impossible but, due to our ignorance, very difficult. Perhaps we cannot know more about the future than we do, and thus will always know much less about the future than the present and the past. There is an explanation for this asymmetry, and furthermore we do know something about the future, enough to make our references to it have a point and on occasion be successful.[18]

There is no logical connection between the view that the future does not already exist and the view that the future is indeterminate. [For it is possible to hold that although the future does not exist what will happen in the future is completely determined by what is happening now.] Yet Geach, while holding that the future does not yet exist, and that it is not now completely 'present in its causes', nevertheless holds that God has perfect control over the future. So while Prior claims that since an omniscient being could know only what is knowable, and what is future,[19] and while at times Geach appears to take the same line, as

---

[18] For a development of this argument see Mellor, *Real Time*, ch. 2.

[19] Prior, 'Formalities of Omniscience', 26 ff.

when he says that 'I do say that God doesn't know the way
things definitely will turn out, but only because I hold that
there is no such thing to be known',[20] he also couples this
with claims about God's control of the universe and the utter
trustworthiness of his promises.

Thus among the theses which Geach wishes to maintain is
not merely one about omniscience, that God knows in
advance all the possibilities,[21] but also that God will be
absolutely faithful to his promises;[22] that God does not
know the way things definitely will turn out;[23] and that God
has perfect control over the future.[24]

By the first of these Geach appears to mean something like
the following. We can suppose, following Prior,[25] that to
know all possibilities is to know all possible worlds, in the
sense of the possible future outcomes of the present world.
Or, more strongly, for God to know all possibilities is for
him to know all the possible courses of events that are
consistent with his original creative fiat, all possible future
outcomes. (In a similar, though more picturesque way, Storrs
McCall supposes sets of mutually compatible possible future
events comprising 'a sheaf of maps of the future', some of
which are discarded as events proceed.)[26]

By the claim that God does not know the way things
definitely will turn out Geach means that it is false that 'God
knows all that is to come to pass', but that it is true that God
knows all that does come to pass. For, according to Geach, all
that is to come to pass does not in fact come to pass. So, in
Prior's words, Geach's view is that omniscience is knowledge
at every moment of whatever at that moment will be.[27]

How does Geach argue for the consistency of the four

---

[20] Geach, 'The Future', 215.
[21] Ibid. 215.
[22] Ibid. 217.
[23] Ibid. 219.
[24] Ibid. 215.
[25] 'Identifiable Individuals', in *Time and Tense*, 69.
[26] 'Temporal Flux', *American Philosophical Quarterly* (1966), 280–1.
[27] Prior, 'Formalities of Omniscience', 30.

theses? For the first to be consistent with the third it must be taken to mean that God knows all possible outcomes, but not which of all possible outcomes will be the actual outcome. For if he knows which of all possible outcomes is (or is to be) actual then he knows the future, which is inconsistent with the third of Geach's claims.

But if God does not know which of all possible outcomes will be actual, how can God be said to have perfect control over the future? For he does not, according to the first claim, know which of all the future possibilities will be actual until it is actual. It looks as though the first and third theses, and the second and fourth, are consistent but that the set is inconsistent.

However, Geach offers an explanation of his view of omniscience in terms of the analogy of a man's knowledge of his future free action.[28] 'God's knowledge of the future comes solely from, indeed consists in, his perfect control over the future.' That is, God does not *learn* what will happen any more than a free agent learns what he is going to do.

Geach would wish to say this because God knows all the possibilities and is not thwarted or driven to improvisation.[29] But this last move will not save the analogy. It is fatally flawed. For, as we noted earlier, it does not follow simply from the fact that God knows all possibilities that he can do whatever he will. What he needs to know, in addition to all these possibilities, is which possibilities will be actual, which will be actualized by the relevant agents. But if he knows this, as according to Geach he does, because he perfectly controls the future, then he knows the actual course of events, he knows the future.

Alternatively, if God has to wait to see which possibilities are actualized by the relevant agents before responding to them in such a way as to ensure his total control of the future, then this implies a division in the divine will into antecedent

[28] 'The Future', 215.
[29] Ibid.

and consequent will, something that Geach elsewhere does not favour.[30]

We may conclude therefore that the analogy of self-knowledge, though helpful in certain respects, does not help us to see how it can be that God has perfect control over the future while not knowing the way things definitely will turn out. Adopting the thesis of an indefinite future seems to create insoluble problems for the traditional Christian view of God's determinate control over his creation.

This chapter began with an inquiry as to whether thinking of God as being in time provides a more satisfactory account of divine omniscience than that defended in a previous chapter. We have seen that it does not, particularly if this view is coupled with the belief that human beings are capable of indeterministically free actions. We have noted that certain philosophers such as Swinburne and Ward are prepared to countenance a modified view of omniscience for precisely this reason.

We have seen, in addition, that such views lead to difficulties in connection with divine providence. For even if it is possible to argue that what is future to us is indeterminate, it is not possible to couple this with a belief in the divine control of the future. So that in so far as theism requires belief in divine providence the indeterminacy of the future, a future indeterminate to both God and his human creatures, is inconsistent with it.

These problems illustrate a claim made earlier, that developing a satisfactory concept of God is partly a matter of straight philosophical argument but also partly a matter of judgement as to which difficulties are least disadvantageous. Faced with the triad of propositions

(1) God is omniscient.
(2) God is in time.
(3) Human beings are (indeterministically) free

some have argued, as (in rather different ways) have Prior,

---

[30] 'An Irrelevance of Omnipotence', *Philosophy* (1973) 332.

Geach, Swinburne, and many others, that (2) and (3) are both essential to theism, and that (1) can be accepted in only an appropriately modified form. But it is possible to maintain, alternatively, that (1) is true and (2) and (3) false and moreover that (1) can be true in its unattenuated sense only if (2) and (3) are false.

Because I deny the compatibility of divine foreknowledge and human libertarian freedom I do not have the problem of wrestling with *how* God can foreknow what is free. Those who do have this problem currently favour some version of the doctrine of God's middle knowledge, his knowledge of what free agents would do in certain circumstances, as a solution to it.[31]

---

[31] See e.g. Kvanvig, *Possibility of an All-knowing God*, ch. 4; an excellent discussion of the issues in Robert M. Adams, 'Middle Knowledge and the Problem of Evil', *American Philosophical Quarterly* (1977); and 'Plantinga on the Problem of Evil', in *Alvin Plantinga*, ed. James E. Tomberlin and Peter Van Inwagen, together with Plantinga's 'Reply' in the same volume.

8

Divine Foreknowledge and Fatalism

THE results of the previous two chapters may now be brought together. In Chapter 6 it was argued that Boethius' way of reconciling divine foreknowledge with human freedom by denying that God's knowledge is strictly speaking *fore*knowledge is unsuccessful. The use of the concept of divine foreknowledge by us allows the recognition of truths such as that it was true yesterday that God timelessly knows that p, where p is some statement describing an event or action in the future, just as it makes sense to say that it was true yesterday that $2 + 2 = 4$. Even if this argument seems somewhat forced, it cannot fail to be noted that if God is timelessly eternal and if he knows all things, past, present, and future to us that knowledge is unchangeable by anything which happens in time. And further, if God is omniscient he is essentially so, and thus nothing could happen to bring it about that any of his beliefs is false, since this would in effect be to bring it about that God no longer exists. This is an argument that has been used by Pike, and though challenged, seems valid. Moreover it is an argument which does not depend upon God being in time, or timeless, but is valid under either supposition.[1]

In Chapter 7 we considered one alternative taken by those who eschew timelessness. Certain philosophers are happy to

[1] 'Divine Omnipotence and Voluntary Action', *Philosophical Review* (1965), reprinted in Steven M. Cahn (ed.), *The Philosophy of Religion* (1970) and incorporated into ch. 4 of *God and Timelessness*. This argument has been criticized by Plantinga in *God, Freedom and Evil* (1975) and replied to by Pike, 'Divine Foreknowledge, Human Freedom, and Possible Worlds', *Philosophical Review* (1979). It is discussed further by Stephen T. Davis, 'Divine Omniscience and Human Freedom', *Religious Studies* (1979), Joshua Hoffman, 'Pike on Possible Worlds, Divine Foreknowledge and Human Freedom', *Philosophical Review* (1979), and by Plantinga, 'On Ockham's Way Out'. Kvanvig, *Possibility of an All-knowing God*, 92 argues that Pike's argument entails non-theological fatalism.

surrender God's knowledge of the future and to adopt views which cast doubt upon his providential rule of it, but this seems to require a radical reconstruction of the concept of God. In Keith Ward's words, according to the classical view,

God's creation is consequent upon his knowledge, which depends in part on creaturely acts, which presuppose that creation has already taken place. The only break from this vicious circle is to conceive of divine creation as a gradual and temporal process, depending partly on possibilities in his own being and partly on creatures. In a strictly limited sense, God can be changed from without.[2]

If such a concept of God were one of the consequences of denying divine timeless eternity then this would provide another reason for maintaining timeless eternity, though in fact, as we have noted, such a consequence does not follow from a denial of timeless eternity alone, but from that denial together with the assertion of freedom in an indeterministic or agent-causal sense. Given such a commitment to human freedom theists such as Swinburne and Ward must maintain that God is in time because such views of freedom, though not entailed by the view that God is in time, entail it.

So God's foreknowledge is incompatible with human freedom. In this chapter it will be shown that this does not involve a further consequence, logical fatalism, while in the next chapter it is argued that the adverse consequences for human responsibility of denying indeterminism are considerably exaggerated.

It is well to remember that 'fatalism' can mean a number of different things. Possibly the strongest form of fatalism is the view that everything that happens does so as a matter of logical necessity, a less strong view being that only some events occur logically necessarily. Coming somewhere in between these two is the view that certain events are fated by God or the gods even though human agents do not want

---

[2] Ward, *Rational Theology*, 152. There is no vicious circle if God may know what is future to us.

these events to happen, and even resist their happening. A further view is that all events are necessitated by God. We are now to consider one version of this final view, namely that all events are necessitated by the divine foreknowledge of them, and to examine whether this view is equivalent to logical determinism.

It is sometimes said that the argument considered in Chapter 6 for the logical incompatibility of divine fore-knowledge and human freedom can be easily transformed into an argument for logical determinism or fatalism. The argument in question is that since whatever is past is necessary, and whatever is entailed by what is necessary, is itself necessary, and since *p* is known entails *p* is true, then if God knew yesterday that I will mow the lawn tomorrow, his knowledge is past, and so necessary, and what it entails, what I will do tomorrow, is likewise necessary. And so I am not free not to mow the lawn. This is an argument.

for what we might call 'theological determinism'; the premise is that God has foreknowledge of the 'acts and wills of moral agents' and the conclusion is that these acts are necessary in just the way the past is. Clearly enough the argument can be transformed into an argument for *logical* determinism, which would run as follows. It was true, eighty years ago, that I will mow my lawn this afternoon. Since what is past is now necessary, it is now necessary that it was true eighty years ago that I will mow my lawn today. But it is logically necessary that if it was true eighty years ago that I will mow my lawn today, then I will mow my lawn today. It is therefore necessary that I will mow my lawn—necessary in just the sense in which the past is necessary. But then it is not within my power not to mow; hence I will mow freely.[3]

Philosophers such as Plantinga then proceed to claim, by means of an argument to be considered shortly, that divine foreknowledge is compatible with human freedom, and

---

[3] Plantinga, 'On Ockham's Way Out', 238–9. Plantinga cites Jonathan Edwards as an example of a theological determinist. See also Susan Haack, 'On a Theological Argument for Fatalism', *Philosophical Quarterly* (1974).

hence that divine foreknowledge does not entail logical determinism.

I shall argue first that such an argument depends upon holding a particular view of what a proposition is, and second that those who are committed to the thesis that divine foreknowledge is incompatible with human indeterministic freedom are not necessarily committed to logical determinism or fatalism, where this is understood as the thesis that whatever happens cannot (as a matter of logic) not have happened.

To begin with it is necessary to distinguish between two concepts of divine foreknowledge, to be called O-foreknowledge and A-foreknowledge respectively. If X O-foreknows that p then X knows that p but not as a result of bringing it about that p is true. There is a contingent connection between the foreknowledge of p and the making of p true; O-foreknowledge results from possessing evidence which ensures the truth of p, or from some other factor. By contrast if X A-foreknows that p then he knows that p as a result of ordaining or effectively willing or otherwise ensuring that p is true. At the very least X's A-foreknowing that p is causally necessary for the truth of p and perhaps it is causally sufficient as well.

This distinction, or one very like it, is well recognized in the literature on the question of divine foreknowledge and human freedom. Thus Augustine, Anselm, Aquinas, and Calvin (to look no further) may be said to be expressing the idea of A-foreknowledge in the following passages:

And with respect to all His creatures, both spiritual and corporeal, He does not know them because they are, but they are because he knows them. For He was not ignorant what he was about to create, therefore He created because he knew; He did not know because he created.[4]

Since God is believed to know or foreknow all things, does His knowledge derive from the things He knows or do the things

---

[4] Augustine, *On the Trinity*, xv. 13.

derive their existence from His knowledge? If God derives His knowledge from things, it follows that they are prior to His knowledge and thus are not from Him, for they cannot come from God except through his knowledge.[5]

God's knowledge is the cause of things. For God's knowledge stands to all created things as the artist's to his products. . . . For it follows logically that if certain things are going to happen, God foreknows them; but the things that are going to happen are not themselves the cause of God's knowledge.[6]

Since he [God] foresees future events only by reason of the fact that he decreed that they take place, they vainly raise a quarrel over foreknowledge, when it is clear that all things take place rather by his determination and bidding.[7]

Furthermore, certain writers, such as Augustine, have not scrupled to use the term 'fatalism' as a characterization of such a view, provided that this term is correctly understood.

We neither deny an order of causes wherein the will of God is all in all, neither do we call it by the name of fate, unless fate derived of *fari*, 'to speak', for we cannot deny that the scripture says: 'God spake once, these two things I have heard, that power belongeth unto God, and to Thee, O Lord, mercy, for Thou wilt reward every man according to his works' (Ps. 62; 11, 12). For whereas He says: 'God spake once', it is meant that He spake unmoveably and unchangeably, that all things should fall out as he spoke, and meant to have them.[8]

By contrast O-foreknowledge is referred to with approval by the majority of contemporary writers and by historical figures such as Daniel Whitby and James Arminius.

God's prescience has no influence at all on our actions. . . . Should God by immediate revelation, give me the knowledge of the event

---

[5] Anselm, *On Foreknowledge, Predestination and the Grace of God.* In *Trinity, Incarnation and Redemption*, ed. and trans. Jasper Hopkins and Herbert W. Richardson, 166.

[6] Aquinas, *Summa theologiae* 1a. 14. 8. A brief discussion of Aquinas's views on this point may be found in Norman Kretzmann, 'Goodness, Knowledge, and Indeterminacy in the Philosophy of Thomas Aquinas', *J. of Philosophy* (1983).

[7] John Calvin, *Institutes of the Christian Religion* III.xxiii.6.

[8] Augustine, *City of God*, v. ix.

of any man's state or actions, would my knowledge of them have any influence upon his actions? Surely none at all.[9]

Free knowledge is also called 'foreknowledge', as is likewise that of vision by which other beings are known; and since it follows a free act of the will, it is not the cause of things; it is, therefore, affirmed with truth concerning it, that things do not exist because God knows them as about to come into existence, but that he knows future things because they are future.[10]

The precise extent to which *A*-foreknowledge is a *causal* notion is sometimes not altogether clear. For example, Augustine distinguishes between foreknowledge and predestination.

Predestination . . . cannot exist without foreknowledge, although foreknowledge may exist without predestination; because God foreknew by predestination those things which He was about to do . . . Moreover, He is able to foreknow even those things which He does not Himself do,—as all sins whatever. Because, although there are some which are in such wise sins as that they are also penalties of sins . . . it is not in such a case the sin that is God's, but the judgment.[11]

Augustine here countenances the possibility that there are states of affairs which God foreknows but does not predestinate. And if for Augustine all that God foreknows he *A*-foreknows, then there are states of affairs which God knows without learning, but which he does not cause. Yet Augustine may mean that while God predestinates all things, he does not predestinate evil things *as* evil, but under some other description. Nevertheless, he foreknows them as evil. Yet the distinction between foreknowledge and predestination would remain.[12]

The distinction between the two kinds of foreknowledge is one of explanatory priority. Does God foreknow the truth

[9] Daniel Whitby, *Discourses on the Five Points*, Disc. VI. ch. I.

[10] J. Arminius, *Writings* (trans. J. Nicholls), i. 448–9.

[11] Augustine, *On the Predestination of the Saints*, ch. 19.

[12] For a recent discussion of this and other points see Gillian Evans, *Augustine on Evil*.

of some proposition, that Jones will do *X*, because it will be true, or will that proposition be true because God foreknows it? Except in rare cases, for instance, a person's knowledge of his own intentions, all human foreknowledge depends upon what will be true. It is because of the way in which, it is judged, things will turn out that a human being may be said to foreknow; his foreknowledge does not ensure the truth of what is foreknown.

While modern philosophers of religion take note of *A*-foreknowledge they almost invariably discuss the problem of divine foreknowledge and human freedom in terms of *O*-foreknowledge.[13]

With the distinction between *A*-foreknowledge and *O*-foreknowledge in mind, let us return to the argument for the incompatibility of divine *O*-foreknowledge and human freedom from the necessity of the past. This argument is not specifically theological. It does not depend for its cogency on God being the foreknower: anyone else who foreknew would do equally well. Furthermore its cogency does not depend upon anything epistemological either, for as we noted there is an equally cogent argument in which the necessity of a truth about the past is ensured not by God's (or someone else's) foreknowing that *p*, but by *p* being true in the past. For if it was true ten years ago that I would sit at my desk this morning, then it is now necessary that I am sitting at my desk this morning, since the former proposition entails the latter.

While the argument for theological determinism can be transformed into that for logical determinism they are none the less somewhat dissimilar arguments, in that while the reason for believing that God foreknew yesterday what I will do tomorrow is (presumably) that an omniscient God exists,

[13] See e.g. Kenny, *God of the Philosophers*, Part Two, Ward, *Rational Theology*, 129–35, and Anthony O'Hear, *Experience, Explanation and Faith*, 189. Kvanvig notes *A*-foreknowledge and regards it as inadequate, *Possibility of an All-knowing God*, 118–21. By contrast Geach maintains that God's knowledge is practical, not observational, *Logic Matters*, 324.

the reason for believing that it was true ten years ago (and so was necessary) that I would sit at my desk this morning is (presumably) that I am sitting at my desk this morning. But perhaps this is irrelevant, or there may be some other reason for believing the truth of the proposition in question. Perhaps the reason has to do with the immutable nature of propositions: if it is true that I am at my desk on 1 March 1987 then it always was true that I am at my desk on 1 March 1987, for though sentences can change their truth value, propositions cannot. But whatever the reason in general it seems that this argument for the incompatibility of divine foreknowledge and human freedom is true only if a parallel argument of a fatalistic kind is true: both rely crucially upon the two principles of the necessity of the past and of the argument $[Np . N(p \supset q)] \supset Nq$.

The claim that the cogency or otherwise of the arguments for fatalism and for the incompatibility of divine foreknowledge and human freedom turn upon the exact nature of a proposition is borne out by a consideration of the most effective counter-argument to theological determinism to date, that which rests upon a distinction between 'hard' and 'soft' facts, facts which are wholly about the past and facts which are partly about the past and partly about the future. It is argued that while

Helm was at his desk in 1980

is wholly about the past and so expresses a 'hard' fact. So (as we noted in Chapter 6) such a statement as

It was true that Helm will be at his desk in 1999

is not strictly about the past, it does not express a 'hard' fact, for it entails a proposition,

Helm will be at his desk in 1999

which is about the future.

Plantinga has shown,[14] and others have suggested, that

[14] Plantinga, 'On Ockham's Way Out', 247; see also John Martin Fischer, 'Freedom and Foreknowledge' and Kvanvig, *Possibility of an All-knowing God*, 100–16.

there are difficulties with the distinction in that it is hard to identify genuinely 'hard' facts, a fact that is strictly about the past. Thus suppose we say that 'Caesar died and his body rotted away in 44 BC' is true. This implies such statements as 'Caesar's heart will not restart' and 'Caesar will not require any more breakfasts' and these statements are about a time or times future to 44 BC, though not, of course, about any one time in the future. Perhaps it is true of any action completed in the past that it entails the non-occurrence of some state of affairs at a time future to the action's completion-date. If so, then any completed action is 'soft', since completion implies truths about the future. But if completed actions, the most promising candidates for 'hard' facts, are in fact 'soft' facts, what is the distinction worth?

A similar problem afflicts the notion of the 'immediate present' as introduced by Alfred J. Freddoso,[15] who argues that there are present-tense propositions which are temporally independent. Thus the truth or falsity of 'David is sitting' (when uttered) is 'wholly independent of considerations about the past or future'. But as normally understood does not the truth-value of 'David is sitting' depend upon the truth of 'David existed at least a moment ago'? For as normally understood 'David' names a continuant.

But not only that: it would appear that there cannot be any statements of the form '*A* correctly believes that *p*', where *p* is a future-tense sentence, which are wholly about the present, the time of the utterance. Further, 'God foreknows that *p*', cannot be temporally indifferent as defined by Freddoso[16] because there are times when expressions of that form are true and times when they are false. That is, in Freddoso's words, the truth-value of such expressions does 'temporally depend on what is true or false at other moments'.[17]

Despite such difficulties let us suppose that the distinction between 'hard' and 'soft' facts can be successfully exploited in

[15] 'Accidental Necessity and Logical Determinism', *J. of Philosophy* (1983).
[16] Ibid. 272.
[17] Ibid. 273.

an attempt to disarm the argument for theological determinism from the premiss that the past is necessary. This distinction, and any argument for the compatibility of divine foreknowledge and human libertarian freedom which depends upon it, in turn rests upon a modification of the classical notion of a proposition as a timeless bearer of truth or falsity.

In a discussion about the relevance of whether propositions or sentences are the bearers of truth to the issue of fatalism Susan Haack claims[18] that it has no relevance to the issue. If, she says, the point of the argument is meant to be that 'now true' cannot be applied to propositions then any true proposition is now true.

But this is not quite the point. Rather, if truth is applied strictly to tensed sentences, it is being applied to something which has some of the logical characteristics of an *event*, and which can be said to be about some particular time, since events occur at particular times. The event in question is necessarily either an uttering or inscribing, something datable, but a proposition can be true or false without a sentence expressing it being assertible; for example, *All human life is annihilated.*

Haack suggests an alternative diagnosis: 'not that "now true" is senseless, but that it is misleading, because *it* is responsible for introducing the worry about fatalism, which would not have arisen had Aristotle stuck to the plain future tense.'[19] But the point is not that 'It is now true that there will be a sea-battle tomorrow' is different from 'There will be a sea-battle tomorrow', but that 'There will be a sea-battle tomorrow' is different from 'There is a sea-battle in 846 BC' in that the former can be said to be about the future but the latter can never be. 'It was the case that there will be a sea-battle tomorrow' makes sense, whereas 'It was the case that there is a sea-battle in 846 BC' scarcely makes any sense at all.

---

[18] *Deviant Logic*, ch. 4, p. 83.
[19] Ibid.

The occurrence of a sea-battle is tenselessly, or tense indifferently true of 846 BC. So,

Helm is at his desk in 1999

understood as a true proposition, one whose verb is understood tenselessly or tense indifferently, is no more about the future than it is about the past. It is unambiguously about 1999. To be about the future the expression would itself have to be regarded as an event occurring at a particular time, as itself having a date of occurrence, and the date mentioned in the expression, 1999, would then refer to a time after the time of the inscribing or uttering of the expression.

So that anyone who holds that the proper bearers of truth and falsity are abstract propositions, and not statements or utterances employing tensed sentences, cannot argue that the prima facie logical incompatibility between divine fore-knowledge and human freedom can be met by employing a distinction such as that between 'hard' and 'soft' facts, since that distinction requires the rejection of such a notion of a proposition.

At least it does if by 'proposition' one is referring to what is possibly true or false. According to some usages the term 'proposition' is used to refer to the meaning of a sentence in the abstract, where no context is assumed. It is what the English sentence 'The window is open' and the French sentence 'La fenêtre est ouverte' have in common. This differs from the sense of 'proposition' already used in this chapter. According to that sense a proposition is a fact or possible fact. Thus if it is a fact or possible fact that Smith is bald this fact or possible fact can be expressed by Smith saying 'I am bald' or by someone else saying 'Smith is bald'. These two expressions have different meanings, but under the circumstances envisaged they express the same proposition. The same fact or possible fact may not only be expressed by different sentences having different meanings but some facts or possible facts may be expressed by sentences some of which are tense-indifferent and some of which are not. Thus the fact of Smith's being ill in 1984 can be conveyed by the proposition *Smith is ill in 1984* or by the utterance by Smith in 1984 'I am ill'.

This can be further illustrated from Plantinga's argument. We shall suggest that this argument, based on the distinction between 'hard' and 'soft' facts, is only plausible because examples of what God knows used in the argument, such as

> God knew eighty years ago that Paul will mow his lawn in 1999,

express what God knew in terms of a tensed sentence about a particular time. By contrast propositions understood as timelessly true or false are, as such, not about the past exclusively, nor the present, nor the future. And what God knew eighty years ago, according to the argument discussed and defended in Chapter 6, is that some proposition p which is not exclusively about our past, or our present, or our future, is true. What makes this proposition necessary, accidentally necessary, is that it is true that God knew it yesterday and this, being past and so accidentally necessary, ensures the accidental necessity of what is known.

By contrast, one can only deploy the distinction between 'hard' and 'soft' facts in any sense which is relevant to this argument by admitting as items of God's knowledge expressions which are tensed. This can be illustrated from Plantinga's argument, as follows.

Take the expression:[20]

(*a*) Paul correctly believes that the sun will rise on 1 January 2000.

Such expressions, according to Plantinga, are 'equivalently abut the future', and it is not true that expressions about the past corresponding to them, such as

(*b*) Paul correctly believed that the sun will rise on 1 January 2000,

---

[20] Plantinga refers to these as 'propositions' but I avoid using this term in order to avoid possible confusion between tensed sentences and timelessly true or false propositions.

will be accidentally necessary, from now on. But expression (*a*) is only equivalently about the future because it has a future tense with an index to a time after the present time, the time when (*a*) is uttered, enunciated or otherwise expressed. Hence the argument which appeals to God's knowledge being a 'soft' fact depends upon employing expressions which have a future tense. But given the alternative view of propositions as tense-indifferent then what God correctly believed yesterday is that the sun is, was, or will be rising on 1 January 2000. And what is thus believed is no more about the past than it is about the future or the present except that when prefixed by 'It was correctly believed eighty years ago that' the whole expression becomes accidentally necessary. So:

> Eighty years ago God believed that Paul will mow his lawn in 1999

ought to be understood as

> Eighty years ago God believed that Paul is, was, or will be mowing his lawn in 1999.

What this shows is that Plantinga's argument is only plausible because what God foreknows is relativized to some observer or agent in the present and so the truth of what God foreknows is not a timeless proposition. But what is past (and so accidentally necessary) is God's knowledge of what Paul is doing at a particular date, regardless of whether that date is now past, present, or future relative to some moment in time. The propositions which are the objects of God's knowledge do not become true or false. They are timelessly true.

So Plantinga's argument against logical determinism or fatalism depends upon a special, and controvertible, notion of a proposition. If one cannot use this sort of argument then the argument against the incompatibility of divine foreknowledge and human freedom fails to convince.

Perhaps a more fundamental question, supposing that the distinction between 'hard' and 'soft' facts can be made out, and its relevance to the argument established, is whether

God's belief that Jones will do x is, unlike our belief, a 'hard' fact. For if it is, then this provides a powerful argument against the compatibility of divine foreknowledge and human freedom, since all God's beliefs about what will happen are then to be reckoned to be 'over and done with', accidentally necessary.

In support of the incompatibility of divine foreknowledge and human freedom Fischer defends the view that for every 'soft' fact there must be a 'hard' fact, a host on which the 'soft' fact is parasitic.[21] Thus in our belief that Jones will do x the belief becomes knowledge upon Jones doing x, not otherwise. So the belief is the 'hard' fact on which the knowledge is parasitic. In the case of God's belief that Jones will do x, however, there is no 'hard' fact, no belief of God which becomes knowledge if Jones does x and remains belief if he does not. So, according to Fischer, God's belief that Jones will do x must itself be reckoned to be a 'hard' fact. So God's beliefs are, unlike our beliefs, 'hard' facts, wholly about the past, and so the incompatibility between divine foreknowledge and human freedom is upheld.

It is not satisfactory to reply to this, as Kvanvig does,[22] that a plausible candidate for the host 'hard' fact is God's believing the truth. For either this belief of God's amounts to a disposition, a disposition to believe whatever turns out to be true, in which case it is hardly a 'hard' fact of the appropriate kind, or it is the possessing of the actual belief that Jones will do x, in which case this is a 'hard' fact about what Jones will do, and incompatibilism will survive unscathed. And even if Kvanvig's reply is satisfactory, and the 'hard' fact is God's disposition, this would serve to differentiate God from the usual human case.

So God's belief is a 'hard' fact, whereas the corresponding human belief is a 'soft' fact. God's believing the truth is an inappropriate candidate for the 'hard' host to the 'soft' parasite of God's belief that Jones will do x.

[21] Fischer, 'Freedom and Foreknowledge', 76–7.
[22] Kvanvig, *Possibility of an All-knowing God*, 112.

Kvanvig finally raises a general objection to utilizing this principle that for every soft fact there is a hard fact lurking beneath.[23] He cites the case of a proposition expressing some soft fact: *It was the case yesterday that it will rain tomorrow.* There is nothing, he claims, on which this is ontologically dependent. But surely the example is irrelevant in that it does not consist of anything other than a reformulation of a truth about the future as one about the past by the prefixing of 'It was the case yesterday . . .'. Fischer could reply that the examples that he is interested in are propositions which express beliefs held in the past, or other facts which formed part of the world's history then.

In Chapter 6 I used an appeal to tenses in arguing for the incompatibility of divine foreknowledge and human freedom. In the present chapter I have used the idea of a tenseless or timeless proposition to discount the idea that the distinction between 'hard' and 'soft' facts can defeat theological determinism. Am I not trying to have things both ways?

What the argument of Chapter 6 shows is that our talk of divine foreknowledge is our own inevitably tense-based recognition of what God timelessly knows. For God to foreknow that p is not for him to know that p expresses an event that will happen in his future, it is for us to ascribe to God a knowledge of the truth of p which may contain within it the description of some event which is due to occur after the time we ascribe that knowledge to God. But what God foreknew is something that is capable of being expressed in tenseless form, for that is how he knows it. The timelessness of God's knowledge is ontologically prior to any recognition of his knowledge by time-bound creatures. The common crucial assumption in both arguments is the centrality of timeless truths.

So far we have seen that there are serious objections to Plantinga's and others' attempts to show that divine

---

[23] Ibid. 114.

foreknowledge and human freedom are compatible. But such a consequence may appear to commit us to logical determinism or fatalism, for the difficulties that there are with reconciling divine foreknowledge and human freedom appear to strengthen the hand of the fatalist. What is the theist who does not wish to be a fatalist to do? It is here that the aforementioned divine *A*-foreknowledge becomes relevant.

For what divine *A*-foreknowledge shows is that if God *A*-foreknows that *p* this is a logically necessary and sufficient condition for *p*'s being true. So that if it is now the case that I am writing with pen and ink and God *A*-foreknew that I would, then I write because he foreknew, and he did not foreknow because I was to write. *A*-foreknowledge is not to be analysed in terms of contingent truth, but contingent truth in terms of *A*-foreknowledge.

It can be seen that *A*-foreknowledge's compatibility or otherwise with human freedom cannot be answered in terms of tensed bearer of truth. If God *A*-foreknows that I will mow my lawn tomorrow then this is necessary and sufficient for me bringing it about that I will mow the lawn tomorrow, just as God's *A*-foreknowing that I am mowing the lawn on 2 March 1987 is a necessary and sufficient condition for this. God's *A*-foreknowledge is sufficient and necessary for the truth of whatever is *A*-foreknown, no matter how whatever is foreknown is expressed.

It is equally clear that *A*-foreknowledge is not logically equivalent to fatalism, because *p* is true only if God *A*-foreknows *p*, and since *p* follows only if God *A*-foreknows that *p*, *p* is not logically necessarily the case unless God's *A*-foreknowledge of *p* is logically necessarily the case. To suppose that God's *A*-foreknowledge that *p* is logically necessary is to suppose a much more controversial thesis, that what God *A*-foreknows he logically necessarily *A*-foreknows. But if God's *A*-foreknowledge of the actual world is not necessitated by the laws of logic alone then logical determinism or fatalism is not equivalent to, and not entailed by, divine *A*-foreknowledge.

So the state of the question is as follows. If only divine O-foreknowledge is under consideration, then perhaps it can be reconciled with human indeterministic freedom and logical determinism or fatalism likewise disproved, if one is also prepared to allow that sentences, uttered on some occasion, with attendant indexicality, can be the bearers of truth, and hence properly expressive of what God knows, and if God's foreknowledge is a 'soft' fact. For this permits one to countenance the idea that some past-tense sentences are wholly about the past, that they express 'hard' facts, while others are partly about the future, expressing 'soft' facts.

An alternative position would be that God A-foreknows human action. This is not equivalent to fatalism, but such a view would be incompatible with human indeterministic freedom. But this would not be a worry if such freedom is in any case logically incoherent, as has frequently been argued. And even if it is not logically incoherent it may be that, for instance, a God who endows men with free will in the sense of liberty of indifference, and who A-foreknows their actions (supposing this to be possible) is as much or as little responsible for any ensuing evil as a God who, though he could A-foreknow an individual who is morally perfect, instead chooses to A-foreknow one who is not.[24]

This chapter concludes the direct argument for divine timeless eternity. In the course of this argument I have attempted to show that only timeless eternity prevents the degeneracy of divine omniscience and divine immutability into the idea of a God who changes with the changing world and who is surprised by what he discovers, and that divine timeless eternity does not commit one to logical determinism

---

[24] While this study does not address the problem of evil directly it should be clear that the celebrated free will defence is not a solution to the problem that is consistent with the denial of human indeterministic or contra-causal freedom. Those who reject such freedom must approach the problem as Augustine did, and hold that 'that evil as well as good exists, is a good', that is, that evil exists for a good reason. (For a similar modern view see Nelson Pike, 'Hume on Evil', *Philosophical Review* (1963) and 'Plantinga on Free Will and Evil', *Religious Studies* (1979).)

or fatalism. I have also argued that God's omniscience, and particularly his *A*-foreknowledge of human action, is incompatible with indeterministic accounts of human action. The only plausible remaining argument for holding that God is in time is that only such a view permits human indeterminism or agent causation and that indeterminism is necessary for human accountability and responsibility. In the next chapter I shall attempt to allay at least some fears on this score.

9
Timelessness and Human Responsibility

ONE clear consequence of the argument of the last three chapters is that the existence of an omniscient, timelessly eternal God is logically inconsistent with the libertarian freedom in any of his creatures, freedom, that is, which requires the absence of causally sufficient conditions for the occurrence of any intentional action.[1] This is partly because such freedom in any creature appears to require an unacceptably reduced concept of omniscience, and also that the main ways of proposing a reconciliation of divine foreknowledge and human freedom appear unsatisfactory, and in any case apply only to O-foreknowledge and not to A-foreknowledge. Thus Boethius' celebrated reconciliation of omniscience with creaturely freedom, even if successful, applies only to O-foreknowledge.

Some famous theologians and philosophers have been surprisingly ambivalent on the question of the incompatibility of divine foreknowledge and human freedom. Thomas Aquinas writes that, 'God not only gave being to things when they first began, but is also, as the conserving cause of their being, the cause of their being so long as they last. . . . He not only gave things their operative powers when they were first created, but is always the cause of these in things,' and that, 'the act of sin not only belongs to the realm of being but is also an act, and from both these points of view it somehow comes from God'.[2] Yet at the same time Aquinas

[1] For stylistic reasons only, 'liberty of indifference', 'libertarianism', 'causal indeterminism', and 'agent-causal freedom' are used interchangeably in this chapter, as equivalent to a denial of causal determinism.
[2] *Summa contra Gentiles* 2. 67. 3; *Summa theologiae* 1a 2ae. 79. 2. (Quoted by O'Hear, *Experience, Explanation and Faith*, 218.)

wishes to deny that God is the author of evil, or, more exactly, to deny that he is the author of sin.

Aquinas, like Augustine before him, does not attribute sin[3] to free will, but to a deficiency, *privatio*.

The chief problem with accepting the logical compatibility of divine foreknowledge and human freedom in a non-libertarian sense is its allegedly unfavourable consequences for human responsibility and especially for human sin. For it is alleged that libertarian free will is necessary for personal responsibility and, equally importantly, that it is necessary in order to remove from God the charge that he is the author of sin.

There are two general arguments which, if sound, are often claimed to settle these questions. It has been claimed that the very idea of an uncaused or self-caused responsible human action is self-contradictory or incoherent.[4] If so, then not even God could bring it about that there exist individuals with such powers of free choice; there is no possible world in which such individuals exist.[5] This argument, if successful, would clearly settle the matter, but it will not be used or pursued here, because to do so would take us too far off the subject of divine timelessness. A second general argument, on the other side of the question, is that even though, granted libertarian free will, God would not be directly responsible for evil, he would none the less be indirectly responsible in that he created human beings with a liability to evil.[6] A possibly effective counter-argument to this is to say that since it was logically impossible for God to create individuals with absolutely no character traits whatever, and equally logically impossible for God to create moral agents who invariably or inevitably did what was

[3] See the discussion of Augustine's views in Pike, 'Plantinga on Free Will and Evil'.

[4] See e.g. Jonathan Edwards, *The Freedom of the Will* (1754).

[5] J. L. Mackie, *The Miracle of Theism* (1982); Plantinga *The Nature of Necessity*, and id., *God, Freedom and Evil*.

[6] Plantinga, *The Nature of Necessity*, ch. 9.

right, it is hardly a slur on God that this logical impossibility was not effected. This ground has been gone over pretty thoroughly in recent discussion and there is no sense in tramping over it again.

Instead an attempt will be made to cast doubt on the argument that the incompatibility of divine omniscience and human freedom has unfavourable consequences for human responsibility and sin by arguing *ad hominem* against the views of two philosophers who take a compatibilist position.[7] They hold that human responsibility is compatible with determinism, and also that if God foreknows what will happen human beings cannot be responsible for their actions. For the purposes of this argument, therefore, the truth of compatibilism is assumed, and it will be argued that it does not have the serious consequences, in a theistic context, that are alleged. If this can be established then it is possible to argue as follows: if compatibilism is true, then one reason for maintaining that God exists in time, namely, that otherwise the only creaturely freedom is compatibilism and compatibilism results in God being the author of evil, is no longer valid. Then only one reason for maintaining that God is in time, namely the need to maintain human libertarian free will, remains. It will therefore be concluded that the only valid reason for denying that God is timelessly eternal derives from the need to maintain creaturely libertarianism. This is borne out inductively when the views of various philosophers who hold that God is in time, such as Swinburne, Ward, Lucas, and Plantinga, are examined.

It will be argued that if we suppose that theism is true, and that therefore God ordains and sustains everything by his creative power, then this fact does not provide an additional difficulty for theism. If non-theistic determinism is compatible with freedom then, it will be argued, theistic creation is as well.

Of course such an argument, even if successful, will have

[7] A more general defence of the compatibility of causal determinism and Christian theism can be found in Robert Young, *Freedom, Responsibility and God.*

only a limited appeal. For example it will not be convincing to an incompatibilist, who will in any case not be disposed to accept God's timeless eternity. But it might be expected to have some force with those who think that determinism is true and compatible with responsibility, and who also think that additional difficulties attach to the idea of theistic creation and responsibility. For I shall argue that the cases of theistic creation and determinism are parallel. If the case for compatibilism is unsatisfactory then so is the case for theistic creation and responsibility. But the much stronger claim that *only* if compatibilism is true could theistic creation be compatible with responsibility will not be defended here. For all that is known to the contrary the compatibility of theistic creation and human responsibility, assuming that they are compatible, may depend on considerations that are peculiar to theism. That the compatibilist and theistic creationist cases are precisely parallel would have to be shown by a separate argument.

Because of their prominence in the literature there is no need to rehearse the arguments about the compatibility of determinism and freedom. In arguing for the partial parallelism of atheistic determinism and theistic creation it is not hoped to produce a conclusive argument but to argue for the plausibility of this position in two ways. In the first place some arguments provided by Antony Flew for the claim that there is a crucial difference between atheistic determinism and theistic creation will be rejected. Then it will be argued that if human responsibility is compatible with theistic creation God is not *jointly* responsible, with the creaturely agents, for the agents' actions, nor is God, *pace* Kenny, the author of sin. Finally, I will discuss the extent of God's responsibility.

In a number of places Antony Flew has maintained the thesis that a libertarian view of human action is incompatible with the theistic view of creation. For instance, in *God and Philosophy* he wrote that according to the theistic view of the relation between God and his creation: 'absolutely nothing happens save by his ultimate undetermined determination and with his consenting ontological support. Everything means everything; and that includes every human thought, every human action, and every human choice.'[8] But Flew has nevertheless maintained that even in a universe created and sustained by God the distinction between performing an action voluntarily and under compulsion remains, though the significance of that distinction may well be altered in such a universe.

For it is . . . entirely inconsistent to maintain: both that there is a Creator; and that there are other authentically autonomous beings. Certainly you can without contradiction say: both that we are the creatures of a Creator; and that there is, as there is, an humanly vital distinction between acting of one's own free will and acting under constraint.[9]

Both these views seem to be plausible, and they will not be questioned or discussed further in what follows. Instead, I shall take up one particular implication that Flew draws from them, that while the distinction between actions done voluntarily and those done under compulsion can provide the basis of human responsibility in an atheistic universe, it cannot do so in a theistic universe. He puts the point explicitly as follows:

The situation is different in the purely secular case. . . . The difference is that in that case all human movings are supposed to be, not the movings at one remove of the Great Manipulator, but the latest outcomes of ultimately impersonal causes. Whereas in the former responsibility must at the very least be shared with, if not shifted wholly onto, the supposed Great Manipulator; in the latter there is and can be no one else to blame.[10]

---

[8] *God and Philosophy*, 44. Also 'Divine Omnipotence and Human Freedom', in A. G. N. Flew and A. C. Macintyre (eds.), *New Essays in Philosophical Theology*, 164 ff.); *An Introduction to Western Philosophy*, 233; *Crime or Disease?*, 104, and 'Compatibilism, Free Will and God', *Philosophy* (1973).

[9] *God and Philosophy*, 55–6. Also *Crime or Disease?*, 102–4 and 'Compatibilism, Free Will and God', 242.

[10] *The Presumption of Atheism*, 96.

But the same considerations that lead Flew to defend the compatibility between human freedom and determinism in an atheistic universe are, if sufficient, also sufficient to uphold compatibilism between human freedom and theistic creation. If they succeed in the one case, they do so in the other. So, at least, I shall argue. Since Flew's arguments for compatibilism between human freedom and determinism are set out most fully in his *Crime or Disease?* I shall refer mainly to that work in what follows.

Flew's argument can be set out in three phases. He claims, in the first place, that there is a basic commonsense pre-theoretical distinction between 'movings' and 'motions', between actions done of one's own free will as opposed to those done under compulsion. Then he claims that if we suppose that 'general determinism' is true, the distinction between voluntary and involuntary actions is necessary for any individual to be responsible for his actions. Only with respect to voluntary actions does the question of responsibility properly arise. And as, in fact, there are cases of both voluntary and involuntary acts, the question of responsibility can properly be raised.

But Flew claims thirdly that although voluntariness is necessary for responsibility, it is not sufficient. For it is possible to conceive of a situation in which individuals are caused to act voluntarily. Likewise it is possible that theism is true, and that God is the creator and sustainer of the universe. If so, while the ordinary distinction between voluntary and involuntary action would still obtain, even voluntary actions would be the effect of divine creative and sustaining action. Some distinction between voluntary and involuntary would remain, but it would not have the significance we might otherwise take it to have.[11]

What Flew seems to hold about the distinction under theistic assumptions is that if theism is true God could not hold the individual concerned responsible for his action, since

---

[11] *An Introduction to Western Philosophy*, 242–3.

God is the ordainer of the action. But he may also mean that we, if we knew or believed theism to be true, could not consistently hold ourselves or others responsible for any voluntary actions. He clearly means the first, and he may mean the second. He says that 'a radical reassessment' would be required;

and second, in particular, that it must be absurd and outrageous for the Supreme Judge to base discriminations upon those differences which would concern a human court. For, whereas the prisoners in any worldly dock are beings independent of their judges, creatures have all and only those characteristics fixed by their Creator.[12]

Theists might protest that words such as 'fix', 'manipulate', 'hypnotize', and 'pull the strings' do not properly fit the creator-creature relation any more than thinking of God as the Puppetmaster does.[13] But these questions are not examined here.

Flew proceeds to claim that if we accept 'an atheist and mortalist Determinism . . . it is at least not obvious that any general revision is required'.[14] That is, given atheism, and determinism, voluntariness is both necessary and sufficient for responsibility unless one can show that someone intervened to manipulate someone else to cause him to have feelings of voluntariness. But given theistic creation voluntariness is neither necessary nor sufficient for responsibility. Indeed, given theistic creation it is impossible for men to be responsible for their actions. Responsibility, given such an assumption, has no sufficient conditions. But what are Flew's reasons for making this distinction between the theistic and atheistic cases?

It may be that Flew is appealing to some general principle such as the following:

Each causally determined but voluntary action has only one agent who is responsible for that action.

[12] *Crime or Disease?*, 106.
[13] For Flew's use of these analogies see e.g. *Introduction to Western Philosophy*, 224, 235; *God and Philosophy*, 44.
[14] *Crime or Disease?*, 106.

In the case of atheism and determinism this would be the agent himself, or, if he was manipulated by another agent, the manipulator. In the case of theism it would be the Super-Manipulator, God. But there are a number of things wrong with this principle. In the case where two agents are concerned, it does not enable us to decide which of them is reponsible. It also rules out cases of joint responsibility. And, most importantly of all, it offers no reason why in the atheist determinist case any agent should be responsible for voluntary actions. The principle cited above is not self-evidently true, and carries positive difficulties with it, and so Flew's reasoning must be examined in a little more detail. After looking at what Flew thinks is the crucial difference between theistic and atheistic determinism I shall discuss his arguments for the compatibility of human responsibility and atheistic determinism.

In the atheist determinist case there is the absence of any intentional agency bringing about the voluntary actions of human beings. Flew supposes the case of an individual so manipulating a patient that that patient is caused to do certain actions and caused to want what he does.

If and when such manipulation is performed either without the knowledge and consent of the patient or actually against his wishes, then it is hard indeed to see how he, rather than his manipulator, can properly be held in any degree responsible for the behaviour resulting.[15]

But why is this at all relevant? Because the activity of the manipulator means that he bears at least some of the responsibility for the behaviour. This seems plausible, and has not been denied by theists who have taken determinism to be true. But is not theism a case of total manipulation? Suppose it is. How is what Flew calls an 'atheist and mortalist Determinism' any better placed? According to general determinism there are forces which are causally sufficient for every event, including every voluntary action, that occurs,

<hr/>

[15] Ibid. 102.

and so the causally sufficient forces are responsible for
bringing about the voluntary actions that occur. This is a case
of total causation, even if not of total manipulation.

Flew claims that,

> The crucial difference is that in the former, the theist, there is
> another agent either to share or to monopolise responsibility;
> whereas in the latter, the atheist, there is not. Thus it will not do,
> here any more than anywhere else, to argue directly from
> possibility to actuality: to urge for example that because the
> Cushing demonstration perhaps shows that all my movings could
> in principle be produced by the manipulation of someone else;
> therefore I always in fact am being thus manipulated, albeit
> perhaps by ongoings in my own central nervous system.[16]

While, as we have just noted, there is no *agent* in atheistic
determinism to whom all changes are due, there are *factors* to
which all changes are due. It can be granted that because *A* is
sometimes, or could sometimes be manipulated by an agent,
it does not follow that *A* is always manipulated. Nor does it
follow that *A* is ever manipulated. But unless Flew is going to
claim that it is logically impossible to causally produce
voluntary actions in an individual other than by manipulation of one person by another, it follows from the thesis of
general determinism, that every action, including every
voluntary action, is produced by causally sufficient conditions. Among the immediate conditions may be the agent's
own wantings, but these wantings are themselves the effect of
other causally sufficient conditions.

General determinism does not claim that the antecedent
causal factors manipulate. 'Manipulate' is a piece of anthropomorphism. The causal factors are usually non-intentional
in character, without plans or aims, but causally sufficient for
the bringing about of certain intentional, voluntary actions.
The question of having or not having the agent's consent, or
of going or not going against his wishes, does not arise.
While, under atheism, no person is ultimately responsible for

[16] Ibid. 107.

the factors that are causally sufficient for a voluntary action, it does not follow that nothing is. For what are responsible are the causally sufficient factors, or their causally sufficient antecedents. If Flew's distinction between voluntary and involuntary actions somehow overrides some of the implications of the general determinism he favours, then, by parity of reasoning, it would appear to override God's creative and sustaining activity.

Flew's 'crucial difference' boils down to the objection that God cannot hold his creatures responsible for what they do voluntarily. But if so, this is because it is unfair or immoral for God to blame someone else for what he has ordained that they do, and unfair to be blamed for what one has been caused to do, even though one has done the action voluntarily. But this is also a prima facie objection to atheist general determinism. If there are general philosophical considerations to suppose that atheist general determinism is consistent with the responsibility of voluntary human actions then these general considerations apply to theism. If so, then it is fair to be blamed for what one has been caused or ordained to do, when what one has done was voluntary or intentional. And if it is fair for *A* to be blamed for what he has been caused or ordained to do, when he has done that action voluntarily or intentionally, then it is fair for someone to blame him. And if it is fair to blame him it is presumably fair for God to blame him. The crucial fact for compatibilism is that the causes of a person's action are extraneous to that person, not that the causes are perhaps the intended effects of someone else's actions.

Let us now turn to consider Flew's arguments for the compatibility of atheistic determinism and human responsibility. He argues that even if general determinism is true this does not preclude the possibility that a person has good reasons for what he is doing. That is, it is wrong to think of physical explanations as overruling explanations in terms of human rationality. This seems correct. If the fact that the crops are very dry because of a drought seems to someone to be a good reason for irrigating them then this is a good reason irrespective of how that idea comes into his head. This is because of the relation between the growth of plants and water, and has nothing to do with how human action is determined. But presumably the same consideration holds in the theistic case as well.

Flew also argues that:

it is, simply, wrong to say that, on Determinist assumptions, 'his action did not really depend on him, but was determined by antecedent external circumstances'; and also, but more subtly, wrong to say that 'if I am determined, my will can be left out of consideration as an independent factor, because it can be calculated from other factors already given'. It is ridiculous thus to assume that nothing can really depend on anything which is in turn dependent upon something else.[17]

What this means is that,

   (i) B is causally sufficient for C which is causally sufficient for D

ought not to be confused with

   (ii) B is causally sufficient for D irrespective of whether or not C happens.

It certainly *would* be wrong to confuse these. Causal chains are chains, and cannot be collapsed into one big cause. But how does this help? It cannot be of any help because the chains in question are determinate. The will is an 'independent factor' in the sense of being logically independent, not causally independent. For 'his action did not really depend on him, but was determined by antecedent external circumstances', we are warranted in substituting something like 'his action did depend on him (his wants etc.) which in turn were determined by antecedent circumstances'.

But if, despite what has just been argued, the considerations about causal chains do help the atheist determinist in maintaining compatibilism then they are of equal comfort to

[17] Ibid. 108.

the theist. The theist is only too ready to acknowledge the existence and importance of 'secondary causes'. As, for instance, in the *Westminister Confession of Faith*:

God from all eternity did, by the most wise and holy counsel of his own will, freely and unchangeably ordain whatsoever comes to pass: yet so, as thereby neither is God the author of sin, nor is violence offered to the will of the creatures, nor is the liberty or contingency of second causes taken away, but rather established.[18]

There are two further arguments of Flew's for compatibilism which he provides in *An Introduction to Western Philosophy*. The first of these concerns the widespread belief that determinism entails inevitability. Flew claims that the term 'inevitable' in the context of human activities is elliptical for 'inevitable by whom?' He gives the following example. While an invasion, looked at from the point of view of those invaded, might appear inevitable because they could do nothing about it, it is not inevitable for the invaders, because there was something they could have done about it, namely, refrained from invading.[19] What does this show? One thing that it shows is that 'inevitable' has an epistemic as well as a metaphysical sense. According to Flew's example, for all the ones who were being invaded knew, the invasion was inevitable. But this does not show that the invasion was, or was not, metaphysically inevitable. And if there was literally an alternative line of action for the invader, then there was an alternative outcome for those who were in fact invaded, whatever they may have believed about the situation. The invader's changing his mind about invading guarantees, in those circumstances, that the invasion will not take place.

But even if Flew was right about inevitability, the parallel case for a theist must also succeed. For if his description of the example of the invasion is acceptable to an atheist determinist, there is nothing that a theist would need to deny about it.

In a second argument for compatibilism in *An Introduction*

---

[18] *Westminster Confession of Faith* (1643), III. 1.
[19] *An Introduction to Western Philosophy*, 262.

to Western Philosophy Flew points out that as a matter of logic
it is not possible that any agent should have chosen all his own
original desires, though it is possible to modify desires in the
course of time, and thereby to acquire and lose inclinations.[20]
He uses this as a *reductio* of the idea that responsibility depends
upon being able to choose one's own desires. But why does
the possibility that God has ordained initial desires limit an
individual's responsibility more than if that individual's
desires are the outcome of purely natural factors, if, as a
matter of logic, it is impossible for an agent to choose all his
own desires?

There is one possible difference in the two situations. Even
if God could have instantiated a possible world such that
individuals only did what was morally right, why does this
have a bearing on the problem of responsibility? It does have
a bearing on the problem of the existence of evil, and of its
amount and incidence. But this is a different question, though
it is certainly one that a theist would have to say something
about in order to provide a proposition to show the
consistency of God's omnipotence, benevolence, and the
existence of moral evil. One such possible true proposition
might be: *God allows evil for a good reason.*

But the problem of responsibility would still have
remained even if God had chosen to instantiate a very
different possible world. That is, suppose God had instantiated a possible world such that men only did what was
right. This is possible, given compatibilism. If he had, there
would have been no problem of evil. But if the question of
responsibility is an issue in a created world in which there is a
great deal of evil it is also a question in a created world in
which there are human agents but no evil. There is only a
contingent relationship between the metaphysical relation of
God to his creatures and the existence and amount of evil in
his creation.

If it could be argued (as it is, for example, by Harry G.

[20] Ibid. 269.

Frankfurt[21]) that the freedom and responsibility of a person is compatible with that person's being caused to desire X and being caused to want to desire X by some other person then it would be possible to argue, *a fortiori*, that responsibility is compatible with theistic determinism. But it ought to be stressed that no such attempt to argue this is being made now. Rather what is being defended is the more modest thesis that if the atheistic case is compatible with responsibility then the theistic case is as well. This, in turn, differs from the claim that if theistic creation is compatible with responsibility then determinism must be, and that creation is compatible with responsibility only if determinism is.

But if compatibilism is true, and *a fortiori* the idea of God's creation of the universe and his ordination of all events is consistent with freedom and responsibility, then the idea of God as the puppetmaster is quite misleading, for the puppet is manifestly not free, whereas human beings often are.

Even if compatibilism between freedom and determinism is true, and human beings are free and responsible for what they do voluntarily, it might be argued that given theistic creation God may nevertheless be responsible as well. For it may be that God and A are *jointly* responsible for A's good and evil actions. The idea that God is jointly the author of morally evil actions would be unwelcome to a theist for whom it is a necessary truth that if God exists he is all-good.

But if compatibilism is true then A is free in doing x (when he does x voluntarily etc.) even though there exist causally sufficient factors for the production of x. Moreover,

---

[21] 'The fact that the D/n [Devil/neurologist] causes his subject to have and to identify with certain second-order desires does not, then, affect the moral significance of the subject's acquisition of the second-order volitions with which he is thereby endowed. There is no paradox in the supposition that a D/n might create a morally free agent. It might be reasonable, to be sure, to hold the D/n too morally responsible for what his free subject does, at least insofar as he can fairly be held responsible for anticipating the subject's actions. This does not imply, however, that full moral responsibility for those actions may not also be ascribable to the subject. It is quite possible for more than one person to bear full moral responsibility for the same event or action.' ('Three Concepts of Free Action', *Proc. of the Aristotelian Soc. Suppl. Vol.* (1975), 122.

according to compatibilism *A* is completely free. According to this doctrine, *A* is not partly responsible and the causes of his action partly responsible. The force of the compatibilist view (and its weakness in the eyes of its critics), is that *A* can be completely free, fully responsible for an act for which there are causally sufficient factors, though this is not to say that for every such act he is completely free or fully responsible. He is completely free when, for example, he is doing what he wants to do, when he had the power to do otherwise but chose not to. He has no freedom, or diminished freedom, when he is acting under duress or compulsion of some kind.

If this is accurate then *A* is responsible for certain of his acts and no one else is responsible for the same act, unless, for example, he and someone else jointly perform a voluntary action. And even then, strictly, the partners are each responsible for their individual parts of the total effect of acting together. If it is never true that *A* is responsible for at least some of his acts, and no one else is responsible for those acts, then compatibilism is false. But if compatibilism and theism are both true, then *A* is responsible for those of his actions which are immoral, and God is not responsible for them. Whereas if there is an inconsistency between creation and responsibility then *A* is not responsible at all for what he does, even what he does voluntarily, and God is only and wholly responsible.

There is of course a derivative sense of 'responsible' in which God would be responsible for the evil voluntary actions of his creatures in virtue of the fact that he is the creator and as such is responsible for all that takes place within his creation. In this sense of 'responsible' God would be responsible for any indeterministic events and actions within his creation, even though he could not cause these events or actions himself. But if, given the compatibility between creation and responsibility, *A* does *x* voluntarily then it does not follow either that *A* has not really done *x* (but God has) nor does it follow that God and *A* have performed *x* jointly.

So there is reason to think that the metaphysics of theism adds no problems for the free will and responsibility issue that are not already raised by the thesis of general causal determinism. If the theist is inclined to think, for whatever reason, that defences of theism against the apparent logical inconsistency of theism and moral evil that rest on indeterminism are unacceptable then he needs to focus his attention on the compatibilism–incompatibilism issue, in which no specifically theological matters are raised.

It might appear that whatever the merits of compatibilism within the assumptions of Christian theism, it has the disadvantage of directly implicating God in human evil, since God ordains sets of circumstances which are causally sufficient for evil actions by human beings. It is true that this is a not entirely welcome result, but then it is worth reflecting on what the indeterministic alternative is, supposing indeterminism to be coherent. It is that God O-foreknows evil and does nothing to prevent it. It is certainly not obvious that someone who does something knowing that evil will result while not intending the evil is free from responsibility. So an indeterministic scheme no more frees God from all responsibility than does a deterministic scheme.

In *The God of the Philosophers* Anthony Kenny argues, as many before have done, that the sense of human free will that is necessary in order to reconcile divine foreknowledge and free will is a sense which makes God the author of sin. God's omniscience is preserved only at the cost of his moral character. For divine foreknowledge is only possible given a compatibilist account of determinism and human freedom. He writes:

Anyone who accepts the compatibility of determinism with freedom must agree that agents can be justly blamed and punished for acts which they were predetermined to perform, provided only they had the ability and opportunity to refrain from them. But if the Calvinist system is to be tenable, it must be possible to show not only that human beings can be involved in blame for determined sins, but that God can avoid responsibility for them.

And this seems to be much more difficult to show. For if an agent freely and knowingly sets in motion a deterministic process with a certain upshot . . . If determinism is true, it is comparatively easy to explain how he can infallibly foresee free action, but impossibly difficult to show how he [God] is not the author of sin.[22]

Kenny goes on to argue that God, who knows everything and who is all-good, could not exist in a world in which there is moral evil, not because God could not allow it but because in any world in which God exists and there is moral evil God would be the author of that evil, and hence would not be all-good. Since for God to be God it is essential that he is all-good, God could not exist.

It is certainly the case that the conclusion that God is the author of sin is an unwelcome one even to those theologians and philosophers who are explicitly predestinarian in their theology. For example, the *Westminster Confession of Faith*, having asserted that God freely and unchangeably ordained whatsoever comes to pass affirms that yet God is not the author of sin.[23] Others, equally predestinarian, have wished to distinguish between different senses of the words 'the author of sin', regarding some of these senses at least as acceptable.[24] They have not been ready to allow that 'the author of sin' is synonymous with 'is morally culpable for every sinful action' or with 'is sinful'. And they have not been prepared to allow the inference 'If God is the author of A and ordains B, which is sinful, to follow as a consequence of A then God is the author of B'.[25]

This position raises certain matters of general philosophical interest such as the idea of negative causation and the cogency of arguing that it is possible to ordain something which is sinful but not as sinful. (Is that like prescribing a toxic substance as a medicine and not as an instrument of murder?)

---

[22] *God of the Philosophers*, 86–7.
[23] *Westminster Confession of Faith*, III. 1.
[24] e.g. Aquinas, *Summa theologiae*, 1a 2aer. 79. 2.
[25] Jonathan Edwards, *The Freedom of the Will*, IV. 9.

It is possible to respond in a more direct fashion to the problem Kenny raises by the following argument:

(1) Necessarily, if God exists he is all-good.

That is, in no possible world in which he exists does God do anything with an evil motive or intention or transgress the moral law. (A utilitarian version of (1) would be: in no possible world does God exist and ordain states of affairs that are overall evil).

(2) God exists and ordains whatsoever comes to pass.

(3) Necessarily, if A is a human action then A is causally determined.

That is, the determination of human actions is not contingently true. There is no possible world in which human beings exist and perform undetermined actions. To suppose that there are worlds in which human beings perform undetermined actions, even though none of these worlds is the actual world, would be to raise the question of why God did not actualize such a world. Hence determinism is a logically necessary requirement of human actions.[26]

(4) There are morally evil human actions.

Morally evil actions are deliberate actions which flout the moral law or which are done solely for the sake of causing pain and suffering.

(5) Either God is the morally culpable author of the morally evil human acts or human beings are their sole morally culpable authors.

(6) (1) and the first disjunct of (5) are formally inconsistent.

There is no possible world in which God is all-good and in which he is the author of morally evil human acts.

(7) (1), (3) and the second disjunct of (5) are not formally inconsistent.

---

[26] Here the truth of a proposition which earlier I declined to argue for is assumed.

That is, in order to show a formal inconsistency between these three propositions another proposition or propositions must be added. Which proposition or propositions might these be? Perhaps something along the lines that Kenny himself suggests:

(8) Any agent who freely and knowingly sets up a deterministic process with a certain outcome must be responsible for that outcome.

But anyone accepting (1) and (2) will hardly have his feathers ruffled by (8), for as it stands it is a central tenet of theism or at least that version of it that might be called deterministic-theism. Under such a system *that moral evil happened* is certainly the responsibility of God, but not the doing of the evil. Perhaps we could try

(9) Whenever one person X causes another person Y to do moral evil X does moral evil.

But whatever evil X performs he does not perform the evil which Y performs, since by (9) Y does that evil. But is there any reason why a theist ought to accept (9) as a proper account of the matter, as the truth? Perhaps he ought to accept (10),

(10) Whenever one person X upholds another person Y and knowing that Y will do evil does not prevent Y from doing evil, X does moral evil.

Perhaps. But this raises further disputable questions about actions and omissions. And moreover, it is by no means clear that even if X does moral evil he is doing the same moral evil as Y. Moreover, whether or not X is guilty of moral evil is presumable a matter of what rule or law X has broken, or whether his upholding and permitting of X to act in an evil manner is in furtherance of some greater good for which X's evil act is a logically necessary condition. It is not obvious that either a law has been broken in such a case, or that X's evil act is not a logically necessary condition for the achieving of certain further goods.[27]

[27] As e.g. Augustine held, *Enchiridion*, ch. 27.

If one takes the view that permission of evil is as such incompatible with full moral integrity or uprightness, then this is a view which has implications not only for a theism in which human beings do not have free will, but one in which they do, as was noted earlier.[28]

The search for a further proposition or propositions has led us back in the direction into which earlier I stated that I did not wish to go. But if the upshot of this is that whether a more acceptable proposition or propositions can be provided is problematic then there remains a legitimate area of doubt about Kenny's claim. The search for a further proposition may succeed, but it has not yet succeeded. Moreover, if such a proposition were to be found it would be equally troublesome to a determinist who is an atheist, such as Flew. Thus the onus is on someone who wishes to provide such a proposition to do so, and until one is provided we are free to believe that God's goodness is consistent with his not being the author of evil even in a situation in which libertarianism is ruled out.

In 'Overpower and God's Responsibility for Sin'[29] Nelson Pike argues that in a universe in which there are agents who have liberty of indifference, God (who is omnipotent) has the power to prevent them exercising this responsibility, he has 'over-power', and so he is himself responsible for the exercise of it, for the fact that they act freely, and for the likely consequences of such action (assuming God does not foreknow exactly what his free creatures will do). He argues[30] that Thomas is wrong in concluding that because God is the cause of free will it is the 'middle cause' which is responsible and God not at all. Human beings can, according to Aquinas, be prevented by God from performing morally wrong actions by God acting to bound, that is to restrict their freedom of action to a choice

---

[28] And as has been frequently pointed out, e.g. Jonathan Edwards, *The Freedom of the Will*, IV. 9.
[29] In Alfred J. Freddoso (ed.), *The Existence and Nature of God*.
[30] Ibid. 22.

between limited alternatives, though presumably the limiting of alternatives results in a diminution of agent responsibility. So God would limit the range of choice but still leave alternatives. And so, Pike argues, God is in fact *responsible* for the outcome (and Aquinas is wrong) though God is not to *blame*[31] since the total outcome is morally good. Furthermore, Augustine holds that God is not and cannot be blamed (since he ordains good to come out of evil and is logically incapable of doing evil, since evil is a privation). It follows by Augustine's reasoning that God is not to blame even if he were to force an individual to act (though this would take away that individual's responsibility) and *a fortiori* God is not to blame if compatibilism is true.

Summing up, it is possible to hold both that human beings are responsible even if compatibilism is true and that God, though responsible, is not to blame for bringing about an evil act on the part of a human being if he has a good reason for bringing such an act about, which he must have.

So far in this chapter I have been defending the view that if compatibilism is true then the fact that the sufficient causal conditions for any action are brought about by God does not present an additional difficulty for theism by removing human responsibility and implicating God in evil. God may be 'responsible' for evil in some sense, but this does not mean that he is morally culpable. And in any case even in a supposedly libertarian situation, one, that is, in which God has created individuals with libertarian free will, God is still responsible for the arrangement both in the sense that he has brought about the conditions which make evil possible, and also because he could prevent the evil, if he chose to do so, by a suitable intervention. This fact about such divine responsibility is widely recognized in, for example, discussions of the free will defence.

But this position must not be confused with an even stronger (and more paradoxical) view. In a number of

---

[31] Ibid. 27.

writings[32] James Ross holds the view that God's eternal
ordination is necessary and sufficient for whatever comes to
pass, including the actions of free human beings, and that a
free human decision is also necessary and sufficient. That is,
following Aquinas, Ross supposes two levels of causality
each of which is necessary and sufficient for what occurs. 'For
the same event two chains of causal sufficiency and necessity
are simultaneously present, and simultaneously required.'[33]

In Ross's view it is an inescapable consequence of the idea
of creation that God's creative will is the necessary and
sufficient condition of anything that exists or occurs. But this
very strong proposal[34] meets with the very obvious
difficulty that it appears to undermine human freedom. Ross
argues against this suggestion by maintaining that since for
every free action of Jones, e.g. Jones's freely doing *A*, God's
will that Jones do *A* is the necessary and sufficient condition,
there is no conflict. God does nothing to prevent Jones from
refraining from acting, such as enticing him or compelling
him to do *A*. Rather, the agent's refraining ensures (logically)
that God has chosen that act of refraining. That is, Jones's
freely refraining from *A* entails God's choice of Jones's freely
refraining from *A*. God's choice is the logically necessary and
sufficient condition of the action, and it follows that the
action occurring is the logically necessary and sufficient
condition of God's having chosen the action. 'Metaphysical
causation is "included", logically, in the being or happening
of the dependent thing.'[35]

The problem with this is not with Ross's insistence that
God's will is the necessary and sufficient condition for *A* (that
if *A* occurs God must have willed it), but with whether
anything can provide logically necessary and sufficient

---

[32] For example, *Philosophical Theology*, ch. 6; *Introduction to the Philosophy of Religion*, ch. 3; 'Creation', *J. of Philosophy* (1980); and 'Creation II', in Alfred J. Freddoso (ed.), *The Existence and Nature of God*.

[33] *Philosophical Theology*, 253.

[34] Ross, 'Creation', 614.

[35] Ibid. 618.

conditions for bringing it about that someone else acts freely, in Ross's sense of free, which is equivalent to an agent-causation sense of freedom.[36] Ross says that this is perfectly satisfactory. But is it? This is the *first* issue.

If it is satisfactory from a logical point of view, does this view not have the consequence that it leaves the divine metaphysical cause 'inoperative', so to say? If Jones doing *A* freely ensures that God has willed this, what exactly has God done? What difference does invoking God's decree make here? Does it not become redundant? There seems to be an unsatisfactory symmetry between the cause and the effect since each is the logically necessary and sufficient condition of the other. This is the *second* area of disquiet.

The *third* area of disquiet is another lack of asymmetry, perhaps a consequence of the first lack. Ross's account does not appear to allow for differentiation between God's cause of what Jones is responsible for and God's cause of what *God* is responsible for.

First, then, freedom and responsibility. Ross says, 'God does not make the person act; he makes the so acting person be.'[37] And he wishes to say that while *God causes it that Adam freely sinned*, this is not equivalent to *God causes Adam to sin*. He has two arguments for this non-equivalence.

One is a rather obscure argument about states of affairs[38] in which Ross objects to talking of God bringing about states of affairs on the ground that states of affairs in general are logically posterior to *being* (but logically entailed by it). *That Adam sins* is posterior to *Adam being a sinner*. Suppose this is granted. Does it not follow from it that if God brings about Adam who is a sinner he brings it about that Adam sins? For the equivalence *not* to hold it would have to be the case that there was a logical condition for bringing it about that Adam sins that bringing it about that Adam who is a sinner does not

---

[36] In the later paper Ross endorses R. M. Chisholm's account of human freedom ('Creation II', 131).

[37] 'Creation II', 130.

[38] Ibid. 130–1. See also p. 133.

require. But Ross has excluded such a possibility in claiming that any condition required for Adam sinning is a condition that God must supply, since God is the source of all that exists.

The second argument is that since God causes everything his causation is a condition for liberty, not an impeding of it. 'Nothing possible can be impeded by its necessary conditions.'[39] This may also be granted; but what these necessary conditions are necessary conditions of, according to Ross, is not simply the being of an individual, but his accidents and therefore all that he does freely. In earlier discussion[40] Ross says that we know that it is false that it is impossible to create a character which is free. But do we? By what argument?

The sufficient conditions provided by God's willing that Jones does *A* and Jones willing that he does *A* are 'logically inferior' according to Ross,[41] each implying the other. On one picture Ross presents, Jones's choice is a sufficient condition for his action provided that he continues to *be* long enough to act. But he goes on to say something much stronger than this, that God's choosing that Jones freely writes philosophy is not sufficient for Jones's doing so, except on the condition that Jones, in fact, does so. But in whose hands is this condition? 'For a sufficient condition to be sufficient every necessary condition being fulfilled is necessary'. But does this mean that Jones has it in his power (exclusive of God's power) to fulfil these necessary conditions? Surely on Ross's overall account God's willing Jones is a necessary and sufficient condition for Jones writing philosophy.

It is clear what Ross wishes to say, but not clear that he can consistently say it. Take for example his claim that God's intentional object is the whole being,[42] including Adam and his doings. From this Ross wants to say that God makes

[39] Ibid. 131.
[40] *Philosophical Theology*, 258.
[41] 'Creation II', 132.
[42] 'Creation', 134.

Adam, who sins freely. But *either* God's timeless decision has a timeless effect (clearly not a possibility here) or it has an effect extended in time, and God timelessly ordains all aspects of this temporal sequence. But if God's decision has an effect which is extended in time, and God ordains all aspects of this, it is hard to see how anything could happen and God not ordain and hence share responsibility for it.

So it is not at all clear that Ross has successfully argued that an account of God's creation in terms of necessary and sufficient conditions is compatible with an agent-causation account of freedom and responsibility. I shall argue later that this does not matter.

As regards the *second* area of disquiet one is more inclined to say, of Ross's proposal, that whatever is a cause of everything is a cause of nothing in any normal sense of 'cause'. For suppose that God is the transcendent cause of free human actions, unfree human actions, natural occurrences, and the like. What does this mean? Normally, to say that X is the cause of Y where X and Y are events, is to say that Y happens because X has happened. But if God transcendentally upholds all these categories of event *in the same sense*, in what sense can he be said to be the cause of them? He is not, according to Ross, responsible for free human actions, though he is the transcendental necessary and sufficient condition of such. But then by parity of reasoning, he is not responsible for unfree human actions, or for any event in nature. He is not responsible for anything.

As regards the *third* area of disquiet, Ross's account, even if it is allowed in all its details, does not appear to provide for differentiation between God's cause of what A is responsible for and God's cause of what God is responsible for. While Ross admirably accounts for God's causation of the universe (though some of the consequences which he thinks are avoidable are not) he finds it more difficult to account for God's causation *in* the universe. For if God is the logically necessary and sufficient condition of everything, then he is the logically necessary and sufficient condition of

God does *A*

and

Jones does *A*.

In other words, being unable to find a place for secondary causation, the secondary causation of Jones acting, conditions for his own acting are likewise not specifiable. For if the necessary and sufficient conditions of *God causes the wind to blow* are the creative necessary and sufficient conditions, what is the difference between

God causes the wind to blow

and

The wind blows?

Ross recognizes that the free will defence theodicy is not possible,[43] while allowing the view that God brings it about that creatures freely do only what is right in a sense which does not require compatibilism. What is the difference, for Ross, between God metaphysically calling Jones who does *A* into being, and God efficaciously determining Jones's doing *A*? Ross's theodicy, as Augustine's, is always open to the question of why God did not effectively prevent Adam from falling?

There is, therefore, reason to doubt the consistency of Ross's doctrine of creation with any view of human freedom which is incompatible with determinism. This conclusion, combined with an earlier one, strongly suggests that both divine omniscience and divine creation are incompatible with non-deterministic accounts of human freedom, but that compatibilistic freedom has no additional difficulties in a theistic context than causal determinism has in any case.

So far in this discussion I have tacitly assumed that God is outside time. But the position outlined in this chapter could also consistently be held by anyone who believes that God is in time. He could hold that, for example, God's determina-

---

[43] 'Creation', 618.

tion in time of events in his creation makes for no additional difficulties than those already present in causal determination.

But while there is nothing inconsistent in holding such a view about God in time there would be no reason to maintain it, at least if the argument of the previous chapters is sound. For it has been argued that the only solid reason for maintaining that God is in time, assuming the coherence of the idea of divine timeless existence, is that it makes possible or, more strongly, that it requires, a non-deterministic account of human action.

Finally, there is an objection to the overall value of the argument of this chapter, even supposing that this argument is successful. It is that this chapter has in view causal determinism, and argues that the source of the causal sufficiency of an action is immaterial, given compatibilism, whereas the adverse implication for human responsibility of divine timelessness is that timelessness entails logical determinism. So, it might be objected, the argument of this chapter is beside the point.

An *ad hominem* reply might be that it would have to be shown by an argument which so far has not been produced that logical determinism eliminates responsibility when causal determinism does not. The trouble with such a reply is that in due course an argument might indeed be forthcoming.

It is more satisfactory to argue that according to the Christian theistic view being defended the causal and logical relations of God to his created universe cannot readily be separated. For according to this view God's timeless decree that B occur at t_2, say, cannot be taken in isolation from God's timeless decree of A at t_1, and any causal links that there may be between these events. In short what God timelessly decrees is a complete causal matrix of events and actions. So timeless creation entails determinism. And if so, it has been argued in this chapter, the fact of the ordination of the causal sequence carries no more adverse consequences for human responsibility than determinism *simpliciter* carries.

10
Divine Freedom

ONE main conclusion of the previous chapters is that an important if not overriding reason for holding the view that God is in time is that only such a conception does justice to human free agency. For such agency, in a theistic universe, requires there to be (it is held) real change in God, and change requires time. In addition, divine free agency is also alleged to require real change in God, since for God to be free (according to philosophers such as Swinburne and Ward) requires him not to know the outcome of his free decisions until he has taken them. (It is even claimed by some that such ignorance of the future is essential to God's own health and growth.) It thus turns out, from this perspective, to be a defect of Boethius' 'solution' to the problem of divine foreknowledge and human freedom that human action is never envisaged as being interactive with God's action. At this point Boethius' theology is a kind of Platonic deism.

We have also seen that to avoid the charge of logical fatalism there is need to appeal to divine freedom of some sort.

So freedom, both human and divine, assumes critical proportions. In this chapter an attempt is made to handle this matter head on by asking the question, could a timeless God be free?

It will be argued that God, being timeless, is nevertheless free in a significant sense, though not in any sense that requires him to be unpredictably interactive with his creation. Such freedom does not require that God is in time and it rules out logical fatalism.

All theists unite in ascribing to God certain kinds of freedom. Because he is a necessary being he is free from intellectual and moral decay and weakness, and because he is the omnipotent creator of all he cannot be dominated or coerced by anything that he creates. Many other theists add that, being supremely excellent, he is free from the need to change for the better, to improve or to develop.

These factors provide a definite sense in which God may be said to be free, a sense in which human beings are never free. But is an eternal God free to choose, as human beings sometimes are? Granted that no one or nothing could coerce such a choice, and that all such choices would be the product of God's supremely excellent nature, is an eternal God free to choose between or among alternative possible outcomes? And if he is not free to choose between such outcomes does this matter? Would it be an unacceptable consequence of the idea of God existing timelessly that such freedom is denied to him? These questions divide themselves into two: the first, a problem for any theist, does it make sense to suppose that there are alternative equally optimific (or equally reasonable in some other way) outcomes between which God may choose? If not, does this matter? And second, a problem for divine timeless eternity, does the idea of divine choice make sense if God is eternal?

If God is supremely good then he could only choose those possible outcomes, instantiate those possible worlds, which are consistent with his having this character, since to act inconsistently is a defect which God could not have. And since God is supremely good it must be supposed that God chooses from all possible worlds that world which is the best, the best of all possible worlds, since to suppose that he might choose a world which was less than the best is to suppose that he might do something which was inconsistent with his supremely good nature.

But what if the idea of a best of all possible worlds makes no sense? In 'Must God Create the Best?'[1] Robert Merrihew

---

[1] *Philosophical Review* (1972). See also Bruce Reichenbach, 'Must God Create the Best Possible World?', *International Philosophical Quarterly* (1979). In 'The Problem of Divine Freedom', *American Philosophical Quarterly* (1983), Thomas B. Flint presents a defence of divine libertarian freedom by arguing that it is plausible to suppose that there are no possible situations in which such a God fails to have a choice between alternatives.

Adams argues that there may not be a best of all possible worlds, that for every world there is a more perfect world conceivable. If so, it would be unreasonable on logical grounds to suppose that God must instantiate the best of all possible worlds, but also unreasonable to suppose that he may instantiate a world that is less than the best.

But even if there *is* a best of all possible worlds, Adams goes on to argue, there is another reason why God need not actualize that world, a reason arising from the Judeo-Christian conception of God as essentially gracious. In actualizing a world which exemplified his grace God would not necessarily wrong any of his creatures, for he may create a world none of the inhabitants of which would exist in the best of all possible worlds, all the inhabitants of which are better existing than not existing, and are as happy in this world as in any alternative world in which they could have existed. Given this, and given that God is gracious, Adams argues that God 'might well choose to create and love less excellent creatures than He could have chosen'.[2]

Suppose that Adams is correct in his reasoning. How would this affect the question of divine freedom as sketched above? While, if Adams is correct, God is not 'obliged' (by his nature) to create the best of all possible worlds, supposing such to be a coherent supposition, he is 'obliged' to act in a way that is consistent with his nature or character. We might say that whatever moral ideal or ideals God's character exemplifies or expresses he is 'required' or 'obliged' to act consistently with those ideals.

It may be thought that the necessity of God *having* to choose some definite world, even if that world is not the best of all possible worlds, would diminish his freedom. But how could this be? Such a diminishing of freedom only makes sense if it is possible to call for an explanation of why God *had* to choose one possible world rather than some alternative. But there is no explanation possible, and so no failure of

---

[2] Adams, 'Must God Create the Best?', 324.

freedom. There is no explanation in terms of some principle external to God, of some physical or metaphysical covering law, which explains his action. But it may be said that freedom entails choice, which in turn entails rationality. And may not rationality be a good candidate for the *explanans*? Certainly having a reason of a certain sort may, given a particular view of explanation, explain an action. But if having a reason for doing the action implies the possibility of having a reason for not doing it (in precisely similar circumstances), then the reason is what the action is due to, but that reason does not render it intelligible. God does not have to do what he does by any necessity of nature, nor is he 'free' in the sense that he has liberty of indifference to opt between alternatives. Rather he is free because he acts in accordance with his supremely excellent nature without coercion or hindrance.

So even if Adams's reasoning is faulty in some respect, and it does make sense to suppose a best of all possible worlds, the further objection that in choosing God is somehow constricted or constrained in his freedom of choice is a curious one. There seems to be a species of metaphysical delusion at work in the advancing of such an objection. For the objection supposes that it would be some sort of disability to have a supremely wise and good nature and to 'have to' act in accordance with it. How much finer and freer, the objection implies, to have a nature which would allow the choosing of what is vile and wretched! But the lameness of this line of reasoning is apparent, for it supposes that to act in accordance with a supremely good nature would be a demeaning slavery, whereas (on the view being defended) to act thus is part of God's glory, part of what makes him supremely worshipful.

The difficulties that we have been discussing would apply equally well to a God who exists timelessly eternally. But there may be an additional difficulty for a timelessly eternal God. Can it be that such a God *could* choose between alternative equally optimific outcomes, if it is supposed that such alternatives are possible and consistent with God's supremely good moral nature? Could God choose between *any* alternatives? In the *Summa contra Gentiles* Aquinas argues that the universe is contingent and that God exists timelessly. Can both these positions be held consistently? I shall in due course argue that the universe is contingent and that God's timeless instantiation of it, though it does not involve some of the features of human choices, is a far cry both from Spinozism and from the view that the universe exists as a matter of formal logical necessity. But before this we shall look at Aquinas's position in more detail.

Even though Aquinas has doubts about the idea of there being a best of all possible worlds for God to choose, he does appear to argue that there are equally optimific possible outcomes, perhaps an infinite number of them. And he makes this consideration the basis of an argument for the contingency of what an eternal God wills, the contingency of the universe. Aquinas writes:

God, in willing his own goodness, wills things other than himself to be in so far as they participate in his goodness. But, since the divine goodness is infinite, it can be participated in in infinite ways, and in ways other than it is participated in by the creatures that now exist. If, then, as a result of willing his own goodness, God necessarily willed the things that participate in it, it would follow that he would will the existence of an infinity of creatures participating in his goodness in an infinity of ways. This is patently false, because, if he willed them, they would be, since his will is the principle of being for things, as will be shown later on. Therefore, God does not necessarily will even the things that now exist.[3]

How is this argument to be understood? According to Aquinas, God, in willing to create, can only create those things which are modelled upon or which exemplify his own goodness, which 'participate in his goodness'. But since there are an infinite number of ways in which God's goodness can be exemplified, then it may appear to follow that there

[3] *Summa contra Gentiles*, 1. 81. 4.

would exist an infinite number of creations each participating in God's goodness, exemplifying it in an infinite number of different ways. But this consequence is obviously false as a matter of fact, since there is only one actual world. So, Aquinas concludes, what exists now does not exist necessarily.

What Aquinas appears to be arguing is that it is the necessary singularity of what is actual which ensures that what is actual is contingent. God cannot as a matter of logic actualize all possibilities, even all possibilities which adequately 'participate in his goodness', because Aquinas assumes that there could not be more than one actual universe, and so there must be another explanation of why what exists does in fact exist. An explanation for what exists which appeals to the goodness of God is not sufficient, even though it is necessary. There must be a further factor which accounts for the actualizing of the world which actually exists.[4]

But what could that further factor be? Clearly nothing which makes reference to the goodness of God sufficient, since a similar explanation is available in the case of all other possibilities which would be exemplifications of God's goodness, an infinite number according to Aquinas. The further factor must be, it seems, something besides God's goodness. And it is hard to see what that other factor could be than a mere exercise of God's will.

While Aquinas's first argument concludes that what God creates must be contingent there is no direct appeal in it to divine eternity or immutability. But there is such an appeal in the second argument. Aquinas writes:

Everything eternal is necessary. Now, that God should will some effect to be is eternal, for, like his being, so, too, his willing is

---

[4] It could be argued, as David Lewis claims in a number of writings, that this, the actual world, is one of an infinite number of equally real possible worlds. It is actual only because it is actual *to us*. Other worlds are equally actual to their inhabitants (*Counterfactuals*, ch. 4). Lewis is thus in a position to deny Aquinas's claims that there is and can be only one possible world. The price to be paid for this is Lewis's counterpart theory.

measured by eternity, and is therefore necessary. But it is not necessary considered absolutely, because the will of God does not have a necessary relation to this willed object. Therefore, it is necessary by supposition.[5]

Aquinas is here arguing that while, *if* God wills something then since God's will is eternal his willing is likewise eternal, it does not follow that what is willed is eternal (in the abstract), considered apart from God's willing it. It is 'necessary by supposition', on the supposition, that is, that God has eternally willed it. Had God not eternally willed it then it would not have been, and hence it cannot be regarded as necessary, since if it had been necessary it would have occurred whether or not God had willed it.

If the conclusion of the previous argument is granted then the conclusion of this argument may be granted as well. If what actually exists is logically contingent, then even if it is granted that God has eternally willed what exists the fact that he has eternally willed it does not affect its logical status.

But even here matters are not quite so straightforward. For example, if we suppose with some (Anselm, for instance), that God's existence is itself logically necessary, and if this logically necessary being eternally wills that A, then it looks as if A is itself logically necessary since there is no possible world in which God does not exist, and no possible world in which God exists and chooses some alternative to A. Not, at least, if God's relation to what he chooses is not contingent, a point we shall return to in due course. Suppose, on the other hand, that God's existence is logically contingent, and thus only necessary in some weaker sense than that of logical necessity. Then even if it is logically necessary that if God exists he will choose A, his choice of A is not itself logically necessary. In general we may se that the ontological status of God's existence is transmitted to what he chooses to create unless it can be shown that there is a contingent relation between God's nature and his choice.

But can this be shown? In attempting to address this

[5] *Summa contra Gentiles*, 1. 83. 3.

question it is worth reflecting upon the notion of a choice. Is choice necessarily a temporally causal affair? And, if not, could an eternal God make choices which are contingent? A timelessly eternal God may be said to choose A if

(i)   There is at least one coherent alternative to A;
(ii) God is powerful enough to will A;
(iii) God has a reason for willing A in preference to any alternative.

Given (i)–(iii) God may plausibly be said by us to have chosen A even though there never was a time when he contemplated willing some alternative to A. Rather God eternally contemplates all alternative possibilities and eternally rejects them for good reason. It is impossible for God now or at any time to choose or to have chosen differently. He cannot now undo his choice. This may seem to be a disadvantage until we recollect that it would only be a handicap for someone for whom second thoughts might be better thoughts.

So God's choice of the universe may be contingent in the sense that there are coherent alternative universes which God is powerful enough to have instantiated had he possessed an adequate reason to do so. This argument does not depend on the idea of God choosing between equally optimific outcomes, which would appear to make God's instantiation of any universe an act of pure reasonless will. Rather the argument is that God's freedom consists in the rationality of his choice, in his having a good reason for what he instantiates, not in his having no reason.[6]

The picture frequently sketched (for example by Leibniz), that among all possible worlds God has chosen to actualize one particular possible world, supposes that God 'stands back' from the array of possibilities in order to confer on one

[6] William Mann argues that 'the will of God' is ambiguous as between the power of willing and what is willed. The power of willing is part of God's essence, whereas what he wills is not part of his essence, and so he is free to will what he pleases. This resolution of the ambiguity does not resolve the problem of divine freedom, however. It simply relocates the problem in what God *pleases*. (Mann, 'Simplicity and Immutability in God', 274–6.)

of them the dignity of actuality. And such a picture implies that while God chose *A* he might instead have chosen not-*A*. The 'internal sources' of God's action incline but do not necessitate, but then this seems to suppose there could have been other reasons inclining other ways. But could there? Could there have been a situation in which God chooses neither *A* nor not-*A*, but is contemplating them both along with all other possibilities? Such a 'situation' could only have been a time, and yet by supposition God is eternal and hence necessarily has no time in which to contemplate a range of unactualized possibilities before deciding which, if any, to actualize. So both his contemplation of them and his decision to actualize one of them is one timelessly eternal act. This does not mean that different phases of that act cannot be distinguished, but such a distinction can only be a conceptual, not a temporal distinction. Consideration of possibilities is logically prior to actualizing one of them, but both contemplation and actualization are one eternal act of the divine nature, if God is timelessly eternal.

So provided that the Leibnizian 'picture' is no more than that, and the different phases of the divine choice are understood conceptually, and as not representing different temporal phases, then the idea of an eternal choice is coherent, and the Leibnizian 'picture' does no harm.

In 'Absolute Simplicity', Eleonore Stump and Norman Kretzmann defend a version of the thesis that divine simplicity and eternity are compatible with divine free choice, and the (conditional) necessity of any such choice with the logical contingency of what is chosen.

On the question of whether God's will is necessitated, Stump and Kretzmann closely follow Aquinas in arguing that God's will is free because God wills in accordance with the highest good[7] and there are alternative ways in which the highest good might be exemplified or realized. So there is no absolute necessity to the will of God because there are numerous co-optimific goals for God to choose between.

[7] 'Absolute Simplicity', 265.

The one that God eternally chooses is not necessitated by his nature since he might consistently have chosen an alternative.

Nevertheless God's will, although not absolutely necessitated, is conditionally necessitated in that given that God has eternally chosen to actualize some world he cannot choose not to actualize that world. His act of actualizing is conditionally necessitated by this choice which, because it is eternal, cannot be changed. So given the fact that God chooses to actualize (and he might, consistently with his nature, not have so chosen) he cannot now choose not to, or at any time choose not to.

The problem with such a position is that, as before, when discussing Aquinas, it is hard to see how divine caprice can be avoided. For God is portrayed as actualizing one of a number of co-optimific goals. If we suppose this makes sense, on what grounds could God decide in favour of one rather than another? Clearly, not by reference to their character. There seem to be two alternatives; either he chooses on the basis of some accidental feature of one alternative lacked by all the others, a feature not related to optimificity, or he chooses as a result of pure whimsy. Neither of these alternatives is very appealing.

Stump and Kretzmann confront the dilemma between on the one hand maintaining God's eternal simplicity of choice and on the other maintaining his freedom. From the first horn of this dilemma it appears to follow that

> Because God is eternal and consequently immutable, we cannot accurately say that God could have willed not to create.[8]

From the second horn it appears to follow that

> it might have been the case that God willed not to create.[9]

They attempt to escape both these horns by relativizing the idea of God's eternal simplicity to whatever world God

---

[8] Ibid. 268.
[9] Ibid.

chooses to actualize. *Within* such a world God is eternally simple, he cannot change, his will is necessary by conditional necessity. But *across* such worlds he is not simple, nor eternal, since he chooses between worlds and so has properties, given the actuality of one possible world, that he would not have given the actuality of some alternative possible world.

This is, of course, a considerable modification of Aquinas's view. As Stump and Kretzmann recognize it surrenders the original position that an eternally simple God may freely choose to actualize one of an array of possible worlds, or choose to actualize no world.

But is it necessary to go to such lengths provided that we recognize both that God is not impelled by any law of logic to act as he does, and that his eternal choice of this, the actual world, is made in preference to any alternative for a reason? We can then maintain both God's timeless eternity and also his freedom, though not freedom understood as an 'equi-poised capacity'.

So far I have defended the contingency of the universe on the grounds that it is the outcome of God's reasonable choice, against the view of Aquinas, recently endorsed by Stump and Kretzmann, that contingency results from choice from among equally optimific outcomes.

But did not God have to choose reasonably? And if he did does this not put paid to his freedom and to the universe's contingency? In a sense, yes. But the language of *having to* does not imply constraint in this case. God had to because of who he is and that he did choose is the ultimate explanation of what takes place. Thus to say that God *had to* is to say that no further explanation of what takes place is possible than that it seemed good to the eternal God that these things should be so.[10]

---

[10] Some may regard it as the ultimate blasphemy to suppose that a universe which contains Belsen is the universe that it seemed reasonable to God to create. But the alternatives, such as the view that such horrors are solely due to the depraved wills of God's free creatures (whom he has created and keeps in murderous being), or that Belsen is part of some natural process of evolution which God is powerless to affect, appear to others to be much more blasphemous.

A universe which is in some sense the inevitable outcome of God's choice which is itself in some sense inevitable may conjure up the spectre of Spinozism. But I shall now argue that Spinoza's metaphysics is incompatible with theism and that it is unwarranted to conclude that the only alternative to the idea that the actual universe is one of a number of equally optimific possible universes is Spinozism.

Spinoza's pantheism was not of a crudely reductionist kind. He did not argue that the empirical universe *is* God, thus effectively eliminating all reference to God as traditionally understood. His pantheism is a form of metaphysical monism, the view that the whole of reality stretching out through time is God or nature, and that certain properties apply to this monistic unity which are traditionally applied to God by theists; for example the properties of freedom and eternity. Spinoza applies to the whole of reality, which he regards as one substance,[11] the property of necessary infinity. Its existence follows from its nature, and its existence must be infinite otherwise it would be limited by something else of the same kind which would also necessarily exist, and the absurdity (for Spinoza) of there being two substances with an identical attribute would follow. This infinite substance is God, and God is the only substance. 'God is one, that is only one substance can be granted in the universe, and that substance is absolutely infinite.'[12] God, thus understood, is the first and the efficient cause of everything else[13] acting freely by the necessity of his own nature.

Spinoza denies both intelligence and will to God, on the grounds that such properties require that there are possibilities that God chooses not to actualize. For Spinoza the omnipotence of God is fully exerted in the unfolding of the course of the whole of reality.

The omnipotence of God has been displayed from all eternity, and

---

[11] *The Ethics*, I, Prop. VIII, Note 1.
[12] Ibid. Prop. XIV, Coroll. 1.
[13] Ibid. Prop. XVI.

will for all remain in the same state of activity. . . . Otherwise, we are compelled to confess that God understands an infinite number of creatable things, which he will never be able to create.[14]

God is the cause of all else that exists, but not, strictly, the creator of it (since being the creator supposes intelligence and will).[15] And whatever else exists cannot have the character of a substance since there is only one infinite substance. Rather everything else that exists must be modifications of the attributes of God, 'modes by which the attributes of God are expressed in a fixed and definite manner'.[16] Things are not produced by God, they follow from God.[17] It follows, therefore, that, 'nothing in the universe is contingent, but all things are conditioned to exist and operate in a particular manner by the necessity of the divine nature.'[18] God, and all his modes, exist necessarily, and so all things are conditioned by the necessity of the divine nature, not only as regards the fact but also the manner of their existence.[19]

So by 'God' Spinoza means the whole of reality or nature (not simply physical nature) considered as active, the total process of the whole of reality through space and time; by 'nature' considered as passive Spinoza means what follows from God's nature, all his modes.

Since all that exists exists necessarily, not as the outcome of a divine choice of one set of possibilities among all others, it follows, for Spinoza, that this world, the actual world, is the only possible world:

If things, therefore, could have been of a different nature, or have been conditioned to act in a different way, so that the order of nature would have been different, God's nature would also have

---

[14] Ibid. Prop. xvii Note.
[15] Ibid. Prop. xxv.
[16] Ibid. Prop. xxv, Coroll.
[17] Ibid. Prop. xxviii, Proof.
[18] Ibid. Prop. xxix.
[19] For an interpretation of Spinoza which regards God as in effect the sum total of physical powers in the universe see E. M. Curley, *Spinoza's Metaphysics: An Essay in Interpretation.*

been able to be different from what it now is; and therefore that different nature also would have perforce existed, and consequently there would have been able to be two or more Gods.[20]

It follows from this that the only sort of possibility which Spinoza will countenance with regard to reality is epistemic possibility and impossibility, the postulating of possibilities based upon our ignorance of the nature of things.

A thing of which we do not know whether the essence does or does not involve a contradiction, or of which, knowing that it does not involve a contradiction, we are still in doubt concerning the existence, because the order of causes escapes us,—such a thing, I say, cannot appear to us either necessary or impossible. Wherefore we call it contingent or possible.[21]

And Spinoza is very definite, in a way which we have seen Aquinas is not, that divine eternity implies that God is not distinct from his decrees.

In eternity there is no such thing as when, before, or after; hence it follows solely from the perfection of God, that God never can decree, or never could have decreed anything but what is; that God did not exist before his decrees, and would not exist without them. But, it is said, supposing that God had made a different universe, or had ordained other decrees from all eternity concerning nature and her order, we could not therefore conclude an imperfection in God. But persons who say this must admit that God can change his decrees. For if God had ordained any decrees concerning nature and her order, different from those which he has ordained—in other words, if he had willed and conceived something different concerning nature—he would perforce have had a different intellect from that which he has, and also a different will.[22]

Finally, according to Spinoza, God does not act in accordance with any goal or plan, for that would be to suppose something independent of God which God might act in fulfilment of and 'this is only another name for subjecting

---

[20] *Ethics*, I, Prop. xxxiii, Proof.
[21] *Ethics*, I, Prop. xxxiii, Note 1.
[22] Ibid. Prop. xxxiii, Note 2.

God to the dominion of destiny, an utter absurdity in respect to God, whom we have shown to be the first and only free cause of the essence of all things and also of their existence'.[23] God's creation is not purposive, but exemplary.[24]

Having glanced at some of Spinoza's metaphysical and theological claims (though not at the arguments by which he supports them) we are now in a position to make a comparison between his views and those of a theism which claims that God is timelessly eternal, and to appreciate the essential differences between the two positions.

The basic metaphysical difference between Spinoza and classical theism lies, obviously enough, in theism's ontological dualism, the basic distinction between the creator, who is un-derived, an all-powerful and all-good spirit, and the creation, derived from and dependent upon the creator and composed not only of minds but also of matter.

So that while a theist may agree with Spinoza in a formal sense that God is eternal and free, he means something very different by 'God'. Spinoza denies that God could ever be a cause of the universe since he denies that there could be more than one distinct substance, since no two substances can have any property in common, and for one substance to be produced by another would be for the produced substance to have some of the properties of the producing substance. Spinoza's proof that there cannot be more than one substance is obscure and implausible[25] and in any case it is quite at odds with the position of the theist who holds that God creates substances distinct from himself all of which are not only consistent with his character but some of which also exemplify aspects of it.

It is Spinoza's view that God's omnipotence is maximally exercised, exercised to the fullest possible extent in the universe. This is not quite the view that God is all-powerful in the sense that no other individual besides God has any

[23] Ibid. Prop. xxxiii, Note 2.
[24] Ibid. Appendix.
[25] Ibid. Prop. v.

power whatever. Theism denies both of these positions. The power that creatures have is derived from God, but it is not immediately from God. According to theism I write these words as a result of physical and mental powers given and maintained by God. But this does not imply that it is God who is writing these words.

Consistent with this, and perhaps entailed by it, theists also hold that the creation is an exercise of the divine will and intelligence. God brings things to pass in accordance with his decree or plan. Spinoza also writes of the decree of God, but once again the relation between this and orthodox theism is purely formal or verbal. For while, according to Spinoza, God is the cause of all things, such a cause is not in accordance with a plan but is rather the inevitable, rational unfolding of the whole of reality. The universe unfolds rather like a geometric theorem proving itself.[26] And so Spinoza denies that God can create things by intelligence and will.

Finally, Spinoza denies, as part of his monism, that God acts for a purpose or goal. He says that to suppose such a goal is to subject God to destiny. One might agree with Spinoza to a degree here, if one had to suppose that any goal which God aims at must be imposed upon him, but such an imposition is not necessary. But even if one concedes to Spinoza that creation is not purposive but exemplary,[27] conceding that while creation as such may not have a purpose objects in creation may have purposes, this concession does not touch the monism–theism issue.

So far we have maintained that the actual universe is contingent; that God chooses it in accordance with his own nature, and not because it is one of a number of equally optimific alternatives; and that this is a markedly different position from that of Spinoza.

In what sense can we say there is an alternative to the choice that God has made? Earlier we noted the view that the

---

[26] Ibid. Prop. xvii, Note.
[27] Ibid. Appendix.

universe is contingent in the sense that given that God chose that p he cannot now change to not choosing that p, but it might have been the case from all eternity that he did not choose that p.[28] We might express this view as follows. The existence of the universe cannot be deduced from any set of logical truths. What God actualizes in timelessly eternal fashion is necessitated not by logic but by his own nature. The universe exists because it is the expression of God's intelligence and will, that which accords with his supremely good nature. The universe is contingent, not because God is rationally indifferent to which universe he chooses but because its existence is not deducible from a set of logical truths. Does this mean that the creation is included in God? Certainly the idea of the universe is in the mind of God. But to suppose that the creation is a whole or a part of God would be to suppose that to talk about creation is to talk about God. But this is manifestly unsatisfactory. If Jones disobeys God there are two individuals related. To suppose that in such a situation God really disobeys himself, or that the disobedience is only apparent, would be to maintain something altogether different.

So there is a sense in which a theist (as opposed to a Spinozist) holds that the universe is necessary in only a qualified sense. For according to theism the universe comes about as a result of God's will, the will of an agent, though an agent who is not, and necessarily not, ever undecided what to do. God is necessarily good, but he is not necessarily good as a result of a decision or an act. The necessary goodness of God is not the result of God's agency. To suppose such would be to suppose an incoherence, for how could God's goodness come about as a result of *God's* decision?

One further thing, then, that might be meant by calling the existence of the universe contingent (in an appropriately qualified sense) is that it is not part of God, otherwise God would have spatial parts, and temporal parts. Rather the

[28] In his *Reason and Religion* a view similar to this is attributed by Kenny both to Grosseteste and Wyclif.

universe is an intentional object of God's mind, that object which he has timelessly eternally chosen to actualize. His choice of the universe is thus an eternal determination of his will. If God, *per impossible*, where not to have eternally willed the actualizing of the universe then he would still be God. But if God *per impossible* lacked the property of goodness he would not be God.

This could be put slightly differently; in the case of a timelessly eternal God there is a conceptual distinction between what he is and what he does in that what he is is logically prior to what he does. It makes no sense to think about what God does without logically presupposing the existence of God, even though there is no logically possible situation in which God exists and does not act determinately.

So the earlier objections to Aquinas's arguments in defence of the contingency of the universe do not entail Spinozistic pantheism. It is perfectly consistent with the basic theistic distinction between the creator and the creature to suppose that the actual universe should be the only possible universe.

So there is a sense in which God could have created an alternative universe to the one he has in fact created. If an alternative is conceivable then an alternative is possible. But there is a difference between saying that a state of affairs is internally consistent quite apart from the question of whether God would actualize it and saying that it is possible that God would actualize it. If the question, 'Could God have instantiated a world different from the actual world?' is a question about God's power then the answer must be that if A is a consistent state of affairs then God's power could have actualized it. But that God is sufficiently powerful that he could is not to say that he would. In fact, we know from the actual world that he would not, because he has not. Abstracted from God's will such consistent alternatives are possible. Moreover, the actualizing or non-actualizing of at least some possible worlds cannot be deduced by us from God's character alone. It would make sense to suppose that any of these possibilities should have been actual. About many of such possibilities regarding the future we are now able to say that for all we know they may come to pass. They represent present epistemic possibilities and logical possibilities. But if we were to know everything, or more than we do, then we would see that these possibilities are only abstract. They do not represent real possibilities and never did. The thought that they did was the product of our ignorance.

The theistic view that we are defending has consequences for all empirical possibility rather like those consequences we readily accept in the case of things we know have happened. Given that the letter did arrive we may still consider abstractly its non-arrival and raise in a hypothetical way its non-arrival as a counterfactual possibility. But such an abstract possibility we know must remain forever abstract, unfulfilled. For a theist who believes that God exists eternally and has eternally willed the universe in all its detail, all conditional propositions about empirical matters of fact with antecedents which turn out (for us) to be false are eternally counterfactual, though we do not know, at present, with respect to most conditionals, which are the ones with the true antecedents and which are the counterfactuals.

Reference was made earlier to the 'illusion' that God's necessarily acting in accordance with his supremely good nature is somehow an abridgement of his freedom. It is now clear that there is another illusion which needs to be uncovered, namely that the problem under discussion would somehow be diminished if it were supposed that God were in time and so had time to make up his mind, and to pass from a state of judicious neutrality to a determinate choice of one out of an infinite series of possible choices of worlds. The positing of a temporal series—God in time—does nothing to change the basic logic of the situation. The idea that time can be a substitute for rationality is a fallacy, though one that lacks a name. For a God in time would be as constrained as a timelessly eternal God, not by time but by his own nature and the reasons which are good reasons for an individual with such a nature. And if these reasons are supposed, in the terms of Leibniz's rather dubious distinction, to *incline* but not to *necessitate* God to action, then they will incline but not necessitate God whether he is in time or timelessly eternal. So the idea that the contingency of the universe, its contingency in a stronger sense than we have been prepared to allow in the previous discussion, can be more plausibly maintained by supposing that God is in time is also an illusion.

So to respond to the argument of the earlier part of this chapter merely by positing a God in time does not change anything. More radical proposals would be needed, and we shall now consider two such proposals, one briefly, the other at greater length.

The first proposal is to slacken the requirement about the rationality of God's choices, whether God is considered to be timelessly eternal or in time. On this view it would follow that there is a universe, and in particular this universe, not because God had a good reason to choose or to instantiate this universe but because he had some reason to choose this universe and at least as good a reason to choose some alternative universe which was overridden by whimsy or by an act of Scotist arbitrary will. Alternatively put, that there is this universe is simply by God's choice and for no good reason at all.

The view that God acted freely in the creation of the universe by exercising a pure act of will is a perfectly consistent view. And it is possible to hold such a position whether or not one also holds that God exists in a timelessly eternal state. But it carries the consequence that the whole of the universe exists by the sheer unreasoning will of the creator, and hardly provides a satisfactory vindication of divine freedom, certainly not the sort of vindication which those who appeal to divine freedom usually have in mind.

A second view is that provided by Keith Ward in *Rational Theology and the Creativity of God*. According to Ward the problems in this area, particularly the problem of accounting adequately for the contingency of the universe, arise from the unwarranted assumption that God is self-sufficient.

The basic notion which has controlled the development of the traditional doctrines of God is the notion of self-sufficiency. The primary, all-explaining being must be self-sufficient, since it must be wholly self-explanatory. The difficulty which arises at once is that though the self-sufficient being is postulated precisely in order to account for the existence of the finite, changing and complex entities of the universe, once one has a self-sufficient being, the existence of anything other than it seems to be unnecessary and superfluous. If God is distinguished from the world, opposed to it as simple to complex, eternal to temporal, immutable to changing and infinite to finite, then as we have just seen it is extremely difficult to see how such a God can be related to the world at all. But if God is said to include the world in his own being, either by identity or emanation, it is equally difficult to see how there can be any freedom or contingency in the universe.[29]

Ward's advice is to drop the idea of divine self-sufficiency from theism[30] and to adopt the view that it is necessary for God to create a universe of interacting free agents in order to be a loving being. God must create such a universe, according to Ward, if he is to be loving, if he is to express or convey his love to others.

The distinction between having a disposition to do something and actually doing it is a crucial one here. If this distinction is granted then there is no reason why being loving could not be an essential property of God, and his eternal intention to create the universe an expression of that love. If so then it is not possible for Ward to claim, as he does, that it is only on such an account as his that it is possible to ensure that God is loving.

The basic reason for creation is that it brings about forms of goodness and value which otherwise would not exist. In brief, it makes it possible for God to be a God of love, possessing the properties of creativity, appreciative knowledge and sharing communion, which are the highest perfections of personal being.[31]

---

[29] *Rational Theology*, 81.
[30] Ibid.
[31] Ibid. 85.

Rather, what Ward's position at best implies is that creation makes it possible for God to express his love. The alternative to this would not only be unacceptable on general grounds, it would also be unacceptable to someone such as Ward who stresses the idea of God's growth through time. For if having a creation of interactive beings is necessary for God to be a God of love, and not merely for God to express his love, then God is only contingently a God of love since on this view the universe is a free, contingent creation of a God who lacks the property of love and who needs the universe in order to acquire that property.

A further reason why it is important to focus on the distinction between love as a disposition of God and love as an action is that according to Ward, if he grants this distinction, God needs the universe not in order to be loving but in order to express his love in an appropriate manner, by creating 'forms of goodness and value which otherwise would not exist'.[32] Thus God needs a universe of free interactive beings in order to express his love, and since it is necessary for him to express his love, the universe is likewise necessary.

But if this is so, what advantage as regards divine freedom does this way of thinking have over the idea of divine self-sufficiency which Ward rejects? According to Ward, the universe which God brings into being contains agents who are indeterministically free, and he is quite prepared to accept the consequence of this, namely that God's purposes are from time to time thwarted.[33] This consequence may be regarded by some as an advantage of Ward's position, though it has been argued earlier that this is a mistake. But on the narrower question of divine freedom and sufficiency it is hard to see how a view which holds that the universe is necessary either for God to be loving, or for God to express his love, and yet nevertheless God is free in the creation of such a universe, is a consistent view or one which provides a more satisfactory

[32] Ibid.
[33] Ibid. 83.

solution to the problem of divine sufficiency and freedom than the view outlined in this chapter that God eternally chooses this universe as the expression of his nature.

Incidentally, there is a tendency for Ward, in his criticism of Aquinas, to want to have things both ways. On the one hand he criticizes Aquinas for holding that God is self-sufficient, caricaturing this view as Narcissistic.[34] On the other hand he argues that: 'For Aquinas, then, there is a sense in which the world is interior to God, as directly willed and known by him.'[35] But if God is *self*-sufficient then presumably a consequence of this view is that nothing apart from God is necessary to God. On the other hand if the world is 'interior to God' it is hard to see how it can be maintained that God is self-sufficient.

This objection is also sometimes alleged, from different quarters, to be a difficulty for the view that has been defended in this chapter. If God is self-sufficient, what reason could there be for creating the world? If on the other hand the world is necessary, how can God be self-sufficient?

If God is self-sufficient does he need to create? In one sense, obviously not. If a country is self-sufficient it does not need to import goods. But an individual may be self-sufficient in the sense that nothing else is necessary for that individual's existence and yet he may wish to act or communicate himself, though not because he has a psychological need or deficiency, or some other defect of existence or character such that he has to communicate or create. To want to do something may be a sign not of weakness but of strength, not of deficiency but of fullness. So that it seems to be perfectly consistent with the fact that God does not need anything that he nevertheless wishes to have other beings and creates in accordance with these wishes. And it would be a perverse piece of argumentation which attempted to qualify this by saying, 'Ah, yes, but this means that God *needs* to wish to create.' This is rather like the claim that all human actions are

[34] Ibid. 82.
[35] Ibid. 84.

selfish. There is a sense, a perfectly trivial sense, in which all human actions are selfish, in the sense that all such action is the action of the self who performs it. But there is a non-trivial sense in which what a person does is selfish because it is at the expense of the legitimate interests of others. In the same way there is a trivial sense in which it might be said, from the very fact that God has created the universe and you and me in it, that God needs you and me. Otherwise why would he have created us? But there is another sense in which he clearly did not need you and me, in the sense in which neither you nor I are necessary for God's being God. We may be pretty important people but it would be taking things a bit too far to suppose that our non-existence would result in God's non-existence as well. Although the language may seem rather extravagant to our ears, Jonathan Edwards is expressing a perfectly consistent and intelligible position when he writes that 'a disposition in God, as an original property of his nature, to an emanation of his own infinite fulness, was what excited him to create the world'.[36]

---

[36] *Works*, I, 100.

II

Referring to Eternal God

PRECEDING chapters have been exclusively concerned with a central aspect of the metaphysics of theism. It has been argued that the idea of God as existing in a timeless eternity, though not without difficulties, can be made plausible, at least more plausible than current arguments against the view would indicate, and that it has certain advantages, for example, the advantage of making possible an unattenuated account of divine omniscience.

In the Christian theological tradition metaphysics is but a prelude to worship. But worship presupposes the ability not only to characterize God in a sufficiently adequate and discriminating way, but also to refer to him, for more than one individual to refer to him, and for such referrings to be possible on more than one occasion. So that if a connection is to be established between metaphysics and worship (between *doctrine* and *application*, as a Puritan preacher might have said) then an attempt must be made to say something about the possibility of referring to God. Worship apart, there is need to say something about the epistemological and semantic issues which are legacies of the idea of God's timelessness.

In *Individuals*, P. F. Strawson argues that the basic conditions for the identification of particulars, the provision of 'individuating facts' are based upon a framework of the knowledge of particulars. 'It is a necessary truth that any new particular of which we learn is somehow identifyingly connected with the framework, even if only through the occasion and method of our learning of it.'[1] And this framework of particulars which is necessary for the identification of any particular is, according to Strawson, basically a spatio-temporal affair.

[1] *Individuals*, 24.

Every particular either has its place in this system, or is of a kind the members of which cannot in general be identified except by reference to particulars of other kinds which have their place in it; and every particular which has its place in the system has a unique place there.[2]

Let us suppose that these plausible claims are correct: reference to individuals can only succeed in a framework of spatio-temporal particulars. We may suppose as well that God is a particular, though not, as has been stressed, a spatio-temporal particular. To say that God is a particular is to say that he is an individual of whom qualities, such as wisdom and power, can be predicated, and a sufficient condition of which is that agency can be ascribed to him—he creates and destroys, for example. There are, allegedly, grave difficulties with this idea[3] but the difficulties of supposing that God is *not* a particular, but a universal, and hence something necessarily abstract, seem infinitely greater. Whatever difficulties there are about supposing that a timeless God is a particular are miniscule in comparison with the idea that divinity is wise, or creates. But if God is a universal the problem of reference is speedily settled: by a definition.

According to one kind of sceptic, reference to God is impossible because God is not the sort of thing to which reference can successfully be made:

it is *logically* impossible to specify what 'God' refers to such that we can ascertain what must be the case so that we can distinguish between it being the case that God exists and it being not the case that God exists. To understand the syntax of 'God' (in non-anthropomorphic employments) is to understand that we cannot specify what 'God' refers to in empirical terms. To speak of specifying his effects when we are logically debarred from specifying him makes no sense at all. . . . 'God' is supposed to be some kind of referring expression standing for an infinite, non-spatiotemporal, non-indicable individual, utterly transcendent to

---

[2] Ibid. 25–6.

[3] See e.g. Michael Durrant, *The Logical Status of 'God'* and *Theology and Intelligibility*.

the cosmos. When we reflect on the meanings of these terms, we recognise that it would be logically impossible to verify that such an alleged individual exists. Anything that we could apprehend or could be acquainted with would *eo ipso* not be such a reality.[4]

Here Nielsen links the issue with the wider question of verification, though it can be discussed separately, as it will be discussed here. Antony Flew says something similar. ' "What is it that all these magnificent attributes are supposed conceivably to be the attribute of?"; or "How is it considered that it would be possible to pick out God, in this sense of *God*, as an object of discourse?" '[5] The arguments of Nielsen and Flew are essentially the same: how can God, who is by definition non-spatial and non-temporal (a definition which the earlier chapters of the present study have endorsed), become an object of discourse? Or how could 'God' function as a referring-expression when the conditions for success or failure in reference cannot be satisfactorily established?

Here is a further example of a philosopher voicing such difficulties:

If there is a God, who has thoughts, what makes the thoughts *his* thoughts? If God has no body, then there is no divine bodily behaviour to serve as the basis of attribution to him of thoughts and knowledge.[6]

Even in telekinesis the agent is identified by being a particular body in a particular place: the agent who makes the claims to have unusual powers, and whose predictions are, if he is fortunate, fulfilled, is a normal bodily agent. If we thought that even the lips of the wonder-worker were being operated by telekinesis then all reason to attribute the remote effects to *his* agency would disappear. But in the case of a non-embodied agent whose sphere of immaterial operation is the entire universe there seems no

[4] Kai Nielsen, *An Introduction to the Philosophy of Religion*, 169–70.
[5] *God and Philosophy*, 30.
[6] Kenny, *God of the Philosophers*, 124. See also id., 'The First Person', in Cora Diamond and Jenny Teichman (eds.), *Intention and Intentionality*, 9.

parallel Archimedean point from which the concept of agency can get a purchase.[7]

Even if (as Kenny believes) the God of the Philosophers cannot exist because he is conceptually incoherent, he thinks that the God of religion would be in other difficulties, notably the difficulty of convincingly ascribing agency to a non-embodied agent. So the problem, as Kenny sees it, is that the God of religion, though not conceptually incoherent, faces a philosophical difficulty that is as daunting as any faced by the God of the Philosophers, namely that even if he exists no one could knowingly refer to him.

As a response to these three expressions of scepticism I shall discuss four arguments, the first three of which seem plausible but which finally prove to be unsatisfactory. The last argument will be developed at greater length since it seems to have the greatest promise.

The first two arguments share a common claim, namely that there is in fact no need to respond to the problem raised by Nielsen and the others by providing even a sketch of a theory of reference which would enable 'God' to function as a referring expression for God.

The first of these arguments appeals to the programme of natural theology. If God's existence can be established by argument, particularly arguments which appeal to a feature or features of our experience, then such features will not only serve as premises for the conclusion that God exists, they will also provide the conditions enabling us to refer to God successfully. So that if, say, some version of the argument from design were successful, then the features of the universe which make it plausible to suppose that the universe has one creator also enable us to refer to that creator. God is the one who has created the universe with such and such a form.

There are two problems with such an argument. One is the well-known difficulty of constructing a plausible a posteriori proof of God's existence. And part of the difficulty of this

---

[7] Kenny, *God of the Philosophers*, 126.

enterprise has precisely to do with the fact that the data of experience are so diffuse and ambiguous that they are compatible with a number of different hypotheses, that is they do not unambiguously function as ways of referring to one God.

This leads to a second difficulty. If it could be argued that there is a successful a posteriori proof of God's existence then the argument about reference will be as follows:

> There is a plausible proof of God's existence, therefore it is possible to refer to God.

To which it might be reported

> Since it is impossible to refer to God there can be no plausible proof of his existence.

In other words there is the problem of which has logical priority, the problem of referring to God or the problem of proving his existence. If priority is given to the problem of reference (as Kenny gives it) then this calls in question the programme of natural theology. If priority is given to the programme of natural theology (as, say, Swinburne gives it) then provided that that programme is successful, and the success is achieved in a particular way, by means of an a posteriori proof of God's existence, then the problem of reference is solved.

In addition some have objections to the programme of natural theology which are quite unconnected with the problems about referring to God, and for this reason, if for no other, it would be desirable to try to provide a solution to the problem of reference which would have a more general appeal and would not derive from a particular view of natural theology.

There is a second argument which has been produced for the conclusion that there is no need to provide a theory reference for God. In *Religion and Rationality* Terence Penelhum writes:

The only solution to this problem (viz. the problem of

identification) would seem to be to capitalize on the requirement of God's uniqueness and to say that the normal processes of identification are rendered unnecessary by it. . . . The question is whether we are in a position to admit that if a believer is prompted to refer to God and to ascribe actions or mental states to him or to address him, his reference is sufficient for coherent discourse to occur. I think the reference is roughly intelligible. First, God is not being picked out from other objects, since he is not one of them— even if we are ascribing to him some action upon an object that we can pick out. Second, he is not being picked out from other beings of the same sort as himself, since there are none. The point here is not only that there can only be one deity, but rather that there can not be more than one incorporeal being with mental states and properties.[8]

It is possible that there is in both Penelhum's and Kenny's claims a confusion between the possibility of reference to God and success in reference to God, considered as an incorporeal spirit. Penelhum's argument is that uniqueness is sufficient to ensure referential success. So that someone who, prompted by a beautiful sunset, says that God created all that surrounds him, succeeds in referring to God if by 'God' he means someone who exists and has the unique set of properties which Penelhum mentions. It may not be true that God has created all this, but it is coherent to suppose that he did, and if it *is* coherent then referential success is ensured by God's uniqueness.

This seems to be correct but to be rather *thin*, for what is needed is a theory of reference which will make both positive semantic and epistemological proposals. Penelhum's argument ensures that it is possible to refer to God but not that anyone can ever know that he is referring to God. Success in reference is a purely semantic success, guaranteed by the connotation of 'God'. By virtue of what 'the wisest man' means, and given that there are men, then 'the wisest man' refers to someone, to an actual person. But in saying 'the

---

[8] *Religion and Rationality*, 156–7.

wisest man cannot be happy', though I am referring to an actual person I am not actually identifying a person, I am not knowingly picking one person out from all others.

To say that what is needed is a theory of reference which incorporates a means of actually identifying what is referred to is not to say that the identifying must succeed. That would be to say that 'God' could only be used to refer if there is a God. There must be the prospect of referential failure, of purporting to use 'God' to refer to God, but failing because the means of identifying him are inadequate. But a theory of reference for God, just like a theory of reference for any individual, must provide conditions of referential success even if such conditions are never in fact satisfied. The theorist must give a plausible account of what would have to be the case for us to be able to pick out God even if we fail to do so. This is what is attempted in what follows.

There is a third argument worth considering. In 'Inconceivable?', Robert Gay argues against Kenny that identifiable reference to conscious agency need not be made by means of the identification of something else, a body, but by a place. Non-bodily experiences could be located by learning that they each have a common geographical point of view, a geometrical point or region uninhabited by anybody. Gay suggests that a set of experiences may even be picked out as the one and only set whose *locus* is the entire universe.[9]

There is merit in this suggestion considered as an argument *ad hominem* against Kenny, though the thought that we could pick out, in the sense of empirically identify, a set of experiences whose *locus* is the entire universe seems bizarre. There might be a mind identifiable in thought as the mind whose locus is the entire universe but not identifiable in experience as such. This distinction between the two kinds of identification will be discussed later.

But Gay's argument cannot be employed to answer arguments against the idea of referring to an eternal God

---

[9] R. Gay, 'Inconceivable?', *Philosophy* (1985), 251.

because it would have the consequence that God was both empirically identifiable and identified in thought as an individual located in space and time. Also ruled out is Gay's further suggestion that God might be thought of as having a body not spatially related to this universe.[10]

So in view of the unsatisfactoriness of these proposals, let us return to the beginning and consider Flew's objection once again.

Flew's argument about the identification of God might be expressed in the form of a dilemma:

Either 'God' is to be understood in terms of a set of defining properties, in which case God cannot be empirically identified, *or* other, contingent properties are to be included in an account of 'God' such as *having appeared to Abraham* in which case it is impossible to be sure that it is *God* that has been identified.

The first horn of this dilemma can be expressed in terms of an ambiguity in the notion of identification. To identify can mean, to give the set of properties which is possessed by one particular individual and by no other. Or it can mean to give a set of properties which are sufficient to pick out that individual empirically. The dilemma which confronts any attempt to make identifying reference to an eternal God is that while it is possible to identify God in the first sense, to identify God in this sense will not necessarily involve identifying him in the second sense. But why cannot God be identified by means of his putative actions and the relations into which he is believed to enter with his creation? Could not empirical identification take place in this way? Flew sees a fundamental difficulty here. Discussing the idea that God might be referred to through Christ he says: 'Instead of trying to single out God, you point to the man; statements concerning God you construe as statements about the carpenter's son.'[11] Flew evidently thinks that if God is to be identified only by means of the relations into which he enters

---

[10] Ibid. 254.
[11] *God and Philosophy*, 33.

then God is identical with the sum of these relations. A reductionist or at best an anthropomorphic account of God, an account in which 'God' *means* 'the spatio-temporal individual who acts or who acted in such and such ways' seems inevitable.

So the dilemma of theological reference may be put as follows:

Either 'God' is defined in terms of a set of essential properties, in which case it appears to be impossible ever to identify God empirically, *or* 'God' is defined in terms of a set of empirically identifiable states of affairs, in which case a reductionist or anthropomorphic account of God is inevitable.

It is this dilemma which I shall now scrutinize and to do so I shall begin by treating 'God' as a proper name,[12] using Saul Kripke's account of proper names.[13]

Kripke rejects the idea that proper names such as 'Smith' are equivalent to a set or cluster of definite descriptions[14] though the arguments for this view are irrelevant here. Following Kripke and using his terminology we may say that a proper name such as 'Nixon' designates or denotes the same individual in every possible world (or counterfactual situation) in which that individual exists, though it does not follow from this that in every possible world in which Nixon exists he is called 'Nixon'.

Proper names are what Kripke calls *rigid designators*. They express a property had by the individual named in any possible world in which that individual exists. If proper names are *strongly rigid designators* they name the same individual with respect to every possible world.[15] That is, if

---

[12] 'God' has several of the grammatical features of a proper name: it is usually capitalized in English, and does not normally take an article. For further discussion see the books by Michael Durrant cited n. 3 above, and Nelson Pike, *God and Timelessness*, ch. 2.

[13] *Naming and Necessity*. Originally published as 'Naming and Necessity' in Harman and Davidson (eds.), *Semantics of Natural Language* (Dordrecht, 1972). Page references are to this edition.

[14] For the cluster view, see J. R. Searle 'Proper Names', *Mind* (1958).

[15] Kripke, 'Naming and Necessity', 270.

an individual has a proper name that is strongly rigid then that individual necessarily exists.

By contrast *non-rigid* or *accidental designators* are true of an individual in only some, at least one, of the possible worlds in which that individual exists. Thus definite descriptions are accidental designators. 'The President of France in 1973' is true of Georges Pompidou in this, the actual world. But there are possible worlds in which Pompidou is not the President of France in 1973 but some other individual is. And still other possible worlds in which there was no president of France at all in 1973. However, the fact that being the President of France in 1973 is not true of Georges Pompidou with respect to all possible worlds, but only with respect to some, including this, the actual world, does not mean that we cannot use an accidental designator such as 'the President of France in 1973' to designate Georges Pompidou in other possible worlds than the actual. It is necessary to distinguish between having the property of being President of France in 1973 and being designated 'President of France in 1973'. To suppose that *being the President of France in 1973* was true of Pompidou in every possible world in which Pompidou exists would be to suppose that *being President of France in 1973* forms part of the individual essence of Pompidou, such that any man who failed to be President of France in 1973 could not have been Georges Pompidou.

The point of Kripke's distinction between rigid and accidental designators is that proper names pick out a property had by the individual denoted by that name in every possible world in which that individual exists whereas accidental designators pick out a property had in only *some* worlds in which the individual exists. What property does 'Nixon' pick out? Presumably the property of *being Nixon*, or *being identical with Nixon* or *possessing Nixonhood*. These properties are not to be confused with the property of *being called 'Nixon'*, which is an accidental designator of Nixon.

Kripke draws a further distinction, between *naming* and *fixing the reference*. This distinction is of considerable importance in developing a response to the dilemma of theological reference.

Normally the names of individuals are learned by means of a definite description or a set of such descriptions. In Kripke's view the function of such definite descriptions is to fix the reference of the individual named. So that if we are told that the name of the man we met yesterday on the train is 'Robinson' then the description 'the man whom we met on the train yesterday' serves to direct our attention, in an unambiguous way, to one man, not by naming him but by fixing the reference to him by means of a definite description.

Besides proper names, such as 'Nixon', Kripke also considers common names such as 'gold' or 'heat', and applies the distinction between naming and fixing the reference to these as well. While Kripke's account of proper names has similarities to the views of J. S. Mill, his account of common names is quite different, for Mill claimed that general terms expressed properties. Kripke disputes this, at least in most cases.[16]

Take the case of heat. It would be perfectly normal to fix the reference of the concept of heat by means of certain data derived from perception. When something is hot this fact can be known by a human being through experiencing a certain characteristic sensation when the hot object is touched. A person having this sensation when he touched a given object would have good grounds for concluding that the object in question was hot. But is this what 'heat' means? Clearly not. For the proposition *Object* O *is hot but when touched by an individual* A *that individual does not get the sensation of heat* is not a self-contradiction, nor is A *gets the sensation of heat when he touches* O *but* O *is not hot*. The individual concerned might be someone with senses which are very different from those possessed by a human being, or he might be a human being with impaired senses.

Similarly a surface having a particular colour will mean,

[16] Ibid. 322.

on Kripke's account, that it has the property of reflecting light-waves of a given wavelength. The fact that the colour of the surface appears to change under different conditions, or that the reflecting of the light-waves of a given wavelength might be seen as a different colour by Martians equipped differently from ourselves, would have a bearing on how one fixes the reference of a particular colour, say, bronze, and on what directions one gives to enable others to refer to the colour, but not on the meaning of 'bronze'.

How then can the meaning of 'heat' be given? What does 'heat' mean? Since it is a general term, and not a word for an individual, the meaning of 'heat' is to be found in those properties or features which a hot thing has (in virtue of its being hot) in all possible worlds in which the thing in question is hot. That is, the meaning of 'heat' is to be given in terms of its essential properties. In the case of heat these properties will have to do with the movement of molecules. So that it is a necessary truth that if something is hot then the molecules of that thing move rapidly. This is what 'heat' means, though the reference of 'heat' might be fixed by touching the object in question.

That heat is the rapid movement of molecules represents a scientific discovery, but a discovery of what is in fact a necessary truth because the proposition *heat is the rapid movement of molecules* is true in every possible world in which there is heat.

One objection to the distinction between giving the meaning of 'heat' and fixing the reference of 'heat' is that the concept of heat would be different in the two cases. This would be the objection of a verificationist, for example. The method of verification of heat^1 is different from that of heat^2, hence the meaning of 'heat' is different in each case, though the two cases are perhaps contingently connected in that the concept of heat^2 was arrived at only because of the interest shown in the concept of heat^1.

This would also be the reaction of broader 'criteriological' accounts of meaning in which the teaching of a concept is

non-contingently connected with the criteria for its application. On this view a change in the criteria of application
entails a change in meaning, whereas on Kripke's account
there are different ways of fixing the reference of the same
concept of heat. In the literature criteriological accounts of
meaning are closely connected with the issue of scepticism in
which it is argued that the criteria provide the means of
settling epistemological issues with certainty. But the price of
this is the ruling out of the possibility of a certain sort of
discovery.[17]

Nothing is discovered about heat, on the criteriological
account, when heat is understood in terms of molecular
motion, for then we are referring to a different concept,
heat^2, whereas previously, when we referred to a characteristic sensation, we were referring to heat^1. But surely when it
is discovered that heat is molecular motion what is found out
is that a certain phenomenon that we, given our sensory
apparatus, identify by its characteristic sensations, *is* molecular motion, or that these sensations are caused by
molecular motion which would, in individuals differently
constituted from ourselves, produce a set of different
sensations.

It is now possible to try to apply Kripke's theory of names,
and his distinction between giving the meaning and fixing
the reference, to the problem of theological reference and the
dilemma of reference sketched earlier.

One difficulty over treating 'God' as a Kripkean proper
name is that in normal religious usage 'God' is not purely
referential in its function. Nor, if we modify Kripke's view
somewhat, is it completely satisfactory to say that 'God'
connotes the property of *being identical with God* as 'Socrates'
connotes the property of *being identical with Socrates*. This is
no doubt true, but there's more to 'God' than that. Nor will it
do to say that 'God' refers to the mysterious or incomprehen-
sible or unknowable divine essence. Nor could 'God' be

[17] In 'Dreaming and "Depth-Grammar"', Hilary Putnam discusses the
criteriological approach to meaning from a similar standpoint.

the name of a 'bare particular'. Nor, finally, is it plausible to treat 'God' as an abbreviated definite description or as a shorthand for a 'cluster' of such descriptions, as we saw earlier.

With all these routes blocked off where are we to turn? The suggestion that I shall consider is that 'God' expresses the individual essence of God. What does this mean? It is possible to distinguish between the notion of a general essence (or nature), and that of a particular essence (or nature) as follows. General essential properties are properties which are essential to an individual but which it is possible for more than one individual to possess, whereas individual essential properties are properties which are essential to an individual which no other individual could have.[18] So that, for example, the property of being omniscient is usually regarded as being essential to God and as not being possessed or possessable by anything distinct from God. It is a property unique to God and essential to him. Put in terms of possible worlds what the notion of an individual essential property amounts to is that if an individual *A* has an individual essential property *P* then the proposition *A has P* is true in every possible world in which *A* exists, and nothing distinct from *A* has *P* in any possible world.

So that what I am suggesting is that 'God' may be thought to express the individual essence of God and this consists in a set of properties some of which are shareable (other individuals than God may have them) but the set of which is unique to him. Each of God's individual essential properties may be said to form *an* individual essence of God, and the set of his individual essential properties to form *the* individual essence of God. In what follows I shall usually refer to *the* individual essence of God. Put briefly it might be said that the individual essence of God comprises those properties that are God-making properties or that together comprise the God-hood of God.

As noted previously there are properties that God has that

---

[18] On this distinction see Plantinga, *The Nature of Necessity*, 70.

he might not have had. *Being the creator of the world* is not a part of his nature whereas *being infinitely good* is. So that the notion of an individual essence, as it is being used here, is compatible with the contrast between essential and accidental properties within any given world, and so is incompatible both with the Leibnizian notion of an individual concept and with the pantheism of Spinoza.

So 'God' is not purely referential, nor is its connotation restricted to *being identical with God* and suchlike properties. On the other hand 'God' is not a truncated definite description because no part of the meaning of 'God' consists in properties which God might have had but does not in fact have, since the properties which give 'God' its meaning are all of them properties that are essential to him, properties which if an individual lacked any of them that individual could not be God.

Since the meaning of 'God' is to be given in terms of a set of individual essential properties there cannot be agnosticism about God's nature (which is not to say that that nature is perfectly comprehensible to finite minds), and since the individual essential properties are not empirically manifest properties there is no danger of 'reducing' God to the dimensions of a material object or human being.

Though God does have certain essential properties which are shareable e.g. *being intelligent*, he does not possess certain properties in virtue of which he is a member of the class of gods, except, perhaps the relational property *being an object of worship*. Here we can see the point of saying that God is not a god in the sense in which Smith is a man. There cannot be a divine nature which, like a natural kind, is shareable by more than one individual in the way in which there is human nature, or manhood, of which there are many instances. 'God' is not the name for a natural kind of thing, and *a fortiori* one could not learn to use 'God' as a proper name by being taught that it is the name of a particular case of a kind of thing that one is acquainted with in some way.

If 'God' has a meaning and if that meaning is to be given in terms of individual essential properties possessed by God the set of which is not possessable by any other individual, such as *being eternal*, and *being infinitely wise*, what determines the set of such individual essential properties? Can it be fixed in some non-arbitrary way?

On those theories, such as Searle's, in which a proper name is shorthand for a definite description or for a cluster of such descriptions the question of what determines the set can only be answered in epistemological terms. The set is fixed by those facts, or by what are believed to be facts, which the user of the name has come to believe are true of an individual, and which constitute the identity of that individual, by the accidents of the epistemological situation, by what the user of a name happens to know or believe about the individual so named. It is this accidental character of proper names that is said to constitute one of the virtues of the 'cluster' position by its advocates.

However, on the theory now being developed the meaning of 'God' is not given by the accidents of the epistemological situation of users of the name 'God'. So the answer to the query about what determines the set of God's individual essential properties is simply that the nature of God determines what these are. It follows logically from the nature of God, of who he is, that his nature is constituted by a certain set of individual essential properties. The set is expressive of that nature. Users of 'God' do not fix the set. It is fixed for them by the nature of the individual they use 'God' to refer to.

But this, though true, can only be half an answer. Granted that God, if he exists, has a unique nature, what reason is there to suppose that there is an individual that has this nature? How do we know what God's nature is? These are important epistemological questions and later we shall indicate how they might in principle be answered. But it is important to recognize that however they are answered, and even if they cannot be answered satisfactorily, they are *different* questions from those we have just been thinking about. Whatever

God's nature, it is logically impossible that human beings should decide what that nature is, though perfectly possible that they should come to know what it is.

So, while the meaning of 'God' is given by the set of individual essential properties that God has, reference to God may be fixed by a knowledge of empirically manifest properties had contingently by God.

Such contingent properties will not be certain characteristic sensations such as those sensations had almost universally by human beings in the presence of the rapid movement of molecules. They will typically be certain actions or the effects of certain actions expressed by definite descriptions. Examples of such definite descriptions might be 'the one who made the bush burn', 'the one who led the children of Israel out of Egypt', and 'the one who appeared to Isaiah in the Temple'. These definite descriptions are reference-fixers, in Kripke's sense. They are empirically manifest descriptions contingently true of an individual, if true at all, which if true of an individual serve to identify or pick out that individual from others. Establishing that something or other made the bush burn is not logically sufficient for establishing that God made the bush burn but it is logically necessary and might, given other beliefs and further reference-fixing definite descriptions, be epistemically sufficient.

So at least two questions need to be distinguished. There is the question of what makes it true that God and not some other individual or individuals made the bush burn and led the children of Israel out of Egypt. And there is the question of what evidence would make it reasonable, or certain, to suppose that God did these things. The answer to the first question is that God both made the bush burn and led the children of Israel out of Egypt only when an individual with a certain individual essence did both of these things. The answer to the question of what would make it reasonable to believe this may well be along the lines of the 'cluster' theory. The fact of such a cluster might provide the evidence on which to base the claim that it is known that God did both of these things even though it does not provide the truth-conditions for such a claim.

This account of the meaning of 'God' represents what might be called an 'essentialist variant' of Kripke's view of proper names. In this it resembles his account of mass terms such as 'gold' and terms for physical phenomena such as 'heat'. 'God' has features both of a proper name and a general name in Kripke's sense.

In the case of mass terms such as 'gold' continuity of reference to gold is initially secured by continuity of the original reference-fixing phenomena (certain visual appearances, perhaps, or simple chemical tests), discovery of other phenomena and finally the discovery of the common underlying chemical structure. It is sufficient, therefore, for A to be an instance of gold that A has a certain chemical structure, though under some circumstances, where, for example, there are perceivers with certain senses, the experience of a certain characteristic sensation is sufficient to secure reference to an object as an instance of gold.

The question of what is sufficient to secure continuity of reference to God may be pursued at two levels, as it may in the case of heat or gold. Continuity of reference can be secured, on the one hand, by observing the continuity of whatever factors served, in the first place, to fix the reference. These factors are contingently connected to the substance or phenomenon in question. They could fail to be present, or they could be present under different conditions, in different possible worlds. In the case of God the reference-fixing factors are not fairly constant and repeatable factors, such as the awareness of certain colours under certain circumstances, or they need not be. For reference to God is fixed by reference to his actions and these reference-fixing factors might be expected to be intermittent, and certainly not repeatable in accordance with a set of laws of nature, or capable of being arranged by human beings. While this is another significant difference between reference-fixing in the case of heat, and in the case of God, it is not an insurmountable obstacle to a theory of theological reference. For there is no reason why, provided that the idea of divine activity or speech is allowed in the first place, it should not be possible to decide whether or not an action or utterance is God's, and whether or not two or more actions or utterances on subsequent occasions are to be attributed to the same individual, God, or to some other factor or factors.

The other level at which continuity of reference may be secured is that of the essential properties of the substance or phenomenon, the rapid movement of molecules in the case of heat. Having discovered that heat is the rapid movement of molecules, that that is what 'heat' means, every discoverable case of rapid molecule movement is *ipso facto* a case of heat. Will this sort of approach work in the case of God? Certainly if 'God' means an individual with certain essential properties then whenever reference is made to such an individual then reference is made to God. The lack of parallel with physical cases such as heat, and the difficulty that this brings with it, arises over the fact that it is not possible to discover the essential properties of God in the way in which it is possible to discover the physical basis of the sensation of heat. What this means, in terms of our overall argument, is that if God is an individual having certain essential properties, and if to refer to God is to refer to that individual, then this by itself is of no help with the dilemma of reference. What is needed in order to help with the dilemma is some way of linking reference to God with reference to factors that are empirically manifested, as we have seen. Otherwise how are we able to distinguish between referring to God and merely talking about the concept of God?

Two claims lie at the heart of the dilemma of theological reference. The first claim is that the identification of individuals is necessarily spatio-temporal. The idea of successful identification in thought alone makes no sense for individuals though it might make sense for abstractions or universals. The second claim is about meaning, that to give the identifying-conditions for a referring expression such as

'God', the conditions under which reference to the individual concerned would be known to succeed or fail, is to give the meaning of that referring expression. On the basis of these two claims it has been argued by philosophers such as Nielsen and Flew that 'God' in 'God is F' must refer either to an incorporeal individual (in which case it is agreed on all sides that it is impossible to make identifying reference to such an individual) or to a corporeal individual (in which case we must abandon the meaning of 'God' as traditionally understood, and face the gruesome prospect of embracing some form of reductionism). Having developed an account of the meaning of 'God' it is now possible to argue that while 'God' refers usually to an individual who is incorporeal it does not follow (as the first horn of the dilemma maintains) that it is impossible to make identifying reference to God.

How is it possible to make identifying reference to God? Here we must look at the second horn of the dilemma. Because there is a difference between giving the meaning of a name and fixing the reference to the bearer of the name, it follows that it is possible to make identifying reference to an individual using data that are only contingently true of that individual. If this is so then it is possible to refer to God by his 'empirical manifestations' while not being committed to the view that the set of such manifestations provides the meaning of 'God'.

So Kripke's distinction between giving the meaning and fixing the reference is crucial. Only if this can be upheld is there any hope of breaking the dilemma. For only then is it possible to argue that because the conditions determining the correct reference to A do not determine the meaning of 'A' (the name for A), A can be incorporeal and yet on an occasion or occasions can have its reference fixed by a set of spatio-temporal predicates.

Granted the distinction between giving the meaning and fixing the reference, then how is Flew's question 'What is it that all these magnificent attributes are supposed conceivably to be the attributes of?' to be answered? Let us suppose, as a first possibility, that Flew is raising an epistemological question, in effect asking what empirically identifiable thing all the attributes that he refers to are attributes of. If we suppose this then the previous discussion indicates a way in which the question may be answered. The identifiable thing of which all the attributes are attributes is 'The one who . . .' where what is needed to complete the expression is some definite description or descriptions sufficient to fix the reference, in Kripke's sense. These definite descriptions will typically include a set of spatio-temporal co-ordinates forming a serial 'tradition'.

The individual who enters into certain relations in terms of which the reference to that individual is fixed is not necessarily an individual that has spatio-temporal position but one that has spatio-temporal manifestations. So that by fixing the reference of an individual one individuates that individual, but in the case of theological reference this does not take place (as it does in the case of material objects) by noting the spatio-temporal position of the individual.

So the answer to Flew's question, taken as an epistemological question, is in terms of a set of empirically manifest reference-fixing properties. What the magnificent attributes may be attributes of is the individual who appeared to Moses.

The second way in which Flew's question 'What is it that all these magnificent attributes are attributes of?' might be understood is as a question about the metaphysical identity of God given in terms of a set of individual essential properties.

Does this imply the eliminability of 'God', considered as a singular term? Is it possible to say all that is said by using the word 'God' by using, instead, the set of properties that constitute God's individual essence? The chief difficulty over the elimination of singular terms in ordinary discourse, as this has been urged by Quine, for example, is that the most plausible cases must mention position. If in the sentence 'The table is next to the window' an attempt is made to translate this into a set of properties having co-instantiation this translation will fail unless some device is included to indicate the position of this co-instantiation, and to include this would in effect be to reintroduce singular terms. Similarly, to eliminate tense in favour of an explicit date in effect reintroduces a reference to a unique date. The demonstrative element which was supposedly eliminated has to return.

But these objections do not hold in the case of theological reference. For here it is true both that because God is outside space and outside time as well there are no demonstratives to eliminate, and also that uniqueness is secured by those properties the set of which comprises the individual essence of God.

Suggesting that God's nature or essence consists in the co-instantiation of a set of individual essential properties may appear to raise the spectre of reductionism in theology. For it may seem to carry the consequence that God is nothing 'over and above' certain qualities or properties, and the translation of sentences about individuals into sentences about qualities or properties is the hallmark of reductionist theses, as when material objects are said to be equivalent to sets of qualities or, as in psychological versions of empiricism, material objects are said to be equivalent to sets of sensations. If this is what reductionism is, then the account of theological reference provided here is committed to it. But it is a perfectly innocuous form of reductionism. It does not involve the elimination of God as a transcendent individual, much less does it require God to be identified with a set of human states or values. What makes reductionism important in theology, and a serious charge to have to handle, is that in reductionist theologies the idea of God as the transcendent source of the material universe is eliminated by such language being translated into descriptions of a set of immanent properties or qualities, states of the universe or of individuals in the universe. But the claim that God is equivalent to a set of individual essential properties does not countenance this objectionable kind of reductionism, rather it re-emphasizes that the individual essence of God is ontologically distinct from individuals inhabiting space and time.

So a further answer to Flew's question is that the magnificent attributes that he mentions are attributes which together are constitutive of God. They are inseparable from God. God is not identifiable in thought separately from these magnificent attributes. God does not have an identity separate from them but one that consists of them.

BIBLIOGRAPHY

ADAMS, ROBERT MERRIHEW, 'Must God Create the Best?' *Philosophical Review*, 81 (1972), 317–32.

—— 'Middle Knowledge and the Problem of Evil', *American Philosophical Quarterly*, 14 (1977), 109–17.

ANSELM of Canterbury, *On the Harmony of the Foreknowledge, the Grace of God with Free Choice*, in *Trinity, Incarnation and Redemption*, ed. and trans. Jasper Hopkins and Herbert W. Richardson (New York, 1970).

—— *Monologion*, in *Anselm of Canterbury*, vol. i, ed. and trans. Jasper Hopkins and Herbert Richardson (London, 1974).

AQUINAS, THOMAS, *Summa contra Gentiles*, ed. and trans. Anton C. Pegis (Garden City, NY, 1955).

—— *Summa Theologiae*, ed. Thomas Gilbey (Garden City, NY, 1969).

ARMINIUS, JAMES, *Writings*, trans. J. Nicholls and W. R. Bagnall (London, 1825–75).

AUGUSTINE of Hippo, *City of God*, trans. John Healey (London, 1945).

—— *Confessions*, trans. R. S. Pine-Coffin (Harmondsworth, 1961).

—— *Enchiridion*, trans. J. F. Shaw (Chicago, 1961).

—— *On the Predestination of the Saints*, in *The Anti-Pelagian Writings of St. Augustine*, trans. P. Holmes and R. E. Wallis (Grand Rapids. Mich., 1971).

—— *On the Trinity*, trans. A. W. Haddan (Edinburgh, 1873).

AUNE, BRUCE, *Metaphysics* (Oxford, 1986).

BARR, JAMES, *Biblical Words for Time* (London, 1962).

BATTLES, FORD LEWIS, 'God was Accommodating himself to Human Capacity', *Interpretation*, 31 (1977), 19–38.

BOETHIUS, *The Consolation of Philosophy*, trans. V. E. Watts (Harmondsworth, 1969).

BROWN, DAVID, *The Divine Trinity* (London, 1985).

BRUMMER, VINCENT, 'Divine Impeccability', *Religious Studies*, 20 (1984), 203–14.

CALVIN, JOHN, *Commentary on the Psalms*, trans. J. Anderson (Grand Rapids, Mich., 1979).

—— *Institutes of the Christian Religion*, ed. J. T. McNeill and F. L. Battles (London, 1961).

CASTANEDA, HECTOR-NERI, 'Omniscience and Indexical Reference', *Journal of Philosophy*, 64 (1967), 203–10.

CHARNOCKE, STEPHEN, *Discourses upon the Existence and Attributes of God* (1682) (London, 1853).

COBURN, ROBERT C., 'Professor Malcolm on God', *Australasian Journal of Philosophy*, 41 (1963), 143–62.

CRAIG, WILLIAM LANE, *The Kalam Cosmological Argument* (London, 1979).

CURLEY, E. M., *Spinoza's Metaphysics: An Essay in Interpretation* (Cambridge, Mass., 1969).

DAVIES, BRIAN, *An Introduction to the Philosophy of Religion* (Oxford, 1982).

DAVIS, STEPHEN, 'Divine Omniscience and Human Freedom', *Religious Studies*, 15 (1979), 303–16.

—— *Logic and the Nature of God* (London, 1983).

DESCARTES, RENÉ, *Discourse on Method and the Meditations*, trans. F. E. Sutcliffe (Harmondsworth, 1968).

DUNN, JAMES D. G., *Christology in the Making* (London, 1980).

DURRANT, MICHAEL, *The Logical Status of 'God'* (London, 1973).

—— *Theology and Intelligibility* (London, 1973).

EDWARDS, JONATHAN, *Works,* ed. S. E. Dwight and E. Hickman (London, 1834), including *The Freedom of the Will* (1754) and *The Great Christian Doctrine of Original Sin* (1757).

EVANS, GILLIAN, *Augustine on Evil* (Cambridge, 1982).

FISCHER, JOHN MARTIN, 'Freedom and Foreknowledge', *Philosophical Review*, 92 (1983), 67–79.

FITZGERALD, PAUL, 'Stump and Kretzmann on Time and Eternity', *Journal of Philosophy*, 82 (1985), 260–9.

FLEW, ANTONY G. N., *God and Philosophy* (London, 1966).

—— *An Introduction to Western Philosophy* (London, 1971).

—— *Crime or Disease?* (London, 1973).

—— 'Compatibilism, Free Will and God', *Philosophy*, 48 (1973), 231–44.

—— 'Divine Omnipotence and Human Freedom', in A. G. N. Flew and A. C. Macintyre (eds.), *New Essays in Philosophical Theology* (London, 1955).

—— *The Presumption of Atheism* (London, 1976).

FLINT, THOMAS P. 'The Problem of Divine Freedom', *American Philosophical Quarterly*, 20 (1983), 255–64.

FRANKFURT, HARRY G., 'Three Concepts of Free Action', *Proceedings of the Aristotelian Society Supplementary Volume*, 49 (1975), 113–25.

FREDDOSO, ALFRED J., 'Accidental Necessity and Logical Determinism', *Journal of Philosophy*, 80 (1983), 258–78.

GALE, RICHARD M., 'Omniscience–Immutability Arguments', *American Philosophical Quarterly*, 23 (1986), 319–35.

GAY, ROBERT, 'Inconceivable?', *Philosophy*, 60 (Apr. 1985), 247–54.

GEACH, PETER, *God and the Soul* (London, 1969).

—— *Logic Matters* (Oxford, 1972).

—— 'An Irrelevance of Omnipotence', *Philosophy*, 48 (1973), 7–20.

—— 'The Future', *New Blackfriars*, 54 (1973), 208–18.

—— *Providence and Evil* (Cambridge, 1977).

HAACK, SUSAN, *Deviant Logic* (Cambridge, 1974).

—— 'On a Theological Argument for Fatalism', *Philosophical Quarterly*, 24 (1974), 156–9.

HELM, PAUL, 'Omnipotence and Change', *Philosophy*, 51 (1976), 454–61.

—— 'Time and Place for God', *Sophia*, 24 (Oct. 1985), 53–5.

—— 'God and the Approval of Sin', *Religious Studies*, 20 (1984), 215–22.

HOFFMAN, JOSHUA, 'Pike on Possible Worlds, Divine Foreknowledge and Human Freedom', *Philosophical Review*, 88 (1979), 433–42.

HUBY, PAMELA M., 'Kant or Cantor? That the Universe, if Real, must be Finite in both Space and Time', *Philosophy*, 46 (1971), 121–32.

HUME, DAVID, 'Dialogues Concerning Natural Religion' in *Hume on Religion*, ed. R. Wollheim (London, 1963).

KENNY, ANTHONY, 'The First Person', in Cora Diamond and Jenny Teichman (eds.), *Intention and Intentionality* (Brighton, 1979).

—— *The God of the Philosophers* (Oxford, 1979).

—— *Reason and Religion* (Oxford, 1987).

KHAMARA, E. J., 'Eternity and Omniscience', *Philosophical Quarterly*, 24 (1974), 204–19.

KNEALE, MARTHA, 'Eternity and Sempiternity', *Proceedings of the Aristotelian Society*, 69 (1968–9), 223–38.

KNEALE, WILLIAM, 'Time and Eternity in Theology', *Proceedings of the Aristotelian Society*, 61 (1960–1), 87–108.

KRETZMANN, NORMAN, 'Omniscience and Immutability', *Journal of Philosophy*, 63 (1966), 409–21.

—— 'Goodness, Knowledge and Indeterminacy in the Philosophy of Thomas Aquinas', *Journal of Philosophy*, 80 (1983), 631–49.

KRIPKE, SAUL, *Naming and Necessity* (Oxford, 1980).

KVANVIG, JONATHAN L., *The Possibility of an All-knowing God* (London, 1986).

LEWIS, DAVID, *Counterfactuals* (Oxford, 1983).

LUCAS, JOHN R., *A Treatise on Time and Space* (London, 1973).

MACBEATH, MURRAY, 'Mellor's Emeritus Headache', *Ratio*, 25 (1983), 81–8.

McCALL, STORRS, 'Temporal Flux', *American Philosophical Quarterly*, 3 (1966), 270–81.

MACKAY, DONALD M., 'On the Logical Indeterminacy of a Free Choice', *Mind*, 69 (1960), 31–40.

MACKIE, JOHN L., *The Miracle of Theism* (Oxford, 1982).

MANN, WILLIAM E., 'Simplicity and Immutability in God', *International Philosophical Quarterly*, 23 (1983), 267–76.

MELLOR, DAVID H., *Real Time* (Cambridge, 1981).

—— 'MacBeath's Soluble Aspirin', *Ratio*, 25 (1983), 89–92.

MOLTMANN, JURGEN, *The Trinity and the Kingdom of God* (London, 1981).

MORRIS, THOMAS V., 'Properties, Modalities and God', *Philosophical Review*, 93 (1984), 35–55.

NIELSEN, KAI, *An Introduction to the Philosophy of Religion* (London, 1982).

O'HEAR, ANTHONY, *Experience, Explanation and Faith* (London, 1984).

PENELHUM, T., *Religion and Rationality* (New York, 1971).

PERRY, JOHN, 'The Problem of the Essential Indexical', *Nous*, 13 (1979), 3–21.

PIKE, NELSON, 'Divine Omnipotence and Voluntary Action', *Philosophical Review*, 74 (1965), 27–46.

—— *God and Timelessness* (London, 1970).

—— 'Divine Foreknowledge, Human Freedom, and Possible Worlds', *Philosophical Review*, 86 (1977), 209–16.

—— 'Hume on Evil', *Philosophical Review*, 72 (1963), 180–97.

PIKE, NELSON (cont.) 'Plantinga on Free Will and Evil', *Religious Studies*, 15 (1979), 449–73.

—— 'Overpower and God's Responsibility for Sin', in Alfred J. Freddoso (ed.), *The Existence and Nature of God* (Notre Dame, Ill., 1983).

PLANTINGA, ALVIN, *The Nature of Necessity* (Oxford, 1974).

—— *God, Freedom and Evil* (London, 1975).

—— 'On Existentialism', *Philosophical Studies*, 44 (1983), 1–20.

—— 'On Ockham's Way Out', *Faith and Philosophy*, 3 (1986), 235–69.

PRIOR, ARTHUR N., 'The Formalities of Omniscience', *Philosophy*, 37 (1962), 114–29, reprinted in *Papers on Time and Tense* (Oxford, 1968).

—— 'Identifiable Individuals', *Review of Metaphysics*, 13 (1960), 684–96, repr. in *Papers on Time and Tense* (Oxford, 1968).

—— 'Now', *Nous*, 2 (1968), 101–19.

PUTNAM, HILARY, 'Dreaming and "Depth-Grammar"', in R. J. Butler (ed.), *Analytical Philosophy* (Oxford, 1962).

REICHENBACH, BRUCE, 'Must God Create the Best Possible World?', *International Philosophical Quarterly*, 19 (1979), 203–12.

ROSS, JAMES F., *Philosophical Theology* (Indianapolis and New York, 1969).

—— *Introduction to the Philosophy of Religion* (New York, 1969).

—— 'Creation', *Journal of Philosophy*, 77 (1980), 614–29.

—— 'Creation II', in Alfred J. Freddoso (ed.), *The Existence and Nature of God* (Notre Dame, Ill., 1983).

SCHLESINGER, GEORGE, 'The Similarities Between Space and Time', *Mind*, 84 (1975), 161–76.

SEARLE, JOHN R., 'Proper Names', *Mind*, 67 (1958), 166–73.

SORABJI, RICHARD, *Time, Creation and the Continuum* (London, 1983).

SPINOZA, BENEDICT DE, *The Ethics*, in *The Chief Works of Benedict de Spinoza*, trans. R. H. M. Elwes, vol. ii (London, 1883).

STRAWSON, PETER F., *Individuals* (London, 1959).

STUMP, ELEONORE and KRETZMANN, NORMAN, 'Eternity', *Journal of Philosophy*, 78 (1981), 429–58.

—— 'Absolute Simplicity', *Faith and Philosophy*, 2 (1985), 353–82.

—— 'Atemporal Duration: A Reply to Fitzgerald', *Journal of Philosophy*, 84 (1987), 214–19.

STURCH, RICHARD L., 'The Problem of the Divine Eternity', *Religious Studies*, 10 (1974), 487–93.

SWINBURNE, RICHARD, *The Coherence of Theism* (Oxford, 1977).

TOMBERLIN, JAMES E. and VAN INWAGEN, PETER (eds.), *Alvin Plantinga* (Dordrecht, 1985).

WARD, KEITH, *Rational Theology and the Creativity of God* (Oxford, 1982).

The Westminster Confession of Faith (London, 1643).

WHITBY, DANIEL, *Discourses on the Five Points* (2nd edn., London, 1735).

WOLTERSTORFF, NICHOLAS, 'God Everlasting' in C. J. Orlebeke and L. B. Smedes (eds.), *God and the Good* (Grand Rapids, Mich., 1975).

—— 'Can Ontology do Without Events?', in Ernest Sosa (ed.), *Essays on the Philosophy of R. M. Chisholm* (Amsterdam, 1979).

YOUNG, ROBERT, *Freedom, Responsibility and God* (London, 1975).

INDEX